JOHN AND SEBASTIAN CABOT

Portrait of Sebastian Cabot, from an engraving by Rawle, after the oil painting, now lost, formerly attributed to Hans Holbein the Younger. The Latin inscription at the upper left reads, "Portrait of John Cabot, Englishman, son of John Cabot of Venice, gilded knight, the first discoverer of new lands under Henry VII King of England. The Latin inscription at the upper right reads, "My hope is in God."

JOHN AND SEBASTIAN CABOT

THE DISCOVERY OF NORTH AMERICA

Charles Raymond Beazley

WESTHOLME
Yardley

Originally published by T. Fisher Unwin in 1898.
This edition ©2015 Westholme Publishing

Westholme Publishing, LLC
904 Edgewood Road
Yardley, Pennsylvania 19067
Visit our Web site at www.westholmepublishing.com

ISBN: 978-1-59416-239-8
Also available as an eBook.

Printed in the United States of America

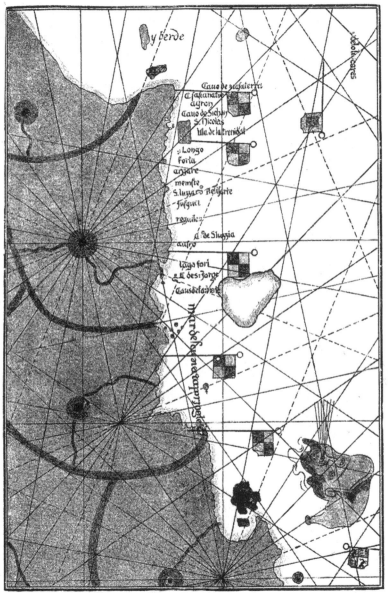

The English discoveries, marked with flags, on Juan de la Cosa's map of 1500.
(*See page 105.*)

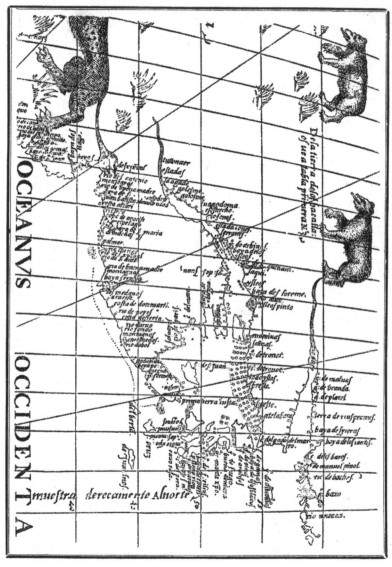

The North American section of the "Cabot" *mappemonde* of 1544. (*See page 218.*)

PREFACE

A GOOD many volumes and essays have already appeared upon the subject of the Cabot voyages; the details of these ventures have already been studied with the greatest minuteness ; and perhaps no events in the history of exploration have been the cause of more perplexing and voluminous controversy. Since the modern Cabot literature began with the appearance of R. Biddle's (American) Memoir in 1831, the educated opinion both of Europe and America has been changed in several important respects. It is no longer possible to speak (with Burke) of Sebastian Cabot as the discoverer of Newfoundland, to the exclusion of his father ; it is no longer possible to exult with Biddle and Nicholls over Sebastian's extraordinary purity of motive and elevation of character. On the other hand, a distinguished scholar has laboured to prove, not merely that

the well-praised Sebastian, being a man and not
a demigod, had his full share of human feelings,
but that among all the treacherous intriguers and
self-advertising nonentities of old time there is
no figure more disreputable than that of John
Cabot's more famous son.   In this statement of
the case, few we imagine will be found to
support M. Harrisse without qualification ; but
no one can work at any part of the story of the
great age of discovery without admiring and
profiting by the admirable industry and close
argument of this eminent student.

The simple facts, so far as they are yet
recovered, present us with two Italians of great
ability,—not unlike Columbus, perhaps still more
like Verrazano, in their careers,—who played an
important part (like so many others of their
countrymen) in the expansion of Europe and
Christendom at the end of the Middle Ages.
Whatever we may say of Sebastian the son,
John Cabot the father certainly gave England
her "title" in the New World, by his discoveries
of 1497 and 1498.   Again, whatever may be
said to Sebastian's discredit in other matters,
he certainly took an important share in bringing
about that voyage of 1553 which opened the

Russian trade by means of the White Sea, gave our merchants their first glimpse of Persia and Central Asia, and was at least one starting point of the Elizabethan revival of trade, discovery, and colonial extension. Of John Cabot we know nothing that is not honourable ; the modern researches in Italian and English archives have " bettered " his reputation more than that of almost any other navigator of the time ; there are few, indeed, among the more shadowy great men of the Tudor age who have won so much from nineteenth-century study. By the necessity of the case the son has lost where the father has gained ; Sebastian's position in the sixteenth century was largely manufactured out of exploits which really belonged to his father ; and as the true proportion has been recovered, the heroic ideal of Peter Martyr and Ramusio has become unrecognisable. Much of the " Sebastianised " history of the early annalists may have been due to their confusion rather than to his misdirection ; but if he had always fairly recognised his father's part and mentioned his father's name, we could not have had such a picture of the first Cabot voyages as is painted for us by the chroniclers in Chapter V. of this volume. Beyond doubt, Sebastian Cabot allowed his father to be defrauded in silence of much of the credit that was justly his ; beyond doubt also Sebastian had small scruple about the Government he served, or the way in which he was prepared to transfer his services. Yet both he and his father did something towards the creation of Greater Britain, and no list of its " Builders " could be complete without a mention of both names. For if only from the fact that Sebastian's life-work is to a great extent inseparable from John's, and that the one is in so many respects the complement of the other, we must join with the discoverer of " Canada " that other figure, so much more fully known to history, in all its weaknesses, the friend of Eden and of Burrough, the first Governor of our Incorporated Company of Merchant Adventurers or of Muscovy.

In preparing this volume, I have had the invaluable advice of Mr. C. H. Coote of the Map Department in the British Museum, who has read all the manuscript, and made many suggestions. His views, it must be said, differ from those expressed here on the birthplace of

Sebastian Cabot, and the part of North America
represented in the map of Juan de la Cosa.
Among modern writings those of M. Harrisse
have been found most helpful ; his French and
English Cabot volumes of 1882 and of 1896 con-
tain the best (though often highly controversial)
treatment as yet attempted of this subject ; the
studies of Deane, Dawson, Tarducci, Desimoni,
and Coote (in the " Dictionary of National
Biography ") may perhaps be considered as next
in value to the work of M. Harrisse ; a full list
of Cabot literature will be found in the two
Appendices to this volume.

One great defect, however, as it seems to me,
may be noticed in almost all treatises on this
question ; and that is in the usual handling of
the evidence. Nowhere, as far as I know, have
the leading documents as a whole been presented
to the reader as the backbone of the *narrative* ;[1]
yet nowhere is a general and accurate view of
the small mass of first-hand testimony more
essential than in the Cabot controversy. This

[1] M. Harrisse, *Jean et Sébastien Cabot*, gives them, not
in the history and biography, but (with a vast mass of
collateral evidence) in what is really a " Mémoire pour
servir."

PREFACE

accordingly has been made the leading feature of the present study. For however much our views may differ on disputable points, all alike must reckon with the original records and start from them ; sometimes it appears hopeless to reconcile the discrepancies that confront us, and we must be content with registering the evidence —carefully excluding from our text, except for purposes of illustration, all second-hand and late testimony, and trusting to future discoveries to clear up some at least of those points which still remain ambiguous.

C. RAYMOND BEAZLEY.

MERTON COLLEGE, OXFORD,
February, 1898.

CONTENTS

CONTENTS

CHAPTER V

CHAPTER VI

CHAPTER VII

CHAPTER VIII

CHAPTER IX

CHAPTER X

CONTENTS

CHAPTER XI

CHAPTER XII

CHAPTER XIII

CHAPTER XIV

CHAPTER XV

CONTENTS

APPENDICES.

John and Sebastian Cabot

CHAPTER I

THE discovery of the North American continent by John Cabot in 1497 was preceded not only by the permanent achievement of Columbus (1492), but by a number of transitory successes in the nature of exploration or settlement by Europeans or Asiatics in that same continent. Other features of an introductory nature are the legendary voyages of St. Brandan and others, and the tradition (so prominent in the later mediæval maps) of islands in the Western Sea. It is also pretty certain that the Portuguese had followed up their well-known exploits on the African coast and among the Atlantic Islands by ventures further westward, ventures, however, which apparently led to no tangible result.

A

And, first of all, we may not find it useless to examine the character of these earlier movements towards 'American' exploration in the history or legend of the Old World.

1. The alleged Chinese discovery of lands to the far east of their country (lands which have been identified with Alaska, with British Columbia, and even with Panama and Mexico) cannot be supposed to have ever reached the ears of Cabot or any other European of his time ; but, if credible, it is the earliest known revelation of any part of America to any one of the nations of 'our continent.' The Celestials' tradition recorded how, at a time answering to the year of Christ 499, a land called Fusang, situated some 32,000 furlongs north-east of Japan, was made known to the Chinese by one Hoei-Sin. This land took its name from its fusang trees, which served the inhabitants for food, fibre, cloth, paper, and timber. The people of this country waged no war and had no armour ; they possessed horses, deer and cattle with horns of wonderful length that could bear an immense weight ; and they used these animals (and especially their tamed stags) to draw their carts, like the reindeer of the Lapps to-day. Among fruits they enjoyed pears and grapes ; among metals, gold, silver, and copper ; but they set no value on any of these except the last. They were ruled by a king, who changed the colour of his garments (green, red, yellow, white, and black) like some of the Tartars, according to a cycle of

years, but who took no part in government for the
first thirty-six months of his reign. Their nobles were
divided into three classes, and the crimes of these exalted
personages were punished with peculiar solemnity.
'They were put under ground with food and drink ;'
a ceremonial leave was taken of them by their friends
and all the people ; and they were left 'surrounded
with ashes.' The men of Fusang punished nearly all
crimes with imprisonment ; for smaller offences they
employed a dungeon in the south of their country ;
but the greater criminals were immured for life in a
northern prison and their children were enslaved.
The marriage ceremonies of this country were much
the same as in China, except that the intending bride-
groom had to serve the family of his betrothed for a
year ; like the Celestials they paid extreme reverence
to parents, and made offerings to the images of
ancestors.

Among other lands to the far east of China were
the Kingdom of Women, and the Lands of Marked
Bodies, of the Dog-headed Men, and of Great Han,
discovered and described, according to the Chinese
annals, in the first half of the sixth century A.D. In
the first-named country the people were erect in
stature and very white in colour, but covered with an
immense growth of hair that reached to the ground.
Their children could walk when little more than
three months old, and within four years they were
fully grown. They fed upon a salt plant like worm-

wood, and fled in terror at the approach of a human being.

In the Land of Marked Bodies there was a race tattooed 'like wild beasts.' After the fashion of the Brahmins of India, the nobles bore upon their foreheads certain lines which showed their rank. As a people they were merry, hospitable, and peaceful, easily pleased with things of small value. The house of their king was adorned with gold, silver, and precious articles, and in traffic they used gems as the standard of value.

In the Dog-headed Land, Chinese mariners, driven out of their course by the winds, found men who had dogs' heads and barked for speech. Among other things they used small beans for food. Their clothing resembled linen cloth; from loose earth they constructed round dwellings with doors or openings like the mouths of burrows. Lastly, the Great Han country was described as very similar to that of the Marked Bodies.

In these curious traditions it is very possible that the Chinese have preserved a record of American voyages on the part of their early Buddhist missionaries similar to the extensive journeyings of these same missionaries at this time to Western and Southern Asia — to Tartary, Afghanistan, and India.

The hairy people of the Land of Women have naturally suggested to many the Ainos of Northern Japan; but the 'Marked Bodies' certainly point rather to the American Indians than to any people of North-eastern Asia ; and those of us who are not prepared to reject the whole Chinese tradition will consider with attention the analogy repeatedly advanced by modern anatomists and physiologists between some of the Tartar tribes and some of the American aboriginals. The same attention may fairly be given to the argument of a striking likeness between certain architectural monuments of Central America and those of Asiatic Buddhism ; to the discovery in North America of fossil remains of the horse, some so recent 'that they must be regarded as coeval with man' ; to the antecedent possibility and even probability of at least occasional transit from Asia to America, and *vice versâ*, in the latitude of the Behring Sea ; to the undoubted achievements of the Vikings in the face of much greater difficulties on the eastern side ; and to the likelihood of an original migration of the human race into the New World from Northern Asia rather than from any other quarter. The Chinese record, if it is to be treated fairly, must not be minimised any more than it must be exaggerated, and if its words and measurements forbid us to identify Fusang with Mexico or Panama, they also require something more extensive than a journey to Japan, which the Chinese of Marco Polo's day reckoned as only 1500 miles from their southern ports, and which is distinctly named in our present narrative as a starting-point for the Land of Marked

Bodies. Nothing has yet been found in Japan to answer to this account of the prison customs of Fusang, the assembly of the people to judge guilty noblemen, the peculiar punishment of the same, the sequence of colours in the royal garments, the use of deer as beasts of burden, and other particulars.

The tin, hammer-shaped coins of the Aztecs have been compared with the shoe-shaped ingots of Sycee silver, current in China ; the copper used so largely in Central America before the European invasion seems once to have been worked as far north as Lake Superior, and traces of Mexican art and influence have been found as far as Tennessee along the course of that migration which, as we may surmise, had crossed from Asia into Alaska ages before Hoei-Sin, which Buddhist travellers of the fifth and sixth centuries may have discovered on its slow progress southwards, and which may have left in its final tropical home some memorials of an intercourse long forgotten with the Old World.

Both in China and in Japan the tradition of an ancient discovery of countries far to the East is said to be very old, very widespread, and very obstinate ; and a modern instance gives some colour to it. In 1833, a Japanese junk belonging to the ' times of ignorance ' was wrecked near Queen Charlotte's Island off British Columbia ; just as in 1832 a fishing smack from the same country with nine men on board, was driven out of its course between Formosa and Tokio, and arrived

safely at the Sandwich Islands. Such undoubted facts
may well encourage those who believe in the sub-
stantial truth of this Chinese claim to American discovery, and a negative argument from an equally
undoubted fact may be added. No one now disputes
that the Norsemen reached the Eastern mainland of
America about A.D. 1000, yet no one can point to a
single proof of their presence or relic of their occupation. Why then should we ask for so much more in
confirmation of the word of Hoei-Sin and his Buddhist
friends than we expect in support of the pretensions of
Red Eric and his house ? Grant that the 'internal'
witness (from consistency and clearness of statement,
absence of fable, and so forth) is far weaker in the case
of the Chinese than in that of the Northmen ; but
this is surely balanced to some degree by the greater
'monumental' and other present-day evidence of the
former claim.

2. A far more important anticipation of the fifteenth-
century successes of Columbus and Cabot was the
Vinland movement of the Norsemen, in the tenth and
eleventh centuries. By way of the Färoes, Iceland,
and Greenland, Viking adventurers pushed on to Newfoundland, Labrador, and Nova Scotia or New England. As early as A.D. 874 the Norsemen had colonised
Iceland. Three years later, Greenland was sighted by
Gunnbiorn, and called White Shirt from its snowfields.
As this country is geographically a part of the North
American continent, the Norse settlements of the tenth

century, conducted by Red Eric and his house, soon led to their natural issue. About 989 one Bjarni Herjulfson, following his father from Iceland to Erics-fiord in Greenland, was driven by storms out West into the Ocean. Before he made his way back again he had sighted two unknown lands :—one was a flat, well-wooded country, the other was a mountainous tract covered with glaciers. Soon after Bjarni's return, Leif Ericson started (about A.D. 1000) with a definite purpose of discovery. He bought Bjarni's ship, manned it with five and twenty men, and set out. First of all he came to the land Bjarni had sighted last, and went on shore. There was no grass to be seen, but great snowy ridges far inland, with snow stretching all the way between the coast and the mountains. Leif called it Helluland or Slabland, and it probably answers to our Labrador. Putting to sea again he came upon another country, flat and well wooded, with a white-sand shore, low lying towards the sea. This Leif ' called after its nature,' Markland or Woodland—the ' Newfoundland ' (in all likeli-hood) of the sixteenth century. Thence driving for two days before a north-east wind the adventurers came to a 'sound' or strait lying between an island and a ness, ' where also a river came out of a lake.' Into this they towed the ship and anchored, carrying their beds out on the shore and setting up their tents, with a large hut in the middle, and so made all ready for wintering there.

As long as Leif remained he saw no frost, and seemed to think that nothing of the sort could happen —where the land was rich in grass, trees, 'self-sown' wheat in the fields, and even wild vines, and where day and night were more equal than in Iceland or in Greenland. The crew were divided in two parts; one worked at the huts and the other explored the country, returning every night to the camp. From the wild vines found by the German Tyrker, Leif's foster-father, the whole district was called Vinland; and here on the shortest day, we are told, the sun was above the horizon from half-past seven to half-past four. By this the latitude has been fixed, in one calculation, to 41° 43′ North, or nearly the position of Mount Hope Bay in New England; and it has been fancifully asserted that the name of 'Hóp' given to the country by the Norsemen, 'from the good hope they had of it,' was found still in use under the form of 'Haup' by the Indians six centuries later—'Mount Hope' being the reversion of the name, on Puritan tongues, to a slightly different form of the original type. On the other hand, Dr. Storm has lately given very weighty reasons for identifying Vinland with Nova Scotia, rejecting some of the details of the Saga and furnishing a correction of his own, which makes Leif the first discoverer of the Western lands, eliminates Bjarni Herjulfson, and compresses together the later ventures of Thorwald Ericson and Thorfinn Karlsefne into one enterprise.

These later ventures, in the original story, were as follows : When Leif returned with his stern-boat full of specimens of the wild vines and trees and self-sown wheat of Vinland, his brother Thorwald was stirred to like adventure ; and he set out with Leif's ship and thirty men, in the year 1002. He came straight to 'Leif's Booths' in Vinland, and stayed the winter there ; in the next spring and summer he coasted along a beautiful and well-wooded land, with a white sandy beach, many islands fringing the shore and shallow water around, but without finding any trace of man or beast, except a wooden corn-barn on an island far to the West. Returning to the Booths for the winter, Thorwald started again eastwards in the spring, and fell in with the mysterious Skraelings (generally identified as Esquimaux) who came in their skin boats ('a countless host from up the fiord,') and 'laid themselves alongside' the Norse vessel. Thorwald was mortally wounded in the battle, and his men returned to Greenland with a cargo of vines and grapes, and the news of their chief's death. On this, Thorstein Ericson, another of Leif's brothers, put out for Vinland, but after beating about in the Ocean for many weeks came back unsuccessfully to Ericsfiord (1004–5). He was followed by the greatest of the Vinland sailors, Thorfinn Karlsefne—'Thorfinn the Predestined Hero,' who made the first and last serious attempt to found a permanent Norse colony in the new lands. According to the Saga he came from Nor-

way to Iceland soon after Thorwald's death, passed on
to Greenland about 1005, 'when, as before, much was
talked about a Vinland voyage,' and in 1006 made
ready to start with one hundred and sixty men and
five women in three ships. The expedition was well
equipped. They had with them ' all kinds of cattle,
meaning to settle in the land if they could.'   Leif lent
them his Booths, and they sailed in 1007. First they
came to Helluland, where they found a quantity of foxes ;
then to Markland, well stocked with forest animals ;
then to an island at the mouth of a fiord unknown before,
covered with eider ducks. They called the new discoveries Stream Island and Stream Fiord, from the current that here ran out into the sea, and hence they sent
off a party of eight men in search of Vinland in a ' stern-
boat.' This (identified by some with the expedition of
Thorwald Ericson) was driven by westerly gales back
to Iceland ; but Thorfinn, with the rest, sailed south
till he came to Leif Ericson's river and lake and corn-
growing islands and vine-clad hills. Here he settled in
peace during one winter, felling wood, pasturing cattle,
and gathering grapes ; but in the spring the Skraelings
came down upon his men, at first to traffic with furs
and sables against milk and dairy produce, and then to
fight. For as neither understood the other, and the
natives tried to force their way into Thorfinn's houses
and to get hold of his men's weapons, a quarrel was
bound to come.

In view of this, Karlsefne fortified his settlement ;

' and at this very time was a child born to him, called Snorre, of Gudrid his wife, the widow of Thorstein Ericson.' The first of native European colonists in America did not fulfil the promise of his birth ; soon after this the whole enterprise was abandoned ; and in the spring of 1008, Thorfinn, though victorious over the Skraelings, and richly laden with Vinland wares, came back to Greenland.

Thus ends the story of the first colonisation of America from Europe, and the Saga, while giving no definite cause for the failure, seems to show that even the trifling annoyance of the Skraelings was enough to turn the scale. Natural difficulties were so immense, men were so few, that a pigmy foe was able to hold the new immigration at bay.

So now, though on Thorfinn's return, the ' talk began to run again upon a Vinland voyage as both gainful and honourable,' and a daughter of Red Eric, named Freydis, won some men over to a fresh attempt in the country where all the house of Eric had tried and failed ; though Leif lent his Booths as before, and sixty colonists, not counting women, were found ready to go—yet the settlement could never be firmly planted in this generation. Freydis and her allies sailed in 1011, reached Vinland, and wintered there ; but jealousy and murder soon broke up the camp, and the remains of the expedition found their way back to Greenland in 1013. From this point the con-nected story of Vinland enterprise comes to an

end. Whether Thorfinn or others made any
more attempts at 'Western planting ;' whether the
account we have of these voyages is really an Eric
Saga, for nearly every Vinland leader is of this family ;
whether the Greenland line of advance on the New
World was accompanied by other similar ventures of
the Norse race, can hardly be proved as yet. We
can only fancy that these suggestions are probable,
in view of the few additional facts that have been
preserved to us of this ' Plantation.' We hear, for
instance, of Are Marson, of Reykianes in Iceland, being
driven by storms far west to White Man's Land,
where he was followed by Bjarni Asbrandson in 999,
and by Gudleif Gudlangson in 1029. This was the
tale of his friend Rafn, the ' Limerick trader,' and of
Are Frode, his great-great-grandson, who called the
unknown land Great Ireland—by some identified with
the Carolinas, by others with the Canaries. Again, in
continuation of the Greenland line of advance, there
are records of Bishop Eric going over from Erics-
fiord to Vinland in 1121 ; of clergy from the
' Eastern Bay ' diocese of Gardar, sailing to lands in
the West, far North of Vinland [1] in 1266 ; of the
two Helgasons discovering a country West of Iceland
in 1285 ; and of a voyage from Greenland to Markland undertaken in 1347 by a crew of seventeen men.
Unless these are pure fabrications, they would seem to

[1] In support of this, a solitary ' American' relic of Norse occupation
has been found on a rock near the entrance of Baffin's Bay.

point to some intercourse (of however slight a kind) between mother and daughter colonies of North-western
Europe and North-eastern America.   Between 980
and 1000, both Iceland and Greenland had become
Christian ; in 1126, the line of the Bishops of Gardar
begins with Arnold ; and the clergy would hardly
have ventured on the Vinland voyage (which was
certainly preserved in twelfth and thirteenth century
Icelandic tradition), if their only object was to
convert an infinitely few Skraelings in an almost
deserted country.

The Venetian, Welsh, and Arabic claims to have
followed the Norsemen in visits to America earlier
than the voyage of 1492, cannot be discussed here.
The Vinland enterprise of the Norseman is a fairly
certain fact ; against all other mediæval claims to the
discovery of a Western Continent, one only verdict
can be recorded—Not proven.

CHAPTER II

3. BUT the achievements of the Vikings in
American discovery were either not communicated
beyond a very narrow circle, or were soon forgotten.
In Cabot's lifetime the Vinland tradition seems to
have been absolutely unknown in Europe ; but it
fared quite differently with those legendary voyages to
the West which go under the names of St. Brandan,
the Seven Spanish Bishops, and so forth.

As we shall see, when Cabot first came to England,
he found the mariners of Bristol ready and willing to
venture far into the Atlantic in the hope of re-discover-
ing the isles of Brandan and of the Seven Cities.

Down to the end of the Middle Ages, and in the

sixteenth century, the former and more famous of these was marked on maps, usually due West of Ireland; it was sighted again and again by determined and devout people who went out to look for it; it was associated with similar discoveries of St. Malo in the sixth century, of the Seven Spanish Bishops in the eighth, of the Basques in the tenth; on the success of Columbus it was turned like the rest into a claim for a prior discovery of America; but it really had its origin in eleventh or twelfth century hagiology, and it obstinately remains in a poetic mirage. It gives us perhaps a picture of the shuddering interest of these missionary travellers in the wildness, the power, and the infinitude of nature, as it could be tested on the Ocean; it rarely gives us anything more definite. Brandan was, in the oldest form of the story, an Irish monk, who died on May 16, 578, in the Abbey of Clonfert, which he had founded. One day, when entertaining a brother monk named Barinth, he listened to the latter's account of his recent voyage in the Ocean, and of an isle called the Delicious, where one Mernoc had retired, with several religious men. Barinth had visited this island, and Mernoc had conducted him to a more distant isle in the West, which was reached through a thick fog, beyond which shone an eternal clearness—this was the promised land of the Saints. [1] Brandan, seized with a

[1] Perhaps St. Kilda (from " Holy Culdees ") the Erse name of which was Hirta or western land.

pious desire to see this isle of the Blessed, embarked in an osier boat covered with tanned hides and carefully greased, and took with him seventeen other monks, among whom was St. Malo, then a young man. After forty days at sea they reached an island with steep scarped sides, furrowed by streamlets, where they received hospitality and took in provisions. Thence they were carried by the winds towards another island, cut up by rivers that were full of fish and covered by countless flocks of sheep [1] as large as heifers. From these they took a lamb without blemish wherewith to celebrate the Easter festival on another island close by—bare, without vegetation or rising ground. Here they landed to cook their lamb, but no sooner had they set the pot and lighted the fire than the island began to move. They fled to their ship, where St. Brandan had stayed ; and he showed them that what they had taken for a solid island, was nothing but a whale. They regained the former isle (of sheep) and saw the fire they had kindled flaming upon the monster's back, two miles off.

From the summit of the island they had now returned to they discerned another, wooded and fertile ; whither they repaired, and found a multitude of birds, who sang with them the praises of the Lord ; this was the Paradise of Birds. Here the pious travellers remained till Pentecost ; then, again embarking, they

[1] Perhaps the Färoes, from Far, "a sheep."

wandered several months upon the Ocean. At last they came to another isle, inhabited by Cœnobites, who had for their patrons St. Patrick and St. Ailbhé ; with these they celebrated Christmas, and took ship again after the Octave of the Epiphany.

A year had passed in these journeys, and during the next six they continued the same round with certain variations (such as their visit to the Island of the Hermit Paul and their meeting with Judas Iscariot), finding themselves always at St. Patrick's Isle for Christmas, at the Isle of Sheep for Holy Week, on the Back of the Whale (which now displayed no uneasiness) for Easter, and at the Isle of Birds for Pentecost.

But during the seventh year especial trials were reserved for them ; they were nearly destroyed by various monsters ; but they also saw several other islands. One was large and wooded ; another flat with great red fruit, inhabited by a race called the Strong Men ; another full of rich orchards, the trees bending beneath their load ; and to the North they came upon the rocky, treeless, barren island of the Cyclops' forges, close by which was a lofty mountain, with summit veiled in clouds, vomiting flames—this was the mouth of hell.[1]

And now as the end of their attempt had come, they embarked afresh with provisions for forty days, entered the zone of mist and darkness, which enclosed the Isle of Saints, and having traversed it, found themselves on

[1] Perhaps Hecla in Iceland ; *cf.* the Olaus Magnus Map of 1539.

the shore of the island they had so long been seeking, bathed in light. This was an extensive land, sown as it were with precious stones, covered with fruit as in the season of autumn, and enjoying perpetual day. Here they stayed and explored the abode of the blest for forty days, without reaching the end of it. But at last, on arriving at a great river that flowed through the midst, an angel appeared to tell them they could go no further, and must now return to their country, bearing with them some of the fruits and precious stones of the land, reserved to the saints against that time when God should have subdued to the true faith all the Nations of the Universe. St. Brandan and his companions again entered into their vessel, traversed afresh the margin of darkness and came to the Island of Delight. Thence they returned directly to Ireland.

The alleged discovery of the Seven Cities (by seven Spanish bishops) is associated with the name of Antillia, as in the inscription on Martin Behaim's Globe, executed for the City of Nuremburg in 1492. "In the year 734 after the birth of Christ, when all Spain was overrun by the miscreants of Africa, this island of Antillia, called also the Isle of the Seven Cities, was peopled by the Archbishop of Oporto, with six other bishops and certain companions, male and female, who fled from Spain with their cattle and property. In the year 1414, a Spanish ship approached very near this island." A somewhat fuller account is given by

Ferdinand Columbus, who also identifies the names of Antillia and Seven Cities as referring to the same spot, but dates the flight from Spain in A.D. 714, and describes how a Portuguese ship professed (but with highly suspicious circumstances) to have discovered the colony in the time of Prince Henry the Navigator.

On these legends we need only remark here that they are certainly in great measure borrowed from Oriental travel romances, with some additions from classical myths and Christian hagiology. Though Brandan is supposed to have sailed in or about 565, no trace is found of his story before the eleventh century, while as to its origin, the voyage of the Lisbon 'Wanderers' (or Maghrurins) as recorded by Edrisi, and those of Sindbad the Sailor, as preserved in the *Arabian Nights*, are clearly related to parts of the Irish legend in the way of original to copy. Thus the Lisbon 'Wanderers' tale of the Isle of El Ghanam (? Madeira), abounding in sheep, recalls St. Brandan's Paschal island, though here the Brandan story may also preserve an independent tradition of the Färoes. Once more the Arabic islands 'Of Birds,' 'Of the Wizards,' and 'Of the Whale,' where Sindbad's companions kindled a fire with even more disastrous results, find their parallels in Brandan's Isles of Pious Birds, of the Solitary Hermit, and of the Great Fish; while, even if his island of Hell's Mouth be admitted as an original Irish reference to Hecla, yet his Isles of Delight and of Paradise may be fairly interpreted as expressions derived from

Classical or Moslem geographers for the lovely climate of the Canary or Fortunate Islands. Even the Griffin of Brandan's story and the Whale that attacks his boat may be borrowed from the Roc and the aggressive sea-monsters of the Sindbad Saga ; while the very number of the years of travel in the Christian legend correspond to the sevenfold ventures of the navigator in the *Arabian Nights*— correspond however in a purely arbitrary manner, as would be the case in a borrowed narrative. We may see this more fully, if it be worth while to multiply instances, in many minor details of Brandan's 'Navigation' —in the empty palace which the saint finds in his first discovered island, the devil who afterwards comes to light in the same palace, the soporific spring in the Isle of Birds, and the speechless man of the Isle of Ailbhé, who only answered by gestures in the Christian narrative, compared with the similar incidents of the second and third voyages of Sindbad. Again the giants who threaten both the Arab and Irish adventurers, by aiming huge blocks of stone at their frail vessels, probably come into both narratives from the Cyclops story of the Odyssey ; the river and precious stones in Brandan's Isle of Paradise recall the bower of the sixth Sindbad voyage; and just as the latter's companions are roasted and eaten by the demon black of Sindbad's third adventure, so on the shore of the Burning Isle one of Brandan's monks is caught away by devils and burnt up to a cinder.

In its final shape the Brandan story aimed at giving

not merely a Christian Odyssey to its readers, but also a picture of monastic life and worship ; and, by thus combining the edifying element with the adventurous, strove to win that popularity which as a matter of fact it gained.

Somewhat similar in design, though less elaborate in execution, was the narrative of Antillia and the Seven Cities, or the tale of the Basque adventurers of 990. So far as these are not purely fantastic, they may refer, like the story of the Portuguese adventurers of 1414, to some distant and imperfect view of the Azores, just as we may discern a possible foundation of fact in the Brandan references to places which may (or may not) correspond to the Färoes, Hecla, and St. Kilda. But all these Spanish variants may, on the other hand (like the Brandan story itself), be based wholly on other narratives, Oriental, Moorish, Classical, and Hagiological ; the semblance of independent explanation in certain details may be accidental and deceptive ; and the Island of the Seven Cities, for example, may be only the transference into Christian phrase of the Western Dragon Island of some Arabic writers, or of the Atlantis of Plato ; with this last Antillia is expressly identified by an inscription of 1455, which says nothing of Spanish bishops and only repeats the tradition of the *Timaeus.*

In any case, what is important for us is to notice the hold which this cycle of legend had gained upon the imagination of Western Europe.   This is a truism of fifteenth-century geography, but in the life of John Cabot we see it exemplified to very practical purpose ; for it is the first stage in our movement towards the discovery of North America, the first incitement of Bristol seamen to the exploration of the Atlantic.

4. A much later myth is the voyage of the Brothers Zeno to Engroneland, Drogeo, and Estotiland about 1390–1400.   Nicolo Zeno, according to this story, being in the service of Henry Sinclair, Earl of Orkney and the Färoes, sailed to Greenland, where he found a settlement of the Order of Friar Preachers.   Nicolo, dying on his return to the Färoes, his brother Antonio, who had joined him from Venice, was 'sent out with a few vessels to the westward,' because in that direction, some of Sinclair's fishermen ' had discovered certain very rich and populous islands.'   Of these one of the said fishermen had given the following account : Six and twenty years ago four fishing boats had been driven by storms to an island called Estotiland, about one thousand miles west from Frisland.   Thence, after many adventures, the castaways came to a country towards the south, called Drogeo, and after that to many other lands, ' increasing in refinement as you go south-west.'   Finally, one of the fishermen escaped and returned to the Färoes.   To discover, and if possible to conquer, Estotiland and the other lands described, Sinclair himself took command of the expedition, on which he required the company and

nautical advice of Antonio Zeno. He did not, however, reach the countries described by the fisherman
(who died before the fleet could sail), but only Icaria
and Trin in the Western Sea. In the latter he settled
down and built a city, sending Zeno back to the
Färoes. This account, put together in the early
sixteenth century by Nicolo Zeno, junior, is obviously
a Venetian claim to a discovery of the New World just
a century before Columbus ; it is professedly derived
from old family papers, of which nothing more is
known, and it bears many traces of being concocted
after the discoveries of 1492–1510. In all probability it is a forgery, and cannot be allowed any real
weight among 'anticipations' of Columbus and the
Cabots.

5. Last, among these foreshadowings of the great
Atlantic discoveries of 1492 and subsequent years, we
must briefly notice the early exploits and more distant,
if fruitless, enterprises of the Portuguese and other
European nations on the 'American track' in the
later Middle Ages. First among these it would be
pleasant to reckon the voyage of the Italian, Lancelot
Malocello, to the Canaries in 1270, and the Genoese
ventures of Tedisio Doria and the Vivaldi in 1281 (or
1291) 'to the ports of India to trade there'—expeditions which mark the commencement of the new
age of maritime discovery ; but we must not lay
stress upon them, for they were essentially attempts to
seek India by the coast way round Africa, not by the

Ocean way across the Atlantic. The same must be said of the Portuguese-Italian voyage of 1341 to the Canaries (described by Boccaccio); of the Catalan voyage of 1346 to the river of Gold, which reached Cape Boyador; and of most of the early ventures of Prince Henry's captains. The discovery of Madeira by Robert Machin [1] from Bristol in the reign of Edward III., if the story is to be credited, has no particular bearing on any definite scheme of exploration—it was at best a romantic accident; but the permanent exploration and settlement of the Canaries by the French Seigneur Jean de Béthencourt, from A.D. 1402, and of Madeira by Zarco and Vaz in the service of Prince Henry, from the year 1420, did push European enterprise somewhat further into the Atlantic, gave it a new and more advanced basis for western expeditions (if such should be attempted), and so far may be considered to have some bearing on the later American discoveries. Much more to our purpose was the exploring movement to the Azores and Cape Verde Islands. Although marked on the Laurentian Portolano of 1351, the Azores or Western islands had been forgotten by nearly all except students of old cartography like Prince Henry himself, when the latter sent out Diego de Sevill in 1427, and Gonçalo Cabral, in 1431, in that

---

[1] A Portuguese sailor, named Machico, existed in Portugal in 1379, and it is possibly after *him* the Machico district of Madeira is named. (Doc. disc. 1894.)

direction. Cabral in his first voyage discovered the Formiga Group, and returning in 1432 made fresh explorations, especially of the island Santa Maria. From about the year 1436 systematic colonisation began under the leadership of Cabral and the patronage of Prince Henry ; the islands first colonised served as centres for the discovery and settlement of others ; and thus St. Michael was found in 1444, Terceira and others a little later (between 1444 and 1450), Flores and Corvo probably between 1450 and 1460. In 1466 there was a fresh movement of immigration from Portugal, when the King conferred the islands upon his sister Isabel, Duchess of Burgundy, and sent out ' many people of all classes ' ; and it was mainly from the Azores as a starting-point that Portuguese expeditions seem to have ventured (though fruitlessly) into the Ocean beyond in the hope of further discoveries. By this extension of Europe (as it were) to the Western islands, two-fifths of the distance between Lisbon and the Delaware was already covered, but the interval still left upon this line was immense, and it was upon a south-west course, from Cape Verde in Africa to Cape St. Roque in Brazil, that the Old World, at least in its central regions, approached most nearly to the unknown and hidden continent so long mistaken for an extension of Asia.

From this point of view the discovery and settlement of the Cape Verde Islands was even more suggestive than similar movements among the Azores.

During his second voyage along the West Coast of Africa in Prince Henry's service, the famous Venetian seaman, Cadamosto, laid claim to the discovery of 'certain uninhabited islands' off Cape Verde (1458). More certainly Diego Gomez and Antonio de Nolli in 1460 sighted those 'islands in the Ocean,' which we know as the Cape Verde Group, and explored the same, calling the chief of them Santiago. De Nolli, outstripping Gomez on his return to Portugal, begged successfully for the captaincy of this isle of Santiago ('which I had found,' says Gomez wrathfully) and kept it till his death. Thus, before the close of Prince Henry's life (1460) exploration had pushed some way into the Atlantic south-west as well as due west from Europe, towards Brazil and the West Indian islands as well as towards the more distant shore of the North American mainland.

Further, on the strength of a very enigmatical inscription in a map of Andrea Bianco, a Portuguese discovery of the north-east corner of Brazil, in or before the year 1448, has again been suggested in recent years, but this is a conjecture which, however possible in itself, is quite lacking in demonstrative evidence.

Rather more certainty attaches to some at least of the expeditions reported by fifteenth-century Portuguese adventurers in search of Western lands. Thus a voyage is said to have been made in 1452 by Diego de Teive and Pedro Velasco for more than 150 leagues west of Fayal in the Azores.

Again in 1462 Gonçalo Fernandes de Tavira is
alleged to have sailed west-north-west of Madeira and
the Canaries ; in 1473 we are vaguely told of certain
attempts to discover land west of the Cape Verde
Islands, and of a western voyage of one Ruy Gonçalves
de Camara in the same year ; similar accounts are to
be found of Fernão Telles in 1475, and of Antonio
Leme in 1476. What may be considered as a more
immediate anticipation of the Cabotian voyages is the
series of attempts made by Pedro de Barcellos and
João Fernandes Lavrador (from the beginning of 1492
down to 1495) to discover land to the north-west, by
order of the King of Portugal. Some weight has
also been attached to a statement of Las Casas that on
his third voyage in 1498 Columbus planned a southern
course from the Cape Verde Islands in search of lands,
especially because, proceeds Las Casas, ' he wished to
see what was the meaning of King John of Portugal
when he said there was *terra firma* to the South,[1] and
for this reason he (Columbus) says that the King of
Portugal had differences with the Kings of Castille,
which were settled by the decision . . . that he . . .
should have 370 leagues to the west beyond the
Azores and Cape Verde, which belong to him . . .
from one pole to the other ; and he (Columbus) also
says that King John considered it certain that inside
those limits he was going to find famous lands. Some
of the more important inhabitants of that island of

[1] Did this refer to Africa or ' America ' ?

Santiago came to see him (Columbus) and said that to the south-west of the island of Fogo, which is one of the said Cape Verde Islands . . . an island was seen, and that King John had a great wish to send an expedition to make discoveries towards the south-west, and that canoes had been known to go from the Guinean coast to the west with merchandise. . . . And he (Columbus) ordered to steer south-west . . . and afterwards due west . . . in which way he would verify the said opinion of King John.'

Once more, Galvano, after speaking of a voyage which took place in 1447, goes on to speak of another (undated but assigned by some critics to the same year) in these terms : 'It is moreover told that in the meantime a Portuguese ship, coming out of the Straits of Gibraltar, was carried westwards by a storm much further than was intended, and arrived at an island where there were *seven cities and people who spoke our language.* . . . The master of the ship is said to have brought some sand . . . from which gold was obtained.' This, however, is obviously a fabulous story, revived from the old Spanish tale of the Seven Bishops and their cities. The strongest argument in favour of the Portuguese claim is certainly that in 1500 Pedro Alvarez Cabral did discover Brazil (or as he called it, the 'Land of the Holy Cross') merely by taking a wide sweep on his course down the West Coast of Africa to the Cape of Good Hope. It is strongly contended (and has been from the beginning) that this was purely accidental, without any thought of following in Columbus's steps—but we cannot be sure of this. The most curious point in this controversy is that the pilots of Cabral's fleet professed to recognise the new land as the same they had seen marked on an old map existing in Portugal—at least, so writes Master John, Bachelor in Arts and Medicine, and Physician and Cosmographer to the King Don Manuel. He accompanied the expedition of 1500 in person, and did not hesitate to declare that the country where Cabral landed was identical with a tract duly marked upon a *mappemonde* belonging to one Pero Vaz Bisagudo, a subject of the King of Portugal. In the same connection a number of still looser and more doubtful assertions exist in Portuguese archives and chronicles. Thus in 1457 the Infant Don Fernando *planned* Atlantic explorations; in 1484 Fernão Domingues de Arco *intended* to look for a reported new island in the West; in 1486 the Portuguese *expected* (possibly on the strength of Columbus's recent suggestions) to find islands and *terra firma* to the West, and *prepared* an expedition [1] under Fernão Dulmo and João Affonso do Estreito, whom Martin Behaim was to accompany; while in 1473 João Vaz da Costa Cortereal was reported (by a now exploded legend) to have actually discovered Newfoundland.

But the character of these stories, or at least of the

[1] We do not know if this fleet ever sailed.

majority, is apparent enough ; no critical student can
pay much more attention to the general run of them
than to the Dieppese claims of French fourteenth-cen-
tury discoveries along the West Coast of Africa ; and
when we come to a definite instance the most certain
and most famous of pre-Columbian Portuguese
ventures into the far West does not inspire much
confidence in other accounts of similar attempts.
When Christopher Columbus proposed the Western
route to India at the Court of John II., he was at
first treated as an unpractical dreamer ; finally his
plan was formally considered, he was induced to
furnish his scheme in writing, and while the Council
pretended to be considering the memoir submitted to
them, a caravel was sent to the Cape Verde Islands,
all unknown to him, to try the route he had suggested.
The Portuguese sailed westwards for several days till
the weather became stormy ; then, as their hearts
were not in the venture, they put back to Europe
with various excuses. They had come to an im-
penetrable mist which had stopped their progress ;
apparitions had warned them back ; the sea, as they
went forward, became filled with monsters, and they
found it almost impossible to breathe. Columbus left
Lisbon soon after this, partly from his disgust at the
trickery that had been put upon him ; but King John
was still disposed to give him a fairer trial, and if the
Spanish monarchs had not come to the front in 1492,
it is possible that Columbus would still have discovered

America in the service of Portugal. It is likely
enough that many attempts were made in the fifteenth
century to discover lands in the far Atlantic, beyond
the Azores and Cape Verdes—by the Portuguese
as well as by the Bristol seamen of 1480 ; it is quite
possible that before 1486 the King of Portugal
really believed in the existence of lands beyond the
Ocean to the South-west, but we have no certain
evidence of actual discovery. Prince Henry and his
followers were for the most part devoted to the South-
east or African route, in their search for India ; all
who believed in the roundness of the world would
have admitted the existence of Western lands (*i.e.*
Asia) if only ships could sail far enough, and even
the less educated were often eager for a search after
the legendary islands of the Atlantic ; but as far
as our authorities can show us to-day, no one in
Columbus's own century anticipated him in his
achievement, or preceded John Cabot in his successful
imitation of Columbus.

CHAPTER III

THE Cabot family is certainly associated with the
commencement of Greater Britain under Henry VII.;
but the best-known name of this family, that of
Sebastian Cabot himself, has sometimes received more
honour than it deserved at the hands of Englishmen.
The difficulty of the subject is really this. Of John
Cabot, the true leader of the expedition of 1497, the
re-discoverer of North America five centuries after
the visits of the Northmen, we have only notices so
few and so fragmentary that they could all be printed
in a few paragraphs; while these notices are often so
obscure and uncertain that an immense amount of
controversy has already been spent upon the problems
they suggest, without any very certain solution of
several, at least, among the points at issue. On the
other hand, as to Sebastian, John Cabot's more famous

son, his career is clouded by suspicions of falsehood and intrigue ; and it is somewhat doubtful if he even accompanied his father in the voyages which he afterwards was supposed to have led. The best years of his life seem to have been spent in the service, not of England but of Spain ; and except for his connection with the North-east venture of 1553, his title as a " Builder of Greater Britain " is shadowy indeed. It will not be any part of this short biography to describe Sebastian Cabot's life in the Spanish service, nor is it possible here to enter minutely into many of the controverted points which gather round the English connections of his family. All we can do is to give as clear a view as possible of that new start of English maritime enterprise which is associated more or less intimately with the House of Cabot from 1497 to 1553.

Recent research seems to have shown pretty clearly that John Cabot was a Genoese by birth and a Venetian by adoption before he settled in England. On the 28th of March, 1476, the Venetian citizenship was conferred on him after proof that he had resided the 'fifteen continuous years' necessary for the enjoyment of this privilege. The Decree of the Senate ran as follows : ' That the privilege of citizenship within and without accrue to John Cabot in consequence of a residence of fifteen years, according to custom ; ' and all the 149 members of the body present on this occasion voted for the decree. The requirement in question dated

from the 11th of August, 1472, and the 'reign' of the
Doge Nicolao Trono ; and may be considered the
counterpart, as regarded aliens, of the privilege of 1313
securing full citizenship to all subjects of Venice born
in the city itself or within the limits of the Duchy
proper.   The exact text of this is of special importance as proving that *continuous* residence was required of
the candidate for citizenship during his fifteen years'
probation :—'Nicolao Trono by the grace of God,
Doge of Venice, &c.   To all and singular our friends.
. . . We wish to make known to you by the present
act that among the things we keep in mind is to
attend with particular care to the interest of our
subjects and faithful friends . . . [And] wishing to
reward merit according to its deserts, we have decided
to decree [as follows] : Whoever has inhabited Venice
for fifteen years or more, and during that time fulfilled
the duties and supported the charges of our Seigniory
as if he had been a citizen and [one of our own]
Venetians, shall enjoy perpetually and everywhere the
privilege of Venetian citizenship and other liberties
. . . enjoyed . . . by . . . other Venetians.'

'Now therefore,' proceeds the document, coming
to the first instance, 'as regards Aloysio Fontana,
formerly of Bergamo, now residing at Venice . . .
it having been represented to us upon true and reliable
proofs diligently examined by the magistrates of our
city, that he has inhabited Venice *continuously* during
fifteen years . . . fulfilling constantly the duties and

supporting the charges of our Seigniory . . . we . . . do admit the said Aloysio Fontana as Venetian and fellow citizen' (August 11, 1472).

As to the phrase 'within and without' (*De intra et extra*) accompanying these grants of citizenship, it may be noticed that the privilege *De extra* denoted the possession of Venetian trading rights in other countries, rights covered by the flag of St. Mark, under which the alien thus naturalised might always sail. To such a man as John Cabot, pretty certainly engaged in trade as well as exploration, the citizenship *De extra* was obviously important, and for that end he had, as required by the decree of Doge Nicolao Trono, 'fulfilled the duties and paid the charges' of the Government 'as if he had been a citizen and one of our own Venetians.' Before leaving this subject we may notice that, besides the Senatorial decree, we have another evidence of John Cabot's Venetian adoption (and so of his original membership of some other state). In the list of seventeen naturalisations occurring in the Republic's Book of Privileges and accompanying the decree of Doge Nicolao Trono, above quoted, the name of our navigator occurs in the thirteenth place with the clause 'The like privilege has been granted to John Caboto, under the above-mentioned Doge' [in 1476]. This list, hurriedly compiled, omits any mention of the original nationality of John Cabot, and implies that he was naturalised under the Doge Giovanni Mocenigo (the 'above-mentioned Doge' of the document in question) instead of under Andrea Vendramin, as the fact really was.

An attempt has been made to prove that Cabot, though not a native of Venice itself, was born in Chioggia, one of the most important of the Lagune Islands; but this only rests upon a memorandum of the later eighteenth century: 'Cabot, a Venetian, a native of Chioggia, discovered North America with English aid.' But by the decree of 1313, still in force throughout the fifteenth century, natives of Chioggia ranked as natives of Venice itself; and, if born there, Cabot would have had no need to apply to the Senate, or to reside fifteen years, to procure naturalisation.

The Genoese origin of our explorer is definitely asserted by several contemporary authorities and implied by others.

For instance, the Spanish Ambassadors in England, Ruy Gonçales de Puebla and Pedro de Ayala, writing home in 1496 and 1498, both refer to him as a Genoese. 'A man like Columbus,' said the former, 'has come to England to propose an undertaking of the same kind (as the enterprise of 1492) to the King of England;' 'the man who discovered the new lands in 1497,' added the latter, writing after the first Cabotian voyage, 'was another Genoese like Columbus.'

A vague inference to the same effect may be drawn from the story of Raimondo di Soncino (the Milanese Ambassador in England), that John Cabot discovering

two islands on his return journey, bestowed one of
them on a 'barber of his from Castiglione of Genoa.'
But as another companion of the navigator's, from
Burgundy, received a grant of the other island found
on this occasion, we cannot ground very much upon
this allusion to the barber.   A little more may, however,
be gathered from the English chronicles of the time.
In the continuation of Thomas Lanquet's *Epitome of
Chronicles*, published in 1559, and probably added by
Robert Crowley, there is a reference to 'Sebastian
Caboto, borne at Bristow, but a Genoway's sonne,'
and a similar statement may be read in Richard
Grafton's *Chronicle*, printed in 1569 ; in Holinshed's
Chronicle (1577), and in John Stow's *Annals* (1580).
Crowley and Grafton, at least, if not Holinshed also,
were living in London at the time of Sebastian Cabot's
second residence there (from 1547), and are likely to
have been tolerably well informed about this point—
at any rate their evidence, with that of Stow and
Holinshed, must be considered to have some corrobo-
rative force.   And the special point of Puebla's testimony is this : He was well acquainted with the
Genoese merchants then resident in England, so
much so that he was accused of receiving bribes
from them to secure their exemption from certain
fines imposed by the Government of Henry VII., and
a commission was sent over from Spain in 1498 to
investigate this charge. Ayala, again, who rather
avoided his Spanish colleague and especially consorted

with the Milanese Ambassador Soncino, must also have had considerable personal acquaintance with the Genoese of the English capital, Genoa then being held by Milan in fief of the French crown ; and at a time when Columbus's success was a subject of universal discussion, his thrice-repeated allusion to John Cabot as likewise of Genoese extraction is surely of great weight.

On the other hand, the letters patent of 1496, the map of 1544, supposed to have been drawn by Sebastian Cabot himself, a copy of which hung at Whitehall in Queen Elizabeth's day, and the manuscript chronicle in the Cottonian Collection from which both Stow and Hakluyt drew so largely, all agree in their reference to John Cabot as a Venetian.   But this is correct enough.   John was a naturalised citizen of Venice ; the Venetian evidence itself, above quoted, decisively proves that he was originally an alien ; and of all alien states or cities, Genoa has evidently the strongest claim.   In default of fresh and better proof favouring another birth-place, we may conclude that John Cabot was a native of Genoa.[1]

Before John Cabot settled in England, we have a few particulars about his movements, mostly transmitted to us by Ayala.   He is said to have visited Mecca as a (? pseudo-Moslem) trader, and to have applied to the Courts of Spain and Portugal for aid in schemes

[1] The claim of the Channel Islands to be the original home of the Cabots rests on nothing reliable.

of discovery ; he is also described as a maker of charts and *mappemondes*. When at Mecca, it is further stated, he was interested in knowing where the spice caravans obtained their supplies ; the answer pointed to lands so far in the East, that Cabot, who believed in the roundness of the earth, was disposed to think them not far from the West of Europe. Like Columbus, he seems to have imagined that the Western route across the Atlantic to Cathay and the Indies would be found shorter than any other ; and before the success of his Genoese fellow-citizen, he tried to win the patronage of Portugal or of Spain, for projects, which in a different way, by a more northern route, and after the discovery of 1492, he carried out under the English flag. These various journeys of our explorer may be fairly set down under the years 1476 to 1491— between his gain of the Venetian citizenship and his (probable) settlement in England. He was bound to reside in Venice from 1461 to 1476—at least for part of every year ; he appears as an English subject in 1496 ; he is described as inducing the Bristol mariners to undertake explorations of their own from 1491 ; these are all the data we have, and they leave us free to suppose that John Cabot was travelling in the Levant and the Spanish Peninsula at the time when Toscanelli was still alive and putting forth his suggestions as to the possibility of the Western route to India ; when Columbus was besieging the Spanish Courts with his applications ; and

when Diego Cam and Bartholomew Diaz were com-
pleting the discovery of the West Coast of Africa.
There is no reason to believe that Cabot had any
share in a very early and remarkable venture of English seamen Westwards—the expedition of 1480 ; but
that venture was inspired by the same ambitions which
stirred both Cabot and Columbus, Toscanelli and
Queen Isabella, and it may have been undertaken in
consequence of a suggestion either from Cabot, from
Columbus, or from some other Italian traveller or
theorist interested in the problem of Western discovery.

On June 15, 1480, according to William of
Worcester, a certain accomplished seaman, called by
the chronicler ' *Magister navis scientificus totius
Angliæ*,' sailed from Bristol with a ship of 80 tons,
equipped at the cost of John Jay, junior, to seek for
the fabulous islands of Brazil and of the Seven Cities ;
but the vessel was beaten about by heavy storms and
returned unsuccessfully on September 18th of the same
year. The ' Magister ' here named is not Cabot, as
some eminent authorities have supposed ; it is one
Thomas Lloyd, Llyde, or Thylde ; and this expedition may possibly be connected with the visit of
Columbus in 1477, when he profited by the practical
knowledge of Bristol seamen, and perhaps gave them in
return some portion of his spirit and some inspiration
to attempt Atlantic discovery.

But when Ayala writes in 1498, speaking of John
Cabot, ' It is seven years since those of Bristol used to

send out, every year, a fleet of two, three, or four caravels to go and search for the Isle of Brazil, and the Seven Cities, according to the fancy of this Genoese'—we are on ground closely touching the life of Cabot himself, and apparently supporting the conjecture that he had lately (say about 1490) settled in England, with his family, ' to follow the trade of merchandises,' and obtain help for his exploring projects. For it was the 'manner of the Venetians to leave no part of the world unsearched to obtain riches' : so Peter Martyr and the ' Mantuan gentleman ' (in Ramusio) learnt from Sebastian Cabot, the son of John.

Further though only conjectural data as to this English settlement of John Cabot's may be derived from Sebastian's statement to Gaspar Contarini, Venetian Ambassador in Spain, in 1522—viz., that he was born in Venice, but brought up in England ; from the information of the same person to the ' Mantuan gentleman,' that he (Sebastian) was rather young when brought to London, but had nevertheless 'some knowledge of letters of humanity and of the sphere ;' from the strong probability that when Henry VII. issued his first patent to the Cabots in March, 1496, Sebastian as a co-grantee with his father, must have been at least of legal age—twenty-one years old ; and from the fact that no earlier reference to an English residence of John Cabot himself can be found than the allusion of Ayala,

which only implies a settlement in or just before
1491.

He had already been (so much at least is probable)
'in Seville and in Lisbon, procuring to find those who
would help him in this enterprise,' as Ayala writes
in 1498 of events plausibly fixed as belonging to the
years 1476–90 rather than to the interval between
John's first and second voyages (1497-8) ; now he
was about to try his fortune with the monarch who
had so nearly secured the services of Columbus.

And here we must say a word about the condi-
tion of geographical theory and achievement, and
the consequent position of an adventurer like
Cabot at this time.   First of all, the ' known
world ' of the Middle Ages, though it had
lately been much extended to the East and South,
had made far slighter advance towards the West.
Yet here too, as we have seen, it had pushed out
a good way into the Atlantic.   The Azores, the
Cape Verdes, the Canary Islands, and the Madeira
Group had all been permanently discovered and
colonised in the course of the fifteenth century ; and
from the Azores in particular fresh expeditions were
being constantly planned Westwards in the latter
years of the same century.   The ultimate cause of
these, as of the Southern movement of Portuguese
exploration, down the West African coast, was no
doubt the conception of the wealth of the far East and
South of Asia, which our Latin world first adequately

realised, through the travels of Marco Polo and others in the thirteenth century. How best to get at the treasure houses of India and Cathay—this was the problem. The direct overland route from the Levant was barred by Moslem jealousy, and made especially dangerous at this time by the political convulsions of Central Asia ; two other ways remained open to those who could rise to the old and now revived beliefs in the rotundity of the earth, and in the insular shape of Africa. Dangerous and terrible as these long unknown tracks might prove, it was still possible (with these assumptions) that ships might sail round Africa to India by the South and East, or across the Western Ocean to Cathay, and the further Indies ' towards the sun rising.'

It is sufficiently well known what the Portuguese (led by Henry the Navigator of the house of Aviz, down to his death in 1460), had done in prosecuting the Southern or African route between 1420 and 1486, from the rediscovery of Madeira to the rounding of the Cape of Good Hope ; it is also well known how, as early as 1484, Columbus was urging the alternative of a Western route to the Indies upon the Court of Lisbon. And we have already given a sketch of the less known Portuguese ventures upon the Atlantic in the fifteenth century—ventures undertaken in the hope of finding lands beyond those West African islands already occupied.

Vague as these records may be, we can perceive

from the evidence quoted in our second chapter, that
the general fact of Portuguese enterprise Westward,
before Columbus, does not admit of doubt, even though
no certain results of the same can now be discerned ;
and both Columbus and Cabot may have known of
this movement, if they did not take part in it, before
the epoch of their great achievements.   The Bristol
merchants who sent out Thomas Lloyd in 1480, were
in pursuit of the same objects — objects which, as
we have already said, were in part suggested by
ancient tradition, in part were due to the recent
revival in physical and geographical interest, and in
commercial and political ambitions.   We should make
a great mistake if we did not connect the exploring
movements of the Europe of this time with every side
of that re-awakening both of internal and external
activity, which is sometimes limited to a period
beginning in the fourteenth century, but which really
starts in the mediæval Renaissance of the eleventh
and twelfth centuries.   Here, however, we must limit
ourselves to the geographical movement, and in this
we may distinguish certain of the elements that
inspired the new activity.   First, there was the old
and true belief (coming down from classical times) in
the roundness of the world.   By sailing far enough
westward from Europe, or the African islands, men
might hope to reach the Eastern Coast of Asia.   Under-
estimating, as did Columbus himself, the true girth of
the world, the hope in question was all the brighter.

Again, there were the ancient and mediæval traditions of land having been discovered far out in the Western Sea, by St. Brandan and others,—traditions which found a very prominent place in the maps of this and even of later time. Unfortunately, these supposed discoveries were, as we have seen, of the most fabulous character, many of the narratives being borrowed from Oriental travel romances, while others were simply religious myths in the style of apocalyptic literature.

On the other hand, as has been pointed out already, the one certain discovery of Western lands by the European race, that of Vinland by the Northmen, had now fallen into apparently complete oblivion ; and we cannot suppose that Cabot, for example, was inspired by a precedent so completely buried. But the ideas we have previously noticed, partly scientific and partly legendary, undoubtedly had their effect upon him as upon Columbus. Similarly, the one may have been moved, as the other was, by the thought that if the Portuguese ' could sail so far south in the discovery of new lands, it might be possible to sail west and find countries also in that direction.' In 1471 the caravels of Affonso V. of Portugal had crossed the equator ; in the first four years of his reign (1482–86) John II. had pushed on the course of exploration to the Cape of Good Hope. Just as in Ptolemy's day, so now, extension of the horizon in one direction led to a certain (if only a theoretical) extension in all.

Thus, the idea of Atlantic or Western enterprise was in the air, even in John Cabot's earlier lifetime ; the great Florentine astronomer Toscanelli had recommended it as early as 1474 ; the Portuguese had, so to say, nibbled at the scheme, perhaps a score of times, before Columbus sailed in 1492 ; the Bristol merchants had made a similar attempt at least as early as 1480 ; possibly Basque and Norman sailors had also made pre-Columbian essays in the same direction. It was a great and obvious line of exploring movement, this Western plunge across the Atlantic, and it was sure to have had a serious trial sooner or later. But it was the most daring of all possible ventures, and if Columbus had not found his path intercepted by the Bahamas, his first Western enterprise would have come to an abrupt end in mutiny and perhaps in death. So immense a voyage as that from Europe to Japan, across unbroken sea, might well have had to wait another century for its fulfilment.

Bearing in mind this widespread awakening in the direction of Atlantic exploration, we shall give up once and for all the futile and evasive inquiry as to who was the first of the fifteenth-century adventurers to start in the direction of the ' American Strand,' or, according to the ideas of that time, in the direction of the Eastern Coast of Asia. Columbus, we see, is but the foremost, the most persistent, and the first completely successful exponent of a movement, a tendency, and a hope, which actually included in its votaries a large number of scientific men, and was really based upon nothing less wide and general than the reawakening of the discovering instinct and of the belief in the roundness of the world. Just the same is true, of course, of John Cabot in a less degree ; and it is perfectly natural to grant the truth of the story, that as early as his visit to Mecca, he thought seriously of a western voyage to Cathay. He had asked, as we have said, where the spice caravans came from ; and pondering over the replies given him, it occurred to his mind that the extreme east of Asia was the very same as the land to the far west of Europe—always assuming (as he did) that the world was round.

But although the success of Columbus in 1492 did not suggest to Cabot the possibility of a venture which had probably occurred to most eminent navigators and scientists of that and of the past generation, as possible in theory if not in practice, yet the great achievement of his brother Genoese did probably suggest to him the policy of securing the patronage of the English Crown as speedily as possible for a similar undertaking. Perhaps he put his trust a little longer in those private enterprises of Bristol citizens westward, which he is said to have directed from 1491 ; but, in any case, he had come to a satisfactory agreement with the Crown early in 1496. On the 5th March of that year his petition was filed and granted. 'To the King our Sovereign Lord, please it your Highness of your most noble and abundant Grace to grant unto John Cabotto, citizen of Venice, Lewis, Sebastian, and Sancto his sons, your gracious Letters Patent under your Great Seal in due form to be made according to the tenor hereafter ensuing ; and they shall during their lives pray to God,' &c.

'The tenor hereafter ensuing' is thus expressed in the letters patent of King Henry VII. 'for the discovery of new and unknown lands' which are affixed to the petition of the Cabots :

'Henry by the grace of God, King of England and France and lord of Ireland, to all to whom these presents shall come greeting. Be it known that we have given and granted, and by these presents do give and grant for us and our heirs to our well-beloved John Cabot, citizen of Venice, to Lewis, Sebastian, and Sanctius, sons of the said John, and to the heirs of them and every one of them, and their deputies, full and free authority, leave, and power to sail to all parts, countries, and seas of the East, of the West, and of the North, under our banners and ensigns, with five ships of what burthen or quality soever they be, and as many mariners or men as they will have with them in the said ships, upon their own proper costs and charges, to seek out, discover, and find whatsoever isles, countries, regions, or provinces of the heathens and infidels whatsoever they be and in what part of the world soever they be, which before this time have been unknown to all

Christians ;—We have granted to them and also to
every of them, the heirs of them and every of them
and their deputies, and have given them licence to set
up our banners and ensigns in every village, town,
castle, island, or mainland by them newly found.
And that the aforesaid John and his sons, or their
heirs and assigns, may subdue, occupy, and possess all
such towns, cities, castles, and isles by them found,
which they can subdue, occupy, and possess as our
vassals and lieutenants, getting unto us the rule, title,
and jurisdiction of the same villages, towns, castles,
and firm land so found. Yet so that the aforesaid
John and his sons and heirs, and their deputies, be
holden and bounden of all the fruits, profits, gains, and
commodities growing of such navigation, for every
their voyage, as often as they shall arrive at our port
of Bristol (at the which port they shall be bound and
holden only to arrive), all manner of necessary costs
and charges by them made being deducted, to pay
unto us in wares or money the fifth part of the capital
gain so gotten ; we giving and granting unto them
and to their heirs and deputies, that they shall be free
from all paying of customs of all and singular such
merchandise as they shall bring with them from those
places so newly found. And, moreover, we have
given and granted unto them, their heirs, and deputies,
that all the firm lands, isles, villages, towns, castles,
and places, whatsoever they be that they shall chance
to find, may not of any other of our subjects be

frequented or visited without the licence of the said
John and his sons and their deputies, under pain of
forfeiture as well of their ships as of all and singular
goods of all them that shall presume to sail to those
places so found.   Willing and most straitly commanding all and singular our subjects as well on land as on
sea, to give good assistance to the aforesaid John and
his sons and deputies, and that as well in arming and
furnishing their ships or vessels as in provision of food
and in buying of victuals for their money, and all
other things by them to be provided necessary for the
said navigation, they do give them all their help and
favour.   In witness whereof we have caused to be
made these our letters patent.   Witness our self at
Westminster, the fifth day of March, in the eleventh
year of our reign [1496].'

In the same month in which John Cabot filed
his petition and obtained his patent, the first information is given us from outside bearing on his life
in England.   On March 28, 1496, the Spanish
sovereigns, Ferdinand and Isabella, reply to a letter
of their senior ambassador in England, Dr. Ruy
Gonçales de Puebla (a letter now lost, but acknowledged as of the 21st of January in the same year),
as follows : 'You write that a person like Columbus
has come to England for the purpose of persuading
the King to enter into an undertaking similar to
that of the Indies, without prejudice to Spain and
Portugal.   He is quite at liberty.   But we believe

that this undertaking was thrown in the way of the King of England by the King of France, with the premeditated intention of distracting him from his other business. Take care that the King of England be not deceived in this or in any other matter. The French will try as hard as they can to lead him into such undertakings, but they are very uncertain enterprises and must not be gone into at present. Besides, they cannot be executed without prejudice to us and to the King of Portugal.' Obviously not, if the claims of the Spanish nation over all new discovered and discoverable lands were to be understood in their widest acceptation, as stretching absolutely from pole to pole, and excluding all other peoples from any access to the Ocean or Oceanic countries west of a certain line. But in practice even Spanish arrogance failed to press this contention, and satisfied itself with asserting its monopoly to the trade and navigation of the regions actually discovered by explorers in the service of the King of Portugal or of the sovereigns of Castille and Aragon. Thus, with rare exceptions, a free hand was given to England, and a little later to France, in the North Atlantic and along the coasts of the present Canada and New England.

NOTE

Anspach, *History of Newfoundland*, 1819, p. 25, makes an important statement about John Cabot's early career in England as follows :—'The Venetians had factories . . . and agents wherever they deemed it advantageous. John Gabota, or Cabot, by birth a Venetian, was employed in that capacity at Bristol ; he had long resided in England ; and a successful negotiation in which he had been employed in 1495 with the Court of Denmark, respecting some interruptions which the merchants of Bristol had suffered in their trade to Iceland, had been the means of introducing him to Henry VII.' Anspach gives no authority for this ; but it is certainly true that in the reign of Edward IV. some Englishmen killed the Governor of Iceland in a brawl ; Christian I., of Denmark, then retaliated by seizing four English vessels, and complaining to Edward IV. ; the latter made no reply ; then Christian sold his prizes, and war resulted between England and Denmark, 1478–91. Cabot may have been employed by Bristol or London shipowners to help them in their recovery of claims against King Christian in this business.

CHAPTER IV

THE VOYAGE OF 1497—CONTROVERTED QUESTIONS—
THE SHARE OF SEBASTIAN — THE NUMBER OF
SHIPS—THE NAME OF THE FLAGSHIP—DESCRIP-
TIONS OF THE VOYAGE BY SONCINO AND
PASQUALIGO—CRITICISM OF THESE ACCOUNTS—
THE QUESTION OF THE LANDFALL

THE letters patent of Henry VII. to John Cabot
and his three sons were issued in March, 1496, but
our navigator does not seem to have started on his
enterprise (thus supported by Royal warrant) till
well on in the next year (1497). Extreme and
perplexing uncertainty hangs over nearly all the
details of this first Cabotian voyage.

First of all we have the question about the share
of John's sons in the actual undertaking. They
are associated with him in the petition and patent ;
did they also accompany him from Bristol to the
new isle ? In after years Sebastian claimed not
only to have gone on the expedition, but to have
commanded it in person, his father being already

dead, as he said to the 'Mantuan gentleman,' in
the famous interview reported by Ramusio : 'When
my father died in that time when news were brought
that Don Christopher Columbus the Genoese had
discovered the coasts of India, whereof was great talk
in all the Court of King Henry the Seventh. . . . I
thereupon caused the King to be advertised of my
device, who immediately commanded two caravels to
be furnished with all things. . . . Beginning therefore
to sail . . . after certain days I found, . . .' &c. Or,
as Ramusio expresses it in his paraphrase of Peter
Martyr d'Anghiera, Sebastian Cabot claimed to have
been 'taken by his father to England, where, after
the latter's death, finding himself extremely rich and
being of high courage, he resolved to discover some
new part of the world as Columbus had done, and
at his own expense equipped two ships.'   But beyond
his own assertions we have no proof that Sebastian, or
either of his brothers, even accompanied John Cabot
in 1497. Pasqualigo and Soncino, in their newsletters after John's return, speak only of the father,
and do not allude to any of his family as sharing in
his achievement ; the grant of Henry VII. from his
Privy Purse was 'to *him* that found the new isle' ;
and in his letters patent for the second voyage of
1498 the King describes the 'londe and isles of late
found' as the discovery of 'the said John Kabotto,
Venetian.' We shall have to deal with this question
somewhat more in detail in connection with the life

of Sebastian himself; here it is enough to say that no sufficient positive proof exists of his having accompanied the venture of 1497, though his companionship with his father is quite possible.

Another doubtful point in this first voyage is the number of ships employed. By the letters patent the Cabots could take five 'upon their own proper costs and charges'—five vessels 'of what burthen or quality . . . they be, and as many . . . men as they will have with them in the said ships.' On the other hand, Peter Martyr and the 'Mantuan gentleman' in Ramusio, copied by Gomara and Galvano, declare (apparently on the direct authority of Sebastian Cabot) that two ships and three hundred men were employed; while again two of John Cabot's Italian acquaintances in London, Lorenzo Pasqualigo and Raimondo di Soncino, report from the explorer's own testimony that he made his discovery with only 'one little ship of Bristol and eighteen men.' This, John must have asserted immediately after his return to London in August, 1497. The *Cottonian Chronicle*,[1] already referred to, and sometimes wrongly quoted as Fabyan's, perhaps offers us a means of reconciling these statements. After mentioning the flagship, it adds : 'with which ship by the King's grace so rigged went three or four more out of Bristol.' Here the difficulty lies in the question whether this detail refers

[1] Cronicon regum Angliæ : ab anno I^{mo}, Henrici III., ad annum I^{num}, Henrici VIII^{vi}. B. Mus. MSS., Cott. Vitellius, A xiv. f. 173.

to the first voyage of 1497 or the second of 1498 ;
all depends on whether the Chronicle's dating 'in
the thirteenth year of Henry VII.' is to be strictly
pressed. If so, the narrative in question belongs to
the time *between* August, 1497, and August, 1498,
or, in other words, to the second voyage ; but, in
the face of the vagueness of reference so constantly
found in English and other chronicles, it is just
possible that the entry here found may belong to the
first expedition, which had properly been brought to
a conclusion before the 'thirteenth year' commenced.

Another vexed question is the name of Cabot's
flagship. In Barrett's *History of Bristol* (1789),
and here alone, is to be found the source of the
famous *Matthew :* ' In the year 1497, the 24th of
June, on St. John's day, was Newfoundland found
by Bristol men in a ship called the *Matthew.*' We
do not know whence Barrett derived this statement,
but till good reason is shown for discrediting it we
may be content to accept the name in question.

Again, as to the dates of the start and the
return, and the duration of the voyage. ' The
beginning of summer,' ' the beginning of May,'
'the 2nd of May,' are all expressions more or less
disputed as referring to this event. Some of them
more probably relate to the second venture of 1498.
Greater certainty attaches to the statement of
Pasqualigo, written on the 23rd of August, 1497,
that John Cabot had lately returned to England

after a voyage lasting three months ; and to the parallel statement of Soncino on the 24th of August: 'They (the explorers) sailed from Bristol, a western port of this kingdom, a few months since.' Once more, a manuscript, said to be in the possession of the Fust family (of Gloucester), dates the departure from Bristol under the 2nd of May, and the return under August 6, 1497 — dates which, at any rate, square with the best evidence otherwise attainable, though they compel us to make some modifications in Cabot's own account of his achievements. Whatever else is doubtful, it is clear that he must have reappeared before the 10th of August, the date of the King's Privy Purse reward 'to him that found the new isle'; while, on the other hand, the contemporary authority, slight as it is, agrees in requiring the start to have been made in the spring or early summer of 1497.

The course of John Cabot's first voyage is clearly described by Soncino and Pasqualigo in those newsletters of theirs to the Duke of Milan and various members of the family of Pasqualigo in Venice, which, however unsatisfactory they may appear to some, are yet our chief authorities, as being absolutely contemporary, as being also coherent and reasonable in themselves, and as having been written to persons whom their correspondents had every reason to keep well informed in such a matter. Pasqualigo's letter to his father and brothers was

written on the 23rd of August ; Soncino's two
despatches to the Duke of Milan bear date of the
24th of August and the 18th of December re-
spectively. The former's facts and figures have been
called the 'gossip of a news-writer,' but it is gossip
which he had every inducement to make as accurate
as possible ; and Soncino's reports to his master are
in the course of serious diplomacy. Certainly the
combined testimony of these witnesses is beyond all
comparison more weighty than the secondary and
largely conflicting testimony of Peter Martyr, of
the 'Mantuan gentleman,' of the legends on
Sebastian Cabot's map, and so forth, which form our
subsidiary line of evidence.

John Cabot then, according to Soncino, first sailed
from Bristol to the West Coast of Ireland ; thence
he proceeded somewhat to the North, and afterwards due West,[1] keeping the North Star on his
right hand. Four hundred leagues from England
—seven hundred leagues according to Pasqualigo—
he struck the new land. He sailed along the coast
three hundred leagues (in the words of the latter
authority), along a country inhabited by natives
who used needles for making nets and snares for
catching game. On this shore the tides surprised
the explorers by their slightness. Soncino adds
that the climate was excellent and temperate ; the
land—'the Land of the Great Khan,' as it was

[1] " East " in original.

confidently styled—was supposed to abound in dye-
wood (Brazil) and silk ; and the sea swarmed with
fish.   On his return, Cabot sighted two large and
fertile islands on the starboard ; one of these (as
already noticed) he bestowed on his Genoese barber,
and the other on a companion from Burgundy.[1]
No inhabitants were seen in the new lands discovered ; but John Cabot himself, in a conversation
with Soncino, soon after his return, declared himself
abundantly satisfied with the produce of the waters,
stating that the sea was full of fish, which were taken
both with the net, and in baskets weighted with a
stone, and that, in a word, so much stock-fish could
be brought thence that England would have no further
need of its old commerce with Iceland.

And here, to get a better view of this enterprise, so
long misunderstood and so often confused with other
voyages, we will take the letters of Pasqualigo and
Soncino in their entirety and see what is the picture
they present.

First of all, on August 23, 1497, within a few days
of John Cabot's return Pasqualigo writes to his family
in Venice : ' The Venetian, our countryman, who went
with a ship from Bristol in quest of new islands, is
returned, and says that seven hundred leagues hence
he discovered land, the territory of the Grand Khan

[1] Mr. G. R. F. Prowse conjectures that this man was really an
Azorean (the Azores were the dowry of the Duchess of Burgundy),
' employed not because of any prior knowledge of Newfoundland, but
for his nautical skill.'

(Gran Cam). He coasted for three hundred leagues and landed ; he saw no human beings, but he has brought hither to the King certain snares which had been set to catch game, and a needle for making nets. He also found some felled trees. Wherefore he supposed there were inhabitants and returned to his ship in alarm. He was there three months on the voyage, and on his return he saw two islands to starboard, but would not land, time being precious, as he was short of provisions. He says that the tides are slack and do not flow as they do here. The King of England is much pleased with this intelligence.

'The King has promised that in the spring our countryman shall have ten ships, armed to his order, and at his request has conceded to him all the prisoners, except such as are confined for high treason, to man his fleet. The King has also given him money wherewith to amuse himself till then, and he is now at Bristol with his wife, who is also Venetian, and with his sons. His name is Zuan Cabot, and he is styled the great Admiral. Vast honour is paid to him ; he dresses in silk, and the English run after him like mad people. So that he can enlist as many of them as he pleases, and a number of our own rogues besides. The discoverer of these places planted on his new found land a large cross, with one flag of England and another of St. Mark, by reason of his being a Venetian, so that our banner has floated very far afield.'

Still more important are the two letters of Soncino

to the Duke of Milan, bearing on the same event. The former, written on August 24, 1497, one day only after Pasqualigo's news-sheet, just quoted, give us a bare allusion to the Cabot voyage of this year ; but the second dispatch, of December 18, contains the most satisfactory and complete account of Master John's great adventure that has come down to us.

'Some months ago,' remarks Soncino, casually, in his August letter (mainly concerned with general politics), 'his Majesty sent out a Venetian, who is a very good mariner and has good skill in discovering new islands, and he has returned safe and has found two very large and fertile new islands ; having likewise discovered the Seven Cities, four hundred leagues from England, on the Western passage. This next spring his Majesty means to send him out with fifteen or twenty ships.'

This is slender enough, but when the ambassador next touches on the subject for the Duke of Milan's guidance, he devotes the whole of a long epistle to its exposition :—

'Most illustrious and excellent my Lord, Perhaps among your Excellency's many occupations, you may not be displeased to learn how his Majesty here has won a part of Asia without a stroke of the sword. There is in this kingdom a Venetian fellow, Master John Cabot by name, of a fine mind, greatly skilled in navigation, who, seeing that those most serene kings, first he of Portugal, and then the one of Spain, have

occupied unknown islands, determined to make a
like acquisition for his Majesty aforesaid.   And
having obtained royal grants that he should have the
usufruct of all that he should discover, provided that the
ownership of the same is reserved to the Crown, with
a small ship and eighteen persons he committed himself
to fortune.   And having set out from Bristol, a
western port of this kingdom, and passed the western
limits of Hibernia, and then standing to the northward, he began to steer eastwards,[1] leaving, after a few
days, the North Star on his right hand.   *And having
wandered about considerably*, at last he fell in with
terra firma, where, having planted the royal banner
and taken possession in the behalf of this King, and
having taken several tokens, he has returned thence.
The said Master John, as being foreign-born and poor,
would not be believed, if his comrades, who are almost all
Englishmen and from Bristol, did not testify that what
he says is true.   This Master John has the description
of the world in a chart and also in a solid globe which
he has made, and he [or, it] shews where he landed,
and that going toward the East [again, for West], he
passed considerably beyond the country of the Tanais.
And they say that it is a very good and temperate
country, and they think that Brazil wood and silks
grow there ; and they affirm that that sea is covered
with fishes, which are caught not only with the net

[1] Or, as we should say, westward.   Soncino probably was thinking
simply of the goal, the Eastern Coast of Asia.

but with baskets, a stone being tied to them in order that the baskets may sink in the water. And this I heard the said Master John relate, and the aforesaid Englishmen, his comrades, say that they will bring so many fish, that this kingdom will no longer have need of Iceland, from which country there comes a very great store of fish called stock fish. But Master John has set his mind on something greater ; for he expects to go further on towards the East [again, for West] from that place already occupied, constantly hugging the shore, until he shall be over against [or, on the other side of] an island, by him called Cipango, situated in the equinoctial region, where he thinks all the spices of the world and also the precious stones originate. And he says that in former times he was at Mecca, whither spices are brought by caravans from distant countries, and that those who brought them, on being asked where the said spices grow, answered that they do not know, but that other caravans come to their homes with this merchandise from distant countries, and these [other caravans] again say that they are brought to them from other remote regions. And he argues thus—that if the Orientals affirmed to the Southerners that these things come from a distance from them, and so from hand to hand, presupposing the rotundity of the earth, it must be that the last ones get them at the North toward the West. And he said it in such a way, that having nothing to gain or lose by it, I too believe it : and, what is more, the

King here, who is wise and not lavish, likewise puts some faith in him : for since his return he has made good provision for him, as the same Master John tells me.   And it is said that in the spring his Majesty afore-named will fit out some ships and will besides give him all the convicts, and they will go to that country to make a colony, by means of which they hope to establish in London a greater storehouse of spices than there is in Alexandria ; and the chief men of the enterprise are of Bristol, great sailors, who now that they know where to go, say that it is not a voyage of more than fifteen days, nor do they ever have storms after they get away from Hibernia.   I have also talked with a Burgundian, a comrade of Master John's, who confirms everything, and wishes to return thither because the Admiral (for so Master John already entitles himself) has given him an island ; and he has given another one to a barber of his from Castiglione of Genoa, and both of them regard themselves as Counts, nor does my Lord the Admiral esteem himself anything less than a prince.   I think that with this expedition will go several poor Italian monks who have all been promised bishoprics.   And as I have become a friend of the Admiral's, if I wished to go thither, I should get an Archbishopric.   But I have thought that the benefices which your Excellency has in store for me are a surer thing. . . .'

In this account, though it does not present more difficulties than might be expected, barring one statement of Pasqualigo's, there are various problems which must be briefly noticed.

First, Soncino reports that the new land is supposed to yield dye-wood and silk, which is quite inconsistent with a discovery of North America ; but this is a difficulty of slight moment. For one thing, as Harrisse has conjectured, the 'dye-wood' may be sumach ; what is much more important, this is only a statement about *supposed* products, and innumerable mistakes of a similar character might be brought together from fifteenth and sixteenth century expeditions.[1]

Cabot's report about the slack tides of his new found coasts quite agrees with the facts, especially as regards the shore from Nova Scotia northward ; his notice of the abundance of fish again confirms in every way the truth of his general account, though it requires to be carefully handled in deciding the question of the landfall.

The two large islands seen on the return journey are probably either two parts of Newfoundland (in our present sense), or some piece of the mainland coast mistaken for an island, and one of the Newfoundland promontories. The snares and net-needles seen upon the shore may point to Esquimaux settlers along some part of the far North-east coast of the

---

[1] Dye-wood was at that time highly valued, and the ordinary view was that all new discovered lands ought to yield abundance of so excellent an article. Thus the wish was often father to the thought—and the assertion.

New World ; it is generally agreed that at the time
of the Norse voyages (five hundred years before)
Esquimaux were to be found as far south as Vinland
(Nova Scotia at least) ; but the reference is surely
vague enough to apply to American Indians of the
shore lands at almost any point.

But when Pasqualigo reports that Cabot, besides
his voyage out and home, coasted three hundred
leagues along the shore of the newly-discovered
country, he seems to be open to the suspicion of great
exaggeration.   True, this exaggeration falls far short
of that in the accounts of Peter Martyr and the
'Mantuan gentleman,' which (probably transferring in
great part to the first voyage the events of the
second) represent, from the evidence of Sebastian
Cabot, that the whole East coast of North America
was skirted by the explorers from a high northern
latitude to about Cape Hatteras if not to Florida
—but even Pasqualigo's statement must be modified.
Nor is there any reason why it should not be.
John Cabot himself may have spoken somewhat
too magniloquently of the scope of his achievements ; three hundred leagues is a very vague
figure ; and we are not disposed to attach any more
importance to it than this—that favoured by wind
and tide the expedition of 1497 did coast along a
considerable extent of shore—but limited always by
the consideration that the whole voyage was accomplished in three months or a little over.

To assume that the voyage really occupied a year and three months, in order to make room for the three hundred leagues of coasting ; to argue that Cabot really started in 1496, immediately after procuring his patent, and was absent from England till August, 1497—is surely gratuitous, and far beyond the necessities of the case, as well as opposed to the best and earliest evidence now obtainable. The fifteen months thus demanded would be as much in excess of the time required for the original description and the three hundred leagues aforesaid, as the 'three months' stated by Pasqualigo fall short of these same requirements. To us it appears that the start in spring or early summer, and the return in August of the same year, 1497, are inexorably required by our authorities ; and this leaves us to the conclusion that the statement about the three hundred leagues of coasting is the one point where we may fairly make a mental reservation.

On Pasqualigo's showing the three months' voyage of John Cabot would have nearly, if not quite, equalled in extent the first eight months' voyage of Columbus. For the sailing ships of that day, it passes belief that a Bristol navigator could reach the mainland of North America, coast nearly one thousand miles along a totally unknown shore (where he would have to contend with many strong currents, sudden winds, and outlying points of danger), and return to Somerset within ninety days, after a journey of about 5,500 miles.

In this question, something again depends upon the position of the landfall, the most eagerly disputed of all the disputed points of this narrative.

The landfall of 1497 (claimed for the year 1494) is placed on Sebastian Cabot's planisphere of 1544 at a point which seems to answer to Cape Breton. On another side, many have argued in favour of Cape Bonavista in Newfoundland, while M. Harrisse supports the old-fashioned opinion that it was at some point in Labrador, more probably between Hamilton Inlet and the Strait of Belle Isle.

We must discuss these claims in turn, beginning with the last, and we must not be surprised if considerable difficulties offer themselves in the way of any precise identification, and if we are thrown back at last upon rather general and uncertain conclusions.

1. Cape St. Louis and the various Labrador sites proposed are not supported, but the reverse, by Cabot's language to Soncino already quoted about the shoals of fish seen by him and his companions.

Master John reached—and left—the New World too early in the year for the 'living slime' of cod and salmon to have 'accumulated on the banks of Northern Labrador'—all his details on this point therefore support a more southern track and landfall.

On the other hand, if the sailing directions given us are to be implicitly trusted, it would need a good deal of southing for Cabot's course, after leaving

Ireland, to have touched the New World very much to the south of Labrador.

2. 'We may take it,' says Sir Clements Markham, 'that Cabot was forced northward (in the deflection mentioned by Soncino) by stress of weather, that he resumed his westerly course as soon as possible, and that he turned his ship's head west, in about the parallel of Blacksod Bay, and held that course across the Atlantic. After passing the meridian of the Azores, there would be westerly variation, and magnetic west would really be west-by-south-half-south. The landfall of the *Matthew* would, under these circumstances, be Cape Bonavista, on the East Coast of Newfoundland.' But granting, as already said, that the amount of southing necessary for this landfall is considerable—there seems no reason why this deflection should not have taken Cabot a little further to the south-west or a little further to the north. It is merely a question of the precise strength of deflection caused by magnetic variation and by current ; there is no definite contemporary authority for any Newfoundland site ; and our modern reconstructions of the navigator's exact course must remain probabilities at best.

What is to be said in favour of Cape Bonavista may equally well be said in favour of several other points close at hand. Is it not better to be content with the general certainty that John Cabot's landfall cannot be appreciably south of Cape Breton Island or appreciably north of the Strait of Belle Isle—at furthest it might be some such point as Hawke Bay on the South Labrador coast? When we are referred to the ' unbroken tradition ' of the Newfoundland colonists that Cabot made his landfall in their country, we can hardly accept this as very conclusive evidence. Leaving out of sight the long interval between the voyage of 1497 and the first permanent settlement of Newfoundland, we must remember that the whole of the fresh discovered lands in the North-West were at first known by the name which has now been handed down to the island we call Newfoundland.

3. The claim of Cape Breton is based upon contemporary authority, so far as we can apply this title to the planisphere of Sebastian Cabot, executed in 1544. But grave doubts attach to the identification. For one thing, Sebastian obviously had very distorted notions about this region ; he tells us there were abundance of white bears on Cape Breton Island (if it be really this which is indicated on his map as the ' Prima Tierra Vista ' ¹) ; he depicts Newfoundland as an archipelago of islets ; his place-names have a suspicious resemblance to those in various French cartographical works based upon the voyages 6f Jacques Cartier, especially the 1541 *mappemonde* of Nicolas Desliens of Dieppe. He also marks a San Juan island

¹ This inscription lies right across the mouth of the St. Lawrence, *beginning* at Cape Breton.

to the westward of the ' Prima Tierra,' which he says was discovered ' on the same day ' (*i.e.*, the Feast of St. John, June 24th), though the nearest actual land that corresponds to this indication lies in the Magdalen Islands, fifty-four miles from the northern point of Cape Breton Island.[1]

M. Harrisse accuses him roundly (1) of inventing the day of the landfall—June 24th—which he contends is equally false with the year of the discovery as stated in his map, viz., 1494 ; (2) of inventing the island of St. John and its name, to tally with the day, June 24th being the Feast of the Nativity of St. John the Baptist ; and (3) of inventing the landfall at Cape Breton in order to give the English Government (whose service he was in 1544 designing to enter, on his desertion of Spain) a claim to original discovery further south than was generally allowed at that time.   For nearly half a century Spanish carto-graphy, under his official superintendence, had placed the landfall of the English explorers several degrees further north than the Prima Vista of the map of 1544. We shall have to return to these points later on when attempting an account of the map in question ; here it will be enough to say that Cape Breton may be accepted as a southernmost point for the Cabotian landfall, as one limit of a line of coast, somewhere in which the adventurers of 1497 must have touched the New

[1] Prince Edward Island, with which ' San Juan ' has also been iden-tified, is still further from Cape Breton.

World—but no more.   The probability is strong against the explorers having been drifted close by Cape Race on their way to Cape Breton without seeing it—the time of year is against it, as regards winds, currents, and atmosphere.   The weather is likely to have been clear at midsummer and the seas setting pretty close into Cape Race, which itself is as likely a point for the Prima Vista as any other.

CHAPTER V

THE VOYAGE OF 1497 CONTINUED—LATER VERSIONS OF THE VOYAGE AS GIVEN BY — 1. PETER MARTYR ; 2. RAMUSIO ; 3. ZIEGLER ; 4. GOMARA ; 5. GALVANO ; 6. THEVET ; 7. RIBAUT ; 8. EDEN ; 9. THE MAP OF 1544

AND now, having tried to gain some idea of the first Cabotian Voyage of 1497 in the light of contemporary evidence, let us see what was the version (or rather the different versions) of this enterprise supplied by Sebastian Cabot in after years. Here we shall find a good deal of matter added to the somewhat meagre details of our first line of evidence, but it will not be always easy to accept the enlarged account of John Cabot's more famous son.

1. First we have the statement, made by Peter Martyr d'Anghiera some time before 1515–16 (when the first three decades of Martyr's history were published), and including the following passage, inserted in the course of a digression on the 'Secret Causes of Nature' :—

'These north seas have been searched by one Sebastian Cabot, a Venetian born, whom, being yet but in manner an infant, his parents carried with them into England, having occasion to resort thither for trade of merchandises, as is the manner of the Venetians to leave no part of the world unsearched to obtain riches. He therefore furnished two ships in England at his own charges; and, first, with 300 men, directed his course so far towards the North Pole that even in the month of July he found monstrous heaps of ice swimming in the sea, and in manner continual daylight. Yet saw he the land in that tract free from ice, which had been molten by [the] heat of the sun. Thus, seeing such heaps of ice before him, he was enforced to turn his sails and follow the west, so coasting still by the shore that he was thereby brought so far into the south, by reason of the land bending so much southward, that it was there almost equal in latitude with the sea called Fretum Herculeum [Straits of Gibraltar], having the North Pole elevate in manner in the same degree. He sailed likewise in this tract so far toward the west that he had the Island of Cuba [on] his left hand in manner in the same degree of longitude. As he travelled by the coasts of this great land (which he named Baccallaos[1]) he saith that he found the like course of the water towards the west [*i.e.*, as before described by Martyr], but the same to run more

---

[1] 'Cod-Fish Country.'

softly and gently than the swift waters which the Spaniards found in their navigation southward. . . . Sebastian Cabot himself named those lands Baccallaos, because that in the seas thereabout he found so great multitudes of certain big fish much like unto tunnies (which the inhabitants called Baccallaos) that they sometimes stayed his ships. He found also the people of those regions covered with beasts' skins, yet not without the use of reason. He saith also that there is great plenty of bears in those regions, which use to eat fish. For plunging themselves into the water where they perceive a multitude of those fish to lie, they fasten their claws in their scales, and so draw them to land and eat them. So that, as he saith, the bears being thus satisfied with fish, are not noisome to men. He declareth, further, that in many places of these regions he saw great plenty of laton among the inhabitants. Cabot is my very friend, whom I use familiarly, and delight to have him sometimes keep me company in mine own house. . . . Some of the Spaniards deny that Cabot was the first finder of the land of Baccallaos, and affirm that he went not so far westward.'

2. The second of these 'Sebastianised' accounts of the achievements of 1497 is from Ramusio, and is expressly given as the version of the 'great seaman' of Seville himself. It is introduced in a dialogue, where a 'famous' but unnamed man (whom the editor of Ramusio has styled the 'Mantuan gentleman,'

and who has been falsely identified by Eden with
Galeacius Butrigarius or Galeazzo Botrigari), addresses,
as follows, a company assembled at Caphi, near
Verona, in the villa of Hieronymo Frascator, Ramusio
himself being among the guests ;—

'And here [after various geographical speculations],
making a certain pause, turning himself towards us,
he said, " Do you not understand to this purpose how
to pass to India toward the north-west wind as did of
late a citizen of Venice, so valiant a man, and so well
practised in all things pertaining to navigations and
the science of Cosmography, that at this present he
hath not his like in Spain, in so much that for his
virtues he is preferred above all other pilots that sail
to the West Indies, who may not pass thither without
his license, and is therefore called Piloto Maggiore—
that is, the Grand Pilot ? " And when we said that
we knew him not, he proceeded, saying that, being
certain years in the city of Seville and desirous to
have some knowledge of the navigations of the
Spaniards, it was told him there was in the city a
valiant man, a Venetian born,[1] named Sebastian
Cabot, who had the charge of those things, being
an expert man in that science and one that could
make cards for the sea with his own hand.   And

[1] Here Eden, in his version of this passage, inserts a marginal note :
'Sebastian Cabot told me he was born in Bristol, and that at four years
old he was carried with his father to Venice, and so returned again into
England with his father after certain years ; whereby he was thought to
have been born in Venice.'

that by this report, seeking his acquaintance, he found him a very gentle person, who . . . showed him many things, and among other a large map of the world, with certain particular navigations as well of the Portugals as of the Spaniards. And that he spake further to him, in this effect : "When my father departed from Venice many years since to dwell in England to follow the trade of merchandises, he took me with him to the city of London while I was very young, yet having nevertheless some knowledge of letters of humanity, and of the sphere. *And when my father died, in that time when news were brought that Don Christopher Colombus the Genoese had discovered the coasts of India,* whereof was great talk in all the Court of King Henry the Seventh, who then reigned ; in so much that all men, with great admiration, affirmed it to be a thing more divine than human to sail by the West into the East, where spices grow, by a way that was never known before ; by which fame and report there increased in my heart a great flame of desire to attempt some notable thing. And understanding by reason of the sphere that if I should sail by the way of the north-west wind I should by a shorter track come to India, I thereupon caused the King to be advertised of my device, who immediately commanded two caravels to be furnished with all things appertaining to the voyage, which was, as far as I remember, *in the year 1496*, in the beginning of summer. Beginning therefore to sail toward

North-West, not thinking to find any other land than that of Cathay, and from thence to turn towards India, after certain days I found that the land ran toward the North, which was to me a great displeasure. Nevertheless, sailing along by the coast to see if I could find any gulf that turned, I found the land still continent to the 56th degree under our pole. And seeing that there the coast turned toward the East, despairing to find the passage, I turned back again and sailed down by the coast of that land toward the equinoctial (ever with intent to find the said passage to India), and came to that part of this firm land which is now called Florida ; where, my victuals failing, I departed from thence and returned into England, where I found great tumults among the people and preparation for the war to be carried into Scotland ; by reason whereof there was no more consideration had to this voyage. Whereupon I went into Spain to the Catholic King and Queen Elizabeth . . . " '

And along with this discourse we may group the well-known passage in the dedication to Ramusio's third volume, where, addressing himself to the same Hieronymus Frascator, at whose house the above-quoted narrative was given, the great compiler says that 'Sebastian Cabot [our countryman],[1] a Venetian,' wrote to him many years before,[2] telling him how he ' sailed along and beyond this land of New France, at

[1] Interpolated by Hakluyt.
[2] Viz., before the date of this dedication, June 20, 1553.

the charges of Henry VII., King of England ; ' how he proceeded a long time ' west-and-by-north ' to the latitude of ' 67½ degrees under the North Pole ; ' and how ' on the 11th of June, finding still the sea open, without any manner of impediment, he thought verily by that way to have passed on still the way to Cathaio which is in the East,' and would have done so, if the mutiny of the shipmasters and mariners had not hindered him and forced him to ' return homewards from that place.'[1]

3. Thirdly, Jacob Ziegler, in 1532, reproduces the narrative of Martyr, to the glorification of Sebastian, in the following shape : ' Sebastian Cabot, sailing from England continually towards the North, followed that course so far that he chanced upon great flakes of ice in the month of July ; and diverting from thence, he followed the coast by the shore, bending towards the South until he came to the clime of the island of Hispaniola, above Cuba—an island of the Cannibals.' He adds that Cabot's falling in with ice in the North proved ' that he sailed not by the main sea, but in places near unto the land, comprehending and embracing the sea in the form of a gulf ' ; and on this passage Eden, who translated Ziegler, has a piece of first-hand information to add—' Cabot told me that this ice is of fresh water, and not of the sea.'

4. Fourthly, Francis Lopez Gomara, who pro-

---

[1] This is apparently the source of Humphrey Gilbert's account in his ' Discourse of a Discovery of a new passage to Cataia.'

bably knew Sebastian Cabot at Seville during his
'Spanish period,' put on record this version of the
case in 1552 : 'Sebastian Cabot was the first that
brought any knowledge of this land [the Far North-
West or " Baccallaos "], for being in England in the
days of King Henry VII. he furnished two ships at his
own charges, or, as some say, at the King's, whom
he persuaded that a passage might be found to Cathay
by the North Sea. . . . He went also to know what
manner of land those Indies were to inhabit.   He
had with him three hundred men, and directed his
course by the track of *Iceland*, upon the Cape of
Labrador, at 58 degrees—*though he himself says much
more*—affirming that in the month of July there was
such cold and heaps of ice that he durst pass no
further ; that the days were very long, and in manner
without night, and the nights very clear.   Certain it
is that at 60 degrees the longest day is of 18 hours.
But considering the cold and the strangeness of the
unknown land, he turned his course from thence to
the West, [his men] refreshing themselves at Baccallaos [Newfoundland, &c.] ; and following the coast of
the land unto *the 38th degree*, he returned to England.'

5. Once more, Galvano, in his *Discoveries of the
World*, written some time before 1557, and giving
(at least in one detail) an apparent indication of some
personal converse with Sebastian, adds his own weighty
testimony to the revised version of the Cabot enterprises,
which on the Continent at least had quite superseded

F

the original : ' In the year 1496 there was a Venetian
in England called Sebastian Cabota [in his version
Hakluyt rightly alters the name to *John* Cabota],
who, having knowledge of such a new discovery as
this was [viz., Columbus's in 1492], and perceiving
by the globe that the islands before spoken of stood
almost in the same latitude with his country, and
much nearer to England than to Portugal, or to
Castille, he acquainted King Henry VII., then King
of England, with the same ; wherewith the said King
was greatly pleased, and furnished him out with two
ships and three hundred men, which departed and set
sail in the spring of the year, and they sailed westward
till they came in sight of land *in* 45 *degrees of latitude
towards the North*,[1] and then went straight northwards
till they came into 60 degrees of latitude, where the
day is 18 hours long and the night is very clear and
bright. There they found the air cold, and great
islands of ice, but no ground in 70, 80, 100 fathoms
sounding, but found much ice, which alarmed them ;
and so from thence putting about, finding the land to
turn eastwards, they trended along by it on the other
tack, discovering all the *river* and bay named Deseado
to see if it passed on the other side ; then they sailed
back again, diminishing the latitude, till they came to
38 degrees towards the Equinoctial line, and from

---

[1] This statement, which almost agrees with the landfall on the
' Cabot ' map, probably came either (1) from Sebastian himself, or (2)
from the *mappemonde* of 1544.

thence returned to England.   There be others which
say that he went as far as the Cape of Florida, which
standeth in 25 degrees.'

6. André Thevet, once again, in his *Singularités
de la France Antarctique*, published in 1558, joins
this chorus of historians with some curious additions
of his own.   From a writer of so slight a value and
so careless a pen these additions are doubly apocryphal,
but if nothing else they are picturesque.   Speaking
of the Cod Fish Land (Baccallaos) he declares : ' It was
first discovered by Sebastian *Babate, an Englishman,*
who persuaded Henry VII., King of England, that
he could easily come this way by the North to Cathay,
and that he would thus obtain spices and other articles
from the Indies equally as well as the King of
Portugal ; added to which he proposed to go to Peru
and America, to people the country with new inhabitants, and to establish there a new England, which
he did not accomplish.   *True it is he put three hundred
men ashore, somewhat to the north of Ireland, where the
cold destroyed nearly the whole company,* though it was
then the month of July. Afterwards Jacques Cartier, as
he himself told me, made two voyages to that country
in 1534 and 1535.'

Is it possible that Thevet, though in the main
apparently reproducing Gomara, with the alteration
of Iceland to Ireland, has preserved in his story of
Cabot's designs and of the three hundred colonists, some
real but elsewhere neglected fact of an early English

attempt at settlement—a fact noticed by Jacques
Cartier, and related to the chronicler ?—or is this, again,
a mere piece of additional gossip, originally set afloat
by Sebastian Cabot himself ?—or, once more, is it a
simple perversion of the old statement in Martyr,
that the crews taken from England numbered in all
three hundred ? For my own part I incline to the
last alternative, as there is nothing certain about this
tradition, except its extreme inconsistency with all
other records, agreeing only (with the secondary
historiographers) in the glorification of Sebastian Cabot.

7. To the same purpose Jean Ribaut (or Ribault),
another French annalist, who wrote at the same time as
Thevet, and whose *Florida* was translated into English
in 1563, refers to the first discovery of the North-West,
and the achievements of former navigators with the
customary word of adulation for the younger Cabot :
' A very famous stranger, named Sebastian Cabota, an
excellent pilot, sent thither by King Henry, the year
1498 . . . who never could attain to any habitation,
nor take possession there of one single foot of ground
nor yet approach or enter into these parts and fair rivers
into the which God hath brought us ' [the French].
Here Ribaut implicitly contradicts Thevet's ambitious
language about a new England and a temporary
colonisation, but the date given by him (1498) has
sometimes been considered as evidence of personal
intercourse between himself and Sebastian. Certainly
this is the earliest explicit reference to the year of

the second Cabotian voyage in sixteenth-century literature (as the date of the original enterprise), although
the same is implicit in the language of Peter Martyr
in his seventh decade, written in 1524, where he says
that Sebastian Cabot discovered the Baccallaos twenty-
six years before.

8. Lastly, Richard Eden, writing about *Florida
and the Baccallaos* in Queen Mary's reign, throws
in a word of his own which unquestionably is derived
from Sebastian himself, Eden's friend as much as
Martyr's : ' Of the which you may read somewhat
in this book in the voyage of that worthy old man
yet living, Sebastian Cabot, in the sixth book of the
third decade.[1]   But Cabot touched only in the north
corner and most barbarous part thereof, from whence
he was repulsed with ice in the month of July.'

Thus all the share of John Cabot in the discovery
of North America, his efforts to rouse the Bristol
seamen between 1491 and 1497, his application to
King Henry VII., his leadership in the initial enterprise of 1497, as well as in the second voyage of
1498, his very name (except as a Venetian trader)
was obliterated from the minds of sixteenth-century
students ; the two voyages, so plainly separated in
the original evidence, were confused in one ; and
Sebastian Cabot stood alone as the first leader of
English exploration to America, associated with vague
but magnificent plans of conquest and colonisation.

[1] Viz., of Eden's translation of Martyr already cited.

9. But in striking contrast to this unanimity of our annalists in falsehood, however unintentional, is the language of the Cabot map of 1544 on the same subject : 'This land [apparently Cape Breton] was discovered by John Cabot, a Venetian, and Sebastian Cabot, his son ; ' and this inscription seems to have been read to good purpose by Hakluyt in 1589, by Michael Lok in 1582, and by Chytraeus in 1565. We shall return to this evidence from maps in a succeeding chapter on the cartography of the Cabots and their voyages. But we may now at once compare a little more closely some typical examples of conflicting evidence in the historians we have quoted.

When examining these accounts we must remember that, before Sebastian enters the Spanish service in 1512, there is great difficulty in tracking his course and identifying or disconnecting him positively with the earlier ventures, associated by tradition with his name. But it is plain that here we have implied or expressed a series of statements which, from the strict contemporary and documentary evidence, we know to be false ; for we should gather from the words of the 'Mantuan gentleman,' of Peter Martyr, and of our other chroniclers, that there was but one original Cabot voyage of discovery under Henry VII., that John had no share in it, and that Sebastian himself, on this single venture (dated under 1496 in one narrative, under 1498 in another, and undated in the rest), discovered and explored the coast line of

Eastern North America from about 36 or even from 25 degrees to 65 (or 67½) degrees north. Further, the 'Mantuan gentleman' has evidently been led to believe that John Cabot was already dead when King Henry VII. authorised the aforesaid voyage of discovery, was dead, in fact, when the news of Columbus's success first reached England—viz., at the end of A.D. 1492. John's occupation, it is not obscurely suggested, was simply commerce—'to follow the trade of merchandises '—as for anything of discovering enterprise, that fell to his son. Once again, to the 'Mantuan gentleman,' Sebastian ascribes his departure from England, and his acceptance of the Spanish service to the 'great tumults among the people, and preparation for the war to be carried into Scotland ; ' while, on the other hand, to Martyr he gave as his reason the death of Henry VII., his patron. Yet not only do the excuses clash, but they are both false. The 'great tumults' and Scottish alarms refer to the year 1497, and the months of June and September; the death of Henry VII. belongs to A.D. 1509 ; and Sebastian was still in the employment of the English government on May 12, 1512.

Lastly (without making much of his loose statement that Ferdinand and Isabella sent him to explore Brazil, whereas he is first associated by name with any Spanish expedition in March, 1514, nine years after the death of Isabella), we see that Martyr was told by Sebastian the exact contrary of what the 'Mantuan gentleman' was informed as to his early life. The former repeats to us that young Cabot was born at Venice, but brought over to England as a child *(pæne infans)*; the latter, on the other hand, emphasises the point that when he came with his father to the country of his first adoption, he was already well forward with his education, 'having some knowledge of letters of humanity, and of the sphere.' While, to crown all, Richard Eden's marginal note, as we have seen, gives the lie to all the continental traditions of his birthplace ; 'Sebastian Cabot told me he was born in Bristol.'

So much for some of the difficulties explicitly contained in our 'Sebastianised' annalists. But what they suggest or involve is still more awkward than what they express. According to the more important of these narratives Sebastian found himself in the month of June (or July) in a region of perpetual day. 'This implies an exploration of Davis Straits to at least 65 degrees north.' He then 'turned his sails,' and coasted the east shore of North America to the parallel of the Straits of Gibraltar, or about 36 degrees north—according to some as far as Florida, or about 25 degrees north. 'In other words, he sailed from about 5 degrees west longitude to 80 degrees, and *vice versâ*,' from 65 degrees north latitude to a point at least 29 degrees to the south of this—round the whole of the North Atlantic, a voyage of more than 6,000 miles, in some three months—and, what is after all the chief point, in totally unknown waters and along a quite unexplored coast.

A word more as to the date apparently assigned for the landfall by Sebastian himself, in the map of 1544, 'in the year of our Saviour MCCCCXCIIII., on the 24th June in the morning.' Nearly all critics now agree in rejecting the year (of 1494) thus given, which is at variance with all the first-hand evidence, and is possibly due to a slip of the pen (IIII. for VII.) if it be not an attempt to increase the family reputation by a new claim, after the lapse of fifty years, when memories had grown dim.

From Puebla's letter of January 21, 1496, giving us our first information about the person 'like Columbus,' who was courting the favour of Henry VII. for similar explorations, down to the letter of Soncino on December 18, 1497, to the Duke of Milan, we have a perfectly clear and consistent series of proofs for the voyage of 1497, begun and ended in the same year, and led by John Cabot himself and by no other—his first great achievement. But some doubt has also been attached to the month (and day) of June asserted above. For one thing John Cabot had certainly returned to London by August the 10th, when he received the King's first reward of £10. Again, Pasqualigo heard that the navigator coasted three hundred leagues along the shore after making land. We have already pointed out that this particular estimate appears to be greatly exaggerated, but some time must be allowed during which the explorers hung off the North American coast, and the narrowest estimate which can be given for this interval would still oblige us to fix the day of 'turning back' as at least not earlier than July 1st —leaving us only about five weeks for the return. This is a possible margin, but the time seems short. It is hypercritical, however, to make a serious difficulty of this ; and if there be one point on which Sebastian Cabot would hardly be misled, on which he would have no particular motive for misleading us, and where his statement might fairly be accepted till positive disproof is forthcoming, it is the day (though not the year) of his father's discovery of North America.

No great confidence can be expressed in the tradition of the lost manuscript once in the possession of the Fust family of Hill 'Court, Gloucestershire, so confidently quoted in the *Encyclopædia Britannica* of 1876. Its details are gratifying in their precision, but the use of the term 'America' shows that at any rate it is not a strictly contemporary document. As to the rest, the particulars given are probable enough, agree with our first-class evidence already quoted, and may embody a genuine local (Bristol) tradition as to the name of the ship and the dates of the start and return :—' This year (1497) on St. John the Baptist's day [June 24] the land of *America* was found by the merchants of Bristol in a ship of Bristol called the *Matthew*, the which said ship departed from the port of Bristol the 2nd of May and came home again the 6th August following.' Thus, for what it is worth, the Fust MS. gives a confirmation of the month and day assigned on the Cabot Map, and with this we will close 'Sebastian's case,' only adding that he never gave the true year (1497) as it is fixed by the Bristol document,[1] but sometimes 1494, sometimes 1496, sometimes apparently 1498, and sometimes suggested an even earlier date than any of these.

[1] As well as by Hakluyt in the final edition of his *Principal Navigations*, and by Clement Adams in the English (1549) re-issue of the 'Cabot' map.

CHAPTER VI

JOHN CABOT'S SECOND VOYAGE—REWARD AND PEN-
SION FROM HENRY VII.—THE SECOND LETTERS
PATENT—VARIOUS ALLUSIONS TO THE VENTURE
OF 1498—EVIDENCE OF LA COSA'S MAP OF
1500—ABSENCE OF ENGLISH NARRATIVES

JOHN CABOT applied for fresh letters patent authorising
a second expedition on the 3rd of February, 1498. In
the interval between this and his return from the
first voyage of 1497 he had received [1] from Henry VII.'s
Privy Purse the famous grant of £10 (at least £120 in
modern money) ' to *him* that found the new isle '—
in order that he might have a good time with it, as
Pasqualigo writes to Italy. On the 13th of December
in the same year the King further bestowed on him
a pension of £20 a year (fully £240 in modern
value) during the pleasure of the Crown. The order
was addressed to Cardinal Morton as Chancellor and
was sealed on the 28th of January, 1498, as follows :—

' Henry by the grace of God King of England,

---

[1] On August 10, 1497.

etc. To the most reverent father in God John, Cardinal Archbishop of Canterbury, Primate of all England, and of the Apostolic See Legate, our Chancellor, greeting. We let you wit that we, for certain considerations us specially moving, have given and granted unto our well-beloved John *Calbot* of the parts of Venice an annuity or annual rent of £20 sterling, to be had and yearly perceived from the Feast of the Annunciation of our Lady last past, during our pleasure, of our customs and subsidies coming and growing [*i.e.*, accruing] in our port of Bristol by the hands of our customs there for the time being, at Michaelmas and Easter, by even portions. Wherefore we will and charge you that under our Great Seal ye do make hereupon our Letters patent in good and effectual form. Given under our Privy Seal, at our Palace of Westminster, the 13th day of December, the 13th year of our Reign.'

In the same connection follows the warrant of the 22nd of February, 1498, for the immediate payment of this pension. John Cabot, it appears, had been unable to obtain the money due to him, because the customs officers of the port of Bristol raised formal difficulties. As the Issue-Warrant recites :—

' Henry by the grace of God King of England, etc. To the Treasurer and Chamberlains of our Exchequer greeting. Whereas we by our warrant under our signet for certain considerations have given and granted unto John Cabot £20 yearly during our pleasure to be had and paid by the hands of our Customers in our port of Bristol, and as we be informed the said John Cabot is delayed of his payment, because the said Customers have no sufficient matter of discharge for their indemnity to be holden at their account before the Barons of the Exchequer,— Wherefore we will and charge you that ye our said Treasurer and Chamberlains, that now be and hereafter shall be, until such times as ye shall have from us otherwise in commandment do to be levied in due form two several tailles, every of them containing £10, upon the Customers of the Revenues in our said port of Bristol, at two usual terms of the year, whereof one taille to be levied as this time containing £10 of the revenues of our said Port upon Richard Meryk and Arthur Kemys late Customers of the same, and the same taille or tailles in due and sufficient form levied ye deliver unto the said John Cabot, to be had of our gift by way of reward, without prest or any other charge to be set upon him or any of them for the same. . . . Given under our Privy Seal at our Manor of Shene the 22nd day of February the 13th year of our reign.'

Thus the delay is remedied, the first payment is made sometime after Easter, 1498, and as late as the summer of 1499 we find John Cabot, on his return from his second voyage, drawing this pension— according to evidence recently brought to light from the Muniments of the Chapter of Westminster. And

before we leave this matter of the pension we may
notice that in these documents just quoted, as in the
second Letter Patent, of February, 1498, there is no
mention of Sebastian nor of any other son or associate
of John Cabot.   All the credit and reward for the
achievements of 1497 are assigned to John, and to
him alone.

The patent for the second voyage authorised John
Cabot, this time unassociated with any co-grantees,
to proceed with six ships at his own cost and under
his own single leadership ; and in the same way
Puebla, Ayala, and Soncino imply that he was entrusted by the King with the sole responsibility of the
second as of the first expedition.   Even the application or petition now bears no other name but that of
the head of the house.   ' Please it your Highness to
grant unto John Kabotto, Venetian, your gracious
letters patents in due form . . . according to the
tenor hereafter ensuing.'

And in exactly the same terms runs the new commission : ' To all men to whom these presents shall
come greeting.   Know ye that we, of our grace
especial, and for divers causes us moving, have given
and granted and by these presents give and grant
to our well-beloved John Kabotto, Venetian, sufficient
authority and power that he by his deputy or deputies
sufficient may take at his pleasure six English ships
in any port or ports or other place within this our
Realm of England or obeisant to that, and if the said

ships be of the burthen of 200 tuns or under, with
their apparel requisite and necessary for the safe conduct of the said ships, and them convey and lead *to
the land and isles of late found by the said John in our
name and by our commandment*, paying for them and
every of them as and if we should in or for our own
cause pay and none otherwise.

'And that the said John by him his deputy or
deputies sufficient may take and receive into the said
ships and every of them all such masters, mariners,
pages, and our subjects, as of their own free will will
go and pass with him in the same ships to the said
Land or Isles without any impediment, let, or per-
turbance of any of our officers, or ministers, or subjects, whatsoever they be, by them to the said subjects
or any of them passing with the said John in the said
ships to the said land or isles to be done or suffered to
be done or attempted. Giving in commandment to
all and every our officers, ministers, and subjects, seeing
and hearing these our letters patent, without any
further commandment by us to them or any of them
to be given, to perform and succour the said John, his
deputy, and all our said subjects to-passing with him
according to the tenor of these our letters patent.
Any statute act or ordinance to the contrary made or
to be made in any wise notwithstanding.'

As already noticed, Sebastian Cabot is not named
in these new patents, nor in any official records
following on the first petition and commission of

March, 1497. But the question of his practical association with his father on either or both of these voyages is another matter, and has been usually argued on the exact reverse of the evidence supplied by the two Letters Patent. From these, and these alone, it would seem more probable that Sebastian went on the first voyage and not on the second—simply because contemporary documents name him in connection with the first and not with the second.

But the accounts of the chroniclers, from Peter Martyr downwards, have usually appeared to fit in better with the second voyage of 1498 than with the first of 1497 ; these accounts were presumably derived from Sebastian Cabot, and, with certain details excepted, look as if they had their source in the evidence of an eye-witness. Again, till recent discoveries showed that John Cabot was alive in 1499, it has been often conjectured that he may have perished in the course of his second expedition, and that his fleet was brought home by his son. And by one of the chroniclers above cited, the date of 1498 is specifically given for Sebastian's great discoveries in the North-West, while no authority whatever, documentary or other, has ever stated or implied (beyond doubt) that Sebastian sailed with his father in 1497. It is probable nevertheless from the petition and authorisation of March, 1496, that not only Sebastian, but also Lewis and Sanctius, accompanied John Cabot in his first enterprise, and there is no ground for supposing that the case was different in the succeeding venture. We have no proof either way, but it must be admitted that the likelihood exists, of this family participation. The mere absence of demonstrative evidence in this detail cannot warrant anything in the way of categorical denial. We shall meet this question again, when we find the English Livery Companies refusing to accept Sebastian Cabot as a leader to the North-West, because he had never been there himself 'albeit he doth make report as he hath heard his father and other speak in time past.'

It is perhaps after all not so much to the venture of 1497 as to the larger enterprise of 1498 that we must refer the entry in the *Cottonian Chronicle* quoted above,[1] which is in all probability the source of the statements in Stow and Hakluyt professedly derived from Robert Fabyan. This genuine contemporary record—a "Chronicle of the Kings of England from the 1st year of Henry III. to the 1st of Henry VIII."—gives the date of 1497 (the 13th year of Henry VII.) to a narrative which other evidence identifies as the story of the second Cabot voyage of 1498. 'This year the King at the busy request and supplication of a Stranger Venetian, which by a chart made himself expert in knowing of the world caused to man a ship with victual and other necessaries for

[1] As a possible solution of the difficulty as to the number of ships engaged in the venture of 1497.

to seek an island wherein the said stranger surmised
to be great commodities ; with which ship by the
King's grace so rigged went three or four more out
of Bristol, the said Stranger being conditor of the said
Fleet, wherein divers merchants as well of London as
Bristol adventured goods and slight merchandises.
Which departed from the West Country in the
beginning of summer, but to this present month came
never knowledge of their exploit.'

The account attributed to Robert Fabyan by Stow
is almost precisely similar. ' 14 Henry VII. This
year one *Sebastian* Gabato, a Genoa's son born in
Bristol, professing himself to be expert in knowledge
of the circuit of the world and islands of the same, as
by his charts and other reasonable demonstrations he
showed, caused the King to man and victual a ship at
Bristol to search for an island which he knew to be
replenished with rich commodities ; in the ship divers
merchants of London adventured small stocks ; and in
the company of this ship sailed also out of Bristol three
or four small ships fraught with slight and gross wares,
as coarse cloth, caps, laces, points, and such other.'

' And so departed from Bristol in the beginning of
May,' adds Hakluyt, ' of whom in this Mayor's time
returned no tidings——' the Mayor in question being
William Purchas, Lord Mayor of London, whose
mayoralty expired on the 28th of October, 1498, and
the mention of whom thus fixes the meaning of the
phrase in the *Cottonian Chronicle* ' this present month.'

Once more, Pasqualigo and Soncino, Puebla and Ayala, add some details of their own to our knowledge of the second as of the first Cabotian enterprise. The King of England, says the first, on this occasion promised to equip for John Cabot no fewer than ten ships, granting the ' Great Admiral,' moreover, the use of as many prisoners as he needed for his crews, those only excepted who were lying under charge of high treason. Soncino makes the number of ships mount to twenty ; while, as we have seen, the letters patent name six, and Puebla and Ayala in their Spanish correspondence, speak of five.

Almost the only additional information, of a contemporary and first-hand character, which we have about the expedition of 1498, comes also from the letters of the last-named ambassadors. ' The King of England,' says Puebla, in an undated communication to the Spanish Court, probably written about the 20–25th July, ' has sent out five armed ships with another Genoese like Columbus to seek for the isle of Brazil and those adjoining to it, and has equipped these ships for a year. They say that they will return about September. By the route which they are going to take, it is evident they seek the same lands that your Highnesses possess. The King has spoken to me several times about it, and he seems to take very great interest in the same. I believe that what they seek is about four hundred leagues distant.'' To the same effect, but more definitely, Ayala writes on July 25th to the 'Catholic Kings' : 'I think your Majesties have already heard that the King of England has equipped a fleet in order to discover certain islands and continents which he was informed some people from Bristol, who manned a few ships for the same purpose last year, had found.   I have seen the map which the discoverer has made, who is another Genoese, like Columbus, and who has been in Seville and Lisbon, asking assistance for his discoveries.   The people of Bristol have, for the last seven years, sent out every year two, three, or four light ships (caravels) in search of the island of Brazil and the Seven Cities, according to the fancy of this Genoese.   The King determined to send out (ships) because the year before [1497] they brought certain news that they had found land. His fleet consisted of five vessels, which carried provisions for one year.   It is said that one of them, in which one Friar Buil [1] went, has returned to Ireland in great distress, the ship being much damaged. The Genoese has continued his voyage.   I have seen, on a chart, the direction which they took, and the distance they sailed, and I think that what they have found or what they are in search of, is what

[1] Probably a corruption of an English name, not Fray Bernardo Buyl, sent with Columbus on his second voyage by commission from the Pope, as has been suggested.   Ruysch, the famous cartographer, who was an ecclesiastic, is supposed on some fairly plausible evidence to have sailed with John Cabot on his second voyage, and it has been suggested, without much probability, that the ' Buil ' here named may be ' Ruysch ' in a corrupted form.

your Highnesses already possess, because it is next
to that which your Majesties have secured by the
convention with Portugal. [Treaty of Tordesillas.]
It is expected that they will be back in the month
of September. I write this because the King of
England has often spoken to me on this subject,
and he thinks that your Highnesses will take great
interest in it. I think it is not further distant
than four hundred leagues. I told him that in my
opinion, the land was already in the possession of
your Majesties; but though I gave him my reasons, he
did not like them. I believe that your Highnesses are
already informed of this matter; and I do not now
send the chart or mappa mundi which that man [John
Cabot] has made, and which, according to my opinion,
is false, since it makes it appear as if the land in
question was not the said islands' [*i.e.*, those possessed
by Spain].

These letters are the main sources of our reliable
information on this enterprise; but it is in the highest
degree probable that King Henry VII.'s grants to
various adventurers at this time are in connection with
the Cabot fleet of 1498. Thus on March 22 (1498),
he lends £20 to Launcelot Thirkill 'for his ship going
towards the new land;' and on April 1st of the same
year £30 to Launcelot Thirkill and Thomas Bradley,
and 40 shillings to John Carter, 'going to the new
isle.' We may notice that there is a certain conflict
of authority about the expenses of the undertaking.

The letters patent imply that the King lent six ships, and that Cabot paid for their maintenance, repair, victual, and so forth, during the voyage ; the *Cottonian Chronicle*, on the other hand, suggests that one ship was both provided and equipped by the King, and that three or four others were provided by merchants of London and Bristol ; the loans above cited would seem to prove that the King advanced considerable aid to others besides Cabot on this venture :—nearly £650 in modern money is lent by him to Thirkill, Bradley, and Carter.

Lastly, we have from Soncino, in the already cited letter of December 18, 1497, to the Duke of Milan, an allusion of some interest. Before starting on his new attempt ' Master John ' told the Milanese Ambassador that his purpose was from the place already occupied to proceed by constantly following the shore till he reached the East and was opposite Cipango [Japan] situated in the equinoctial region. On his previous voyage, as Pasqualigo learnt, he supposed that he had reached the land of the 'Great Khan' [China]. Here ends all our really contemporary evidence about this second voyage. We do not know where John Cabot went (except for the statement of his intentions just quoted), or when he returned (except that from the Hakluyt entry transcribed above, it would seem to have been *after* October 28, 1498). Till lately we did not even know whether he ever returned at all. The recent discoveries in the Westminster Chapter

muniments show us that he did return, and was drawing his pension far on in the next year, 1499; the map
of Juan [1] de la Cosa (A.D. 1500) points to an extensive coasting of the North American (or as La Cosa
probably considered it, the Asiatic) mainland, such as
Sebastian Cabot and others repeatedly and misleadingly
referred to the time of the first voyage. It was probably now, and not earlier, that Cabot ' directed his
course so far towards the North Pole that even in the
month of July he found monstrous heaps of ice swimming on the sea, and in manner continual daylight';
it was now probably that he was ' brought so far into
the South,' that 'it was there almost equal in latitude
with the sea called Fretum Herculeum '; it was now
probably that ' in the latitude of $67\frac{1}{2}$ degrees under the
North Pole, on the 11th of June finding still the sea
open without any manner of impediment, he thought
verily by that way to have passed on ... to Cathaio which
is in the East '; it is to this year, 1498, that we must
refer the still more advanced and more doubtful claim
of having navigated as far South as Florida. Once
more, it was probably now, if ever, that Cabot entered
Hudson's Bay (as he did according to one tradition),
and ' gave English names to sundry places therein.'

---

[1] La Cosa's NW. land S. of the English flags is probably meant for
Asia, just as in Ruysch's Atlas of 1508 the Terra Nova is depicted as a
little piece of land joined on to Asia in about the position of our Corea.
It has also been argued that La Cosa's Map, in this quarter, only shows
the Southern coast of Labrador and not the mainland of North America
to the South of the St. Lawrence.

The famous map of Juan de la Cosa already mentioned (the only contemporary plan which bears closely upon these Cabotian voyages, and the first known design which contains any part of the New World), was executed in 1500, between April and October in that year. It was the work of a Biscayan, the most eminent and skilful of Spanish pilots in this age ; and its 'North-West' coast was probably based in part upon Cabot's chart of the first voyage, supposed to have been sent to Spain some time at least before July, 1498. It is not necessary to confine its information to these earlier data ; in all likelihood La Cosa had before him in 1500 equally full evidence of Cabot's explorations on his second voyage of 1498. On this map we have, west of Cuba, a continental coast line which stretches north to the end of the sheet, adorned with a row of English flags. At the southern end of these flags is the legend 'Sea[1] discovered by the English' ; at the northern is the answering inscription, 'Cape of England.' Between these are twenty inscriptions, presumably derived from Cabot's discoveries. But very little can be gathered from them. They run as follows : 1. Mar descubierta por Ingleses (4th and 5th flags). 2. Cabo descubierto. 3. C. de S. Jorge. 4. Lago fori. 5. Anfro (3rd flag). 6. C. Lucia. 7. S. Lucia. 8. Requilia. 9. Lus-quei.

---

[1] By some this has been conjectured to refer to Verrazano's inland sea, viz., either the Northern Pacific or the Gulf of St. Lawrence, then unnamed.

10. De Lisarte. 11. Meniste. 12. Argare. 13.
Forte. 14. Ro longo. 15. Isla de la Trinidad (2nd
flag). 16. Cabo de S. Juan. 17. S. Nicolas. 18.
Agron. 19. C. Sastanatre. 20. Cabo de Ynglaterra
(1st flag). 21. S. Grigor. 22. I. Verde.

Among these names we notice that one is applied to
a sea, ten to bays or inlets of that sea, eight to capes or
headlands, one to a river, one to a lake, three to islands
—while five saints are indicated in the nomenclature.
The coast depicted seems clearly to indicate, however
much distorted in general direction, a part of the
North American mainland, and not merely as some
have suggested, the south coast of the island of Newfoundland. Correcting the error of inclination, and
assuming a coastline (from the Central American mainland near Cuba) with a main course to the north instead
of the east, most students of this map would probably
conclude that the coast marked by the English flags
represented the eastern shore of the United States
and of Canada from about Cape Hatteras to Cape
Breton or Cape Race. But when we come to examine the names themselves, and endeavour to gain
greater precision from them, we are met with considerable difficulties. Most of them convey no meaning even
to the most laborious students of contemporary cartography, and are found on no other map known to us.
All the identifications with various points on the South
Coast of Newfoundland, proposed by some critics, fall
to the ground in the face of the general impossibility

of scale. The extent of land marked by the English flags is so immeasurably too vast for such limitation that one feels it hopeless to convince the plain man of the correspondence, not merely between Cabo de Ynglaterra and Cape Race, which is possible enough, but also between Isla de la Trinidad and Burin Peninsula, Cabo de S. Jorge and Cape Ray, Cabo descubierto and Cape Breton; still less can we hope to persuade him that the 'deep bay' between the latter indicates the channel between Cape Breton Island and Newfoundland. As pointed out before, it is quite unnecessary to limit La Cosa's data for this coast to those supplied by the *first* voyage of 1497 ; there was abundance of time and opportunity for him to gain full information about the achievements of the second voyage, whose mainland coasting 'to about the latitude of the Straits of Gibraltar,' is in all probability here depicted, though with such strange distortion of general direction.[1]

The names of saints to be found in this part of La Cosa's map might have been expected to afford us some assistance, as it was common enough to name a new-found point, river, inlet, or island, after the saint on whose day it was discovered. But both the voyages of 1497 and 1498 seem to have been accomplished between the beginning of May and the end of November at furthest ; while of the saints here

[1] A distortion partly due no doubt to the 'Asiatic' preconceptions of the draughtsman.

named—St. Gregory, St. Nicholas, St. Lucia, St. George and St. John—the days of St. Nicholas and St. Lucia fall on December 6th and December 13th, that of St. George on April 23rd, that of St. Gregory on March 12th ; the Nativity of St. John the Baptist, June 24th, is, as we have heard already, the day claimed for the Prima Vista. Thus only one of these names gives us any help towards fixing the day of a discovery ; for only one falls within the time fixed by our authorities (and, in the case of the second expedition, by reasonable probability) as that of Cabot's first or second voyage.

It is possible, as Sir Clements Markham has suggested, that the two islands of ' S. Grigor ' and ' I. Verde,' placed to the extreme end of the La Cosa map, beyond the Cabo de Ynglaterra, may represent the present isles of Miquelon and St. Pierre, and correspond to those which Cabot bestowed on his barber-surgeon and his Burgundian (or Azorean ?) companion ; but if so, of course they are wrongly placed, and with the readjustment of direction already proposed it would be more natural to imagine them to be two parts of Newfoundland, which, as the map of 1544 shows us, was only misconceived as a number of islets instead of one large island.

John Cabot then, we may suppose, started on his second voyage in the beginning of May, 1498, attempted to penetrate to Asia by the North-West, was foiled (about June 11th), then coasted along the

East shore of the American mainland to Cape Hatteras,
if not to Florida, and returned to England some time
subsequent to October 28th in the same year, after
a voyage so extensive as to give a pretty thorough
trial to the expectations of its promotors, so ambitious
as to arouse the envy of Spain, and so far successful
as to make his child and heritor, Sebastian, the chief
authority in Europe upon questions of North-West
geography.

We have an interesting confirmation of the safe
return of part, at least, of the expedition in the fact
that Launcelot Thirkill who, as we have seen, almost
certainly accompanied Cabot on his start in May,
1498, again appears in documentary history in 1501.
On the 6th of June of that year he is stated to be in
London, and along with three others is ' bounden in
two obligations' to pay at Whitsunday next £20—
either the King's loan of 22nd of March, 1498, or
another debt—and besides this he is noticed as owing
for ' that day twelvemonth 40 marks for livery of
Flemings' lands.'   On the other hand, Portuguese
explorations of later time professed to have found
certain relics which might indicate the destruction of
part of Cabot's fleet.   In October, 1501, the consort
of Gaspar Corte Real reappeared in Lisbon, from the
North American coast, bringing a piece of a broken
sword, gilded, of Italian workmanship, and relating that
two silver rings of Venetian make had been seen upon
a boy who was a native of the North-West country.

It was probably owing to this second voyage of John Cabot that Ferdinand and Isabella took alarm at supposed English incursions on Spanish privileges, and ordered Alonzo de Hojeda to check the intruders. This order was conveyed to him on June 8, 1501, when he was on the point of starting for the Caribbean Sea; and in this connection we may recall the repeated declarations of Puebla and Ayala that John Cabot in his enterprises was trespassing, had trespassed, or was about to trespass, on the rights of the Catholic Kings, which, in their widest extent, were applied to all new found lands whatever lying west of a meridian drawn one hundred leagues west of the Azores.[1]

Why so little has been recorded in English sources about either of these two first national enterprises in American waters must remain, like much of the later gossip, on which we often have to rely for the Cabotian claims, an unsolved problem,—only made more perplexing by the way in which the two expeditions have evidently been confused. All that can be said is that the national interest in exploration was not really awakened till the North-East adventure of 1553 and the consequent Russian trade; that in the earlier sixteenth century Englishmen only thought of the New Found Land as a cod-fish country; that the King and the merchants who assisted Cabot were probably alike disgusted that he brought back no gold and gems, silks and spices; that the failure to find a

[1] By (3rd) Bull of Alexander VI., May 4, 1493.

North-West passage to the Indies was a disappointment deep enough to make them undervalue what had actually been done ; and that jealousy of the foreigner, who had led these earliest ventures, also contributed towards this extraordinary apathy on our part.

NOTE.

The 'S. Juan' of Cosa's map may refer to St. John the Evangelist, whose day falls on December 27th. This would remove our last help from hagiology towards the interpretation of the questions discussed on pp. 105–8.

CHAPTER VII

SEBASTIAN CABOT : HIS LIFE TO 1512—QUESTION
OF SEBASTIAN'S BIRTHPLACE — ESTIMATE OF
SEBASTIAN'S CHARACTER—ALLEGED VOYAGE OF
1502—ITS POSSIBLE SOURCE—ALLEGED VOYAGE
OF 1508-9

WE have already alluded to certain points in connection
with the life and claims of Sebastian Cabot, and so
far we have arrived at the following results :—Firstly,
various and conflicting statements have been seen to
exist about his birthplace ; but the balance of probability
inclines to Venice, rather than to Bristol. Secondly,
it is certain that he was a co-grantee with his father
in the first letters patent of Henry VII., granted in
March, 1496. Thirdly, it is not equally certain,
but, on the contrary, questionable, whether he actually
accompanied his father on the first voyage of 1497.
This, however, is possible. Fourthly, it is plain that
he had no part in the second patent of 1498. Fifthly,
we cannot be either more or less certain of his share
in the voyage of 1498 that in that of 1497. One

of these points, however, must now be examined a little more closely.

As to the first : Sebastian told Richard Eden that he was born in England, at Bristol, but taken to Venice when he was four years old, and that this was the only foundation for the story of his Italian origin.[1]   On   the   other   hand,   he   told   Gaspar Contarini, the Venetian Ambassador in Spain, in 1522, with equal directness and greater emphasis, that he was ' born in Venice, but brought up in England.' Contarini's successor, Andrea Navagero, in 1524, also describes him as a Venetian, like Ramusio and the ' Mantuan gentleman ' whose interview with Sebastian is reproduced by Ramusio.   Again as late as 1551 the Council of Ten writing to their Ambassador in England, describe him as ' our most faithful Sebastian Cabot,' just as the chief of the Ten in 1522 states that Cabot had declared himself to be ' of our city.' The Twelve Great Livery Companies of London, protesting in 1521 against the employment of Sebastian in a North-West venture, plainly imply that they

---

[1] It is only fair to notice that Eden attaches great weight to this statement, as he obtained it of set purpose from Sebastian with the avowed object of settling finally the true story of his birthplace, and meeting the ' Venetian ' advocates.   But, on his death-bed, Sebastian talked with just as much emphasis to Eden about the divine revelation vouchsafed him for finding the longitude ' yet so that he might not teach any man '—forcing the Englishman to conclude that he was ' somewhat doted.'   It was a natural thing to pass himself off as an Englishman in England ; and his talk is too generally incoherent and suspicious for us to attach much value to the statement about his Bristol birthplace.

H

consider him as of foreign birth; so, apparently, though in vaguer terms, did Peter Martyr, writing in 1515, and Oviedo, who speaks of him as 'by origin Venetian and brought up in the island of England.' Sebastian must have been at least twenty-one in 1496 [1] when Henry VII. granted his first letters patent to the Cabots,—as such letters (in which he appeared as a co-grantee) could not be issued to minors. It is not probable he was born before 1461, when his father's term of probation began for Venetian citizenship: John had to 'keep a residence' in Venice from 1461 to 1476; and we have nothing positive to show us he had removed and settled in England before 1491. The probability therefore is that all his sons were born in Venice. As against this we have only Sebastian's statement to Eden, and Ferdinand of Aragon's allusion to him, on his entering the Spanish service in 1512 [2] as 'Sebastian Caboto, Englishman.' [3]

We have already discussed the question of Sebastian's personal companionship with his father in the enterprises of 1497–8, and expressed our qualified belief in

[1] *I.e.*, born in 1475. In 1535 when figuring as a witness in a Spanish lawsuit, Sebastian declared himself to be ' 50 years old and upwards '— *i.e.* born before 1485.

[2] After a long residence in England, where of late he had been doing work for the Government.

[3] In the same way, Edward Hayes or Haies, writing in 1583 an account of Sir Humphrey Gilbert's expedition to 'Newfoundland,' says : ' The first discovery of those coasts . . . was well begun by John Cabot the father and Sebastian the son, an Englishman born.' To like purpose writes Sir George Peckham, an adventurer with Gilbert, also in 1583 ; and Richard Hakluyt in his *Western Planting*, in 1584.

this, at least as a probability ; but it is unfortunate that
the younger Cabot's words and works occasionally are
the reverse of a support to our belief. For one thing, his
alleged map of 1544 shows an inaccuracy so remarkable
as to Newfoundland, yet so closely corresponding to
certain Dieppese maps of the time (especially one by
Nicholas Desliens, of 1541) that the suspicious critic
might easily persuade himself that the former was
copied from the latter, without any correction from
first-hand knowledge, such as Sebastian should have
possessed, if he had ever accompanied his father to the
New World. Again, the positive disbelief expressed by
our London Livery Companies in 1521, and by certain
Spanish captains, as recorded by Peter Martyr in 1515,
may be discounted by the national jealousy of a
foreigner, which would readily take advantage of any
obscurity of title ; but Sebastian himself uses very
strange language about this matter in 1535, while in
the service of Charles V. He is speaking as a witness
in a lawsuit, and in answer to a question on the
claims of the descendants of Columbus in the New
World, he declares that as regarded Florida, and the
' Baccallaos,' he could not say whether it were all one
continent or no, without any break or sea intervening.
This may well have been interested evidence given by
an official of the Spanish Government, as Cabot then
was, to rebut the claims of the Columbus family
against that same Government. We are far from
pressing this enigmatical utterance of his, and in spite

of ' his ' map we are inclined, as already said, to believe
that he had actually visited the North-West both in
1497 and 1498, but these points we have just noticed
hardly strengthen our confidence.   At any rate of one
thing we may be sure, Sebastian's share, however real,
was unimportant.   He probably did take part with his
father in the actual perils and discoveries of 1497 and
1498.   But as regards these, Henry Stevens's formula
holds good—'Sebastian Cabot *minus* John Cabot = o.'

We have now come to the point at which we lose
sight of John Cabot.   It is clear that he returned
from his second great voyage ; he was drawing the
pension allowed him by Henry VII. in the year 1499 ;
after this we have no glimpse of him ; and although
we cannot now indulge in the pleasant fancies of an
earlier time as to his heroic death in some adventure
of the enterprise of 1498, yet it is probable, from the
language of Peter Martyr and Ramusio (as well as
from the new patent granted to the Anglo-Portuguese
Syndicate on the 19th of March, 1501), that he must
have died soon after—perhaps in 1500.   From this
time Sebastian maintains the fame and credit of the
family.

And here it must be said that, however damaging
appearances may sometimes be for Sebastian's credit, it
is hardly fair to regard him as a mere charlatan, a man
who did nothing but trade upon his father's reputation, a professed cartographer without any real
science, a professed discoverer without any real achieve-

ment.   True the claims made by him or for him to
superiority over, or even to equal eminence with, his
father during his father's lifetime must be dismissed as
fabulous—but in the long period during which he
acted as Chief Pilot of Spain and England,[1] he must
have possessed some attainments to justify his high
position and to keep him in it against the envy and
competition of rivals.   It is difficult to believe that he
could have enjoyed—to so remarkable a degree as he
did—the confidence of Henry VIII., of Cardinal
Wolsey, of Ferdinand the Catholic, of Charles V., of
Edward VI. and his chief advisers, of the Republic of
Venice—if he was simply the clever but absolutely
empty humbug he has been represented.   His instructions for the English enterprise of Chancellor and
Willoughby in 1553 at least show good sense and
practical knowledge of the requirements of such an
expedition.   Charles V. would hardly have saved him
as he did from the almost successful attack of his
enemies after the La Plata voyage if he had not
attached a very high value to his services ; and the
same is shown by the Emperor's anxiety to retain him
in his employ after Sebastian's final removal from Spain
to England (1547).

Students of geography and history like Peter
Martyr and Ramusio, practical men like Contarini, the
Council of Ten, and the contemporary sovereigns and

[1] Here he did not hold this title, but seems to have practically held the
office first technically created for Stephen Burrough in 1563.

chief ministers of Spain and England, seem to have held an exalted opinion of Sebastian's capacities ; and we must not allow too much weight to language which may have been partly inspired by racial and national jealousy.

On the other hand, it must be allowed that the best evidence is very damaging to Sebastian's claims and character ; he seems to have aimed at appropriating his father's credit ; he undoubtedly intrigued with Venice while holding employment and taking pay from the Governments of Spain and England. Further, he gives on various occasions perfectly inconsistent accounts of the same event ; in that age of vague knowledge and vast hopes he cannot be excused from the charge of sometimes trading on the ignorance and credulity of ambitious men, and making pretensions which were either untrue in the light of past fact, or impossible from the standpoint of later achievement and final verification. All that we would plead for is some allowance of possible merit, in face of the great difficulty in otherwise crediting some parts of the success of his life.

A third Cabot voyage under the English flag has been conjectured from Stow's note, professedly drawn from Fabyan's Chronicle under A.D. 1502, the 18th of Henry VII., when there were 'brought unto the King three men taken in the new found Islands by Sebastian Gabato . . . these men were clothed in beast skins, and ate raw flesh, but spake such a lan-

guage as no man could understand them ; of the
which, two were seen in the King's court at Westminster two years afterwards clothed like Englishmen
and could not be discerned from Englishmen.'
But we have no other evidence of such a voyage of
Sebastian Cabot's made at this time. On the other
hand, Henry VII. on March 19, 1501–2, granted new
letters patent for a Western voyage to an Anglo-
Portuguese Syndicate composed of three Englishmen
—Richard Ward, Thomas Ashehurst, and John
Thomas of Bristol ; and three Portuguese—John
Fernandez, Francis Fernandez, and John Gonsalvez of
the Azores.[1] It was probably a venture conducted by
these men which brought over the captive American
Indians referred to by Fabyan and Stow. The rights
of these new grantees are especially guarded by their
letters patent : 'And let none of our subjects drive them,
or any of them, from their title and possession over
and in the said main-lands, islands, and provinces, in
any manner against their will, and let not any
foreigner or foreigners attempt the like, *by virtue or
colour of any previous grant made by us* under our Great

---

[1] Here perhaps is some confirmation of Mr. Prowse's theory about the
Burgundian (= Azorean ?) companion of John Cabot on the voyage of
1497. To this conjecture some additional force is given by Santa Cruz's
derivation of the name of Labrador. 'So called because it was discovered
and indicated by a *labourer* (Lavrador) from the Azores to the King of
England, when he sent out on a voyage of discovery *Anthony* [= John]
Gabot, an English pilot and the father of Sebastian Cabot, at present
Pilot-Major to the Emperor.' See Santa Cruz's *Islario*, fol. 56, written
about 1545.

Seal, or which may be made hereafter with any other places and islands.' This last clause, though struck out with the pen, must have been aimed, in its original form, at the Cabots, the only foreigners who, as far as we know, could have disputed the ground 'by virtue or colour of any previous grant' from the Crown of England; and we may fairly assume that the privileges bestowed in the grants of 1496 and 1498 were now held to be expired. The death of John Cabot was probably the sufficient reason for this new departure.

The Syndicate of Ashehurst and his friends may be supposed to have succeeded in their first venture, of A.D. 1501–2; for letters patent are granted them for a second expedition, this time with another associate, Hugh Elliott of Bristol, on December 9, 1502; a pension is bestowed on Fernandez and Gonsalvez in September of the same year; and other entries of rewards occur at this time in the Privy Purse expenses of Henry VII.[1] (A.D. 1502) referring to this or similar ventures of Bristol seamen. Thus, 'January 7, 1502, to men of Bristol that found the Isle £5'; and again, 'September 24, 1502, to the merchants of

---

[1] Another expedition of this time seems indicated in a gift of £2 on April 8, 1504 'to a prest that goeth to the new island.' On September [?] 25, 1515, we have another entry, of a somewhat similar character, '£5 to Portingals that brought popinjays and cats of the mountain with other stuff [from the new found island] to the King's Grace.' These are not products of the Baccallaos region; they were probably brought from Brazil to Lisbon and thence to England by Portuguese seamen, who were quite unconnected with English explorations.

Bristol that have been in the New-found-Land £20.'
Lastly, there is a reference to the Portuguese asso-
ciates of Ashehurst and Elliott in a warrant issued on
December 6, 1503, for the payment of the pension
already granted to Francis Fernandez and John
' Guidisalvus.'

' Whereas we by our letters patent under our Privy
Seal, bearing date at our Manor of Langley the 26th
day of September the 18th year of our reign, gave and
granted unto our trusty and well-beloved subjects
Francis Fernandus and John Guidisalvus, squires, in
consideration of the true service which they have done
to us to our singular pleasure as captains unto the
New Found Land, unto either of them ten pounds
yearly, during pleasure to be had . . . of the
Revenues . . . of our Customs within our port of
Bristol by the hands of the customers there . . . We
will that ye from henceforth from time to time and
year to year do to be levied several tailles containing
the . . . sum of £20 upon the customers of our said
port . . . unto the time ye shall have from us otherwise commandment by writing.'

No letters patent, so far as we know, were issued by
the English Government for transatlantic ventures
between John Cabot's second commission, granted in
1498, and that issued to Ward, Ashehurst, Thomas,
and their Portuguese companions on March 19, 1501
—so that these grants of January and September,
1502, above noticed, do probably — as that of

December, 1503, does certainly—refer to the new Syndicate.

The grant of January 7, 1502, may also be fairly interpreted to mean that the Syndicate had successfully accomplished its first enterprise, and the warrant of December 6, 1503, notes that the pension to Francis Fernandez and John Guidisalvus or Gonsalvez was originally granted on September 26, 1502, 'in consideration of the true service which they have done unto us to our singular pleasure as captains unto the New Found Land,'—probably on the same expedition as that just referred to, viz., one undertaken in the summer of 1502.

The best evidence, therefore, rather points against a voyage of Sebastian Cabot in 1501 or 1502 ; but this is not the only (alleged) event of his career between his father's death and his entry into the Spanish service in 1512, and we must briefly notice the scattered allusions to other enterprises in this period of his life.

According to a loose statement attributed to Sebastian himself, he was entrusted by Ferdinand and Isabella with the charge of an expedition to Brazil, which is otherwise unrecorded. This must have been before November 26th of the year 1504, when Queen Isabella died—if the story is to be credited—but it must remain a very doubtful matter. As against it, we find Sebastian in the service of the English Government as late as 1512, and referred to in a Spanish document of that year as an Englishman : his wife [1] and household were domiciled in England as late as October, 1512. Appearances are certainly in favour of his having then first, and not before, transferred his services.

Again, some allusions are made by Marc Antonio Contarini, Venetian Ambassador in Spain, in 1536, which have been construed by some as referring to a voyage of Sebastian's in the last year of Henry VII. (1508–9). 'Sebastian Caboto', says Contarini, 'being the son of a Venetian who repaired to England on galleys from Venice, with the notion of going in search of countries . . . obtained two ships from Henry, King of England, father of the present Henry, and navigated with three hundred men till he found the sea frozen. Caboto was forced therefore to turn back without accomplishing his object, with the intention of renewing the attempt. But upon his return he found the King dead, and his son caring little for such an enterprise.'

M. Harrisse considers that Contarini's account from the bearing of all except the last sentence refers to the first transatlantic voyage of 1497. In support of this, he notices especially how the voyage seems to have been made in consequence of, and shortly after, John Cabot's arrival in England with 'galleys from Venice'; how the two ships, the three hundred

---

[1] This first wife must have died soon after ; for soon after entering the Spanish service Sebastian married Catalina Medrano, evidently a Spaniard, who is said to have acquired great influence over him.

men, the frozen sea, all tally with statements made by Sebastian to Peter Martyr and others about the original Cabotian voyage ; and how there exists no other evidence for the claim of such an enterprise in 1508–9.

Yet, unless we are to refuse all the statements emanating from Sebastian himself and not corroborated by documentary evidence, it is perhaps rash to deny the possibility of this story. Contarini is an excellent witness—at any rate to the fact that he was informed exactly as he has recorded—and his suggestion, to our thinking, rests on a somewhat better foundation than the assertion of a Cabotian enterprise in 1501–2.

CHAPTER VIII

Now we come to Sebastian's career in the Spanish service ; and even at the outset, and upon such a simple matter as the time of his removal from England to Spain, we are met by the old difficulties and contradictions. Peter Martyr, his 'very friend,' who probably writes from Sebastian's inspiration, tells us that ' he was called out of England by command of the Catholic King of Castille, after the death of Henry, King of England, the seventh of that name.' He thus implies that Ferdinand invited Cabot to his Court in or about 1509, and that the invitation was immediately accepted. On the other hand, Spanish documents mention the name of Sebastian

Cabot in 1512 for the first time—and mention it 'in terms and under circumstances' which imply that his arrival in the Peninsula was not earlier than the aforesaid year, and was due originally 'to his own initiative.'

Sebastian had just received twenty shillings [= £12] from the Government of Henry VIII. for a map seemingly drawn, in May, 1512, to aid the English troops in their expedition now made against Aquitaine,[1] and he accompanied Lord Willoughby de Brooke to the same parts at this very time. England and Spain, Henry VIII. and Ferdinand, were allied in this attack upon the South of France, and Cabot's opportunity was easy. His English friends seem to have rather helped than hindered his application for Spanish employment; on September 13, 1512, King Ferdinand wrote to Lord Willoughby requesting that 'Sebastian Cabot, Englishman,' might be sent on to confer with him at Logroño, and on the same day corresponded with Cabot direct, on the subject of the North-West navigation. The latter accordingly proceeded to Burgos, where he conferred with Conchillos, the Secretary of Queen Juana, and the Bishop of Palencia, on behalf of the King of Spain, whom he must have persuaded of his capacity to gratify him in the matter of the 'secret of the new land.' For now, as afterwards, Sebastian was commonly supposed to have special

[1] 'Paid Sebastian Tabot making of a card of Gascoigne and Guyon (Gascony and Guyenne) 20s.'

information about the Cod Fish country that his
father had explored, and to be able, if any man
were, to find the Western passage by the North, for
which so eager search was being made. Nine years
later Magellan found such a passage by the South ;
in 1512 hope was equally sanguine, or equally cast
down, about both possibilities, both extremities of
the New World. Only the year before King
Ferdinand had planned to send out Juan de Agra-
monte with Breton pilots on a Western voyage, which
was probably in search of the North-West passage ; now,
with one of John Cabot's sons in his service, he might
take up these plans with better prospect of success.

Thus Sebastian now suddenly appears as an
important person, by his transference to a Court
where discovery and exploration were valued more
highly than in England. On October 20, 1512, he
is appointed a naval captain of Spain, with a salary
of fifty thousand maravedis. On the strength of
this he seems next to have brought over his family
from England to Seville, the Spanish Ambassador
in London aiding him with a loan of money ; and,
now fairly settled in Spain, he is at once consulted
(6th of March, 1514) about a new project of discovery. Fifty ducats were granted him on this
occasion to help him to 'come to Court and consult
with his Highness about the matters of the journey
of discovery ' ;[1] but we hear no more about it,

[1] Las cosas del viaje que ha de llevar a descubrir.

except that Peter Martyr, in 1515, may be alluding
to the same in his words: 'Cabot . . . was made
one of our counsel and assistance, as touching the
affairs of the new Indies, looking daily for ships
to be furnished for him to discover this hid secret
of nature.[1] This voyage is appointed to be begun
in March next, 1516.' We may also suppose that
a further grant of ten thousand maravedis on June 13,
1515, to Cabot, 'fleet captain of matters of the
Indies,' and his appointment as pilot to the King in
the same year, refer to this projected but apparently
unaccomplished North-Western venture.

Next we come to the alleged voyage of 1516–17,
once more in the English service. Ferdinand of
Aragon died January 23, 1516 ; Charles, the new
king, did not reach Spain till the end of 1517 ; and
on February 5, 1518, he appointed Cabot Pilot-
Major of Spain. In the interval between these two
events Sebastian is supposed to have come to England, and made a voyage in the service of Henry
VIII. when that king had reigned seven or eight
years. Richard Eden, in his translation of the fifth
part of Sebastian Munster's *Cosmography*, adds an
epistle dedicatory to the Duke of Northumberland, then (1553) Lord Protector of England, in
which he refers to this abortive attempt as an
instance of the lack of discovering spirit among
some of his countrymen : 'Our sovereign Lord

---

[1] The North-West passage.

King Henry VIII. (says the *Treatise of the New India*), about the same year of his reign,[1] furnished and sent forth certain ships under the governance of Sebastian Cabot, yet living, and one Sir Thomas Perte, whose faint heart was the cause that voyage took none effect.' Again, Ramusio, in the Preliminary Discourse prefixed by him to the third volume of his *Collection of Voyages*, inserts a passage whose general tone exactly corresponds to the one just quoted from Eden, but which we have already noticed as probably intended to refer to the first Cabotian enterprise of 1497.[2] A Thomas Pert, or Spert, yeoman of the Crown, is known to have commanded two ships of the Royal Navy between 1512 and 1517—the *Mary Rose* and the *Great Harry;* but all English references to this voyage narrow themselves down to the statement of Eden, repeated as it is by Sir Humphrey Gilbert, Hakluyt, and others ; and it is certainly remarkable that we

---

[1] *I.e.*, according to context, 1516 or 1517.

[2] 'As many years past it was written unto me by Signor Sebastian Gabotto, our Venetian, a man of great experience and very rare in the art of Navigation and the knowledge of Cosmography, who sailed along and beyond this land of New France, at the charges of *King Henry VII.* of England. And he advertised me that having sailed a long time west-and-by-north beyond those islands unto the latitude of $67\frac{1}{2}$ degrees under the North Pole, and at the 11th day of June, finding still the sea open without any manner of impediment, he thought verily by that way to have passed on still the way to Cathaio, which is in the East; and he would have done it if the mutiny of the shipmasters and mariners had not hindered him, and made him to return homewards from that place.'

have no independent account of so important a venture.

Again, this attempt, if made, would surely discount very much the protest of the Livery Companies, made only five years afterwards, in 1521, when they objected to the demand of Henry VIII. and Cardinal Wolsey for the equipment of an 'American' expedition under Sebastian Cabot, and declared the latter to be an impostor, well known as such, without any real knowledge of the North-West countries or passage, although a glib reciter of the tales of other men.

In support (or criticism) of the alleged fiasco of 1516–17 we may notice that a mutiny causing very similar results occurred in Hugh Elliott's journey of 1502, and that Robert Thorne refers to this in his famous letter of 1527 to King Henry VIII. Robert's father Nicolas had accompanied Elliott on this voyage to the West, and the son declares as to the possibility of their success, that it could not be doubted, 'as now plainly appeareth, if the mariners would then have been ruled and followed their pilot's mind, the lands of the West Indies, from whence all the gold cometh, had been ours, for all is one coast.'

Again, a similar allusion to such a break-down occurs in a curious dramatic poem belonging to the early part of the reign of Henry VIII., and probably written about 1517 or a little later. Speaking of the new land in the West, the work in question (*A new Interlude and a Merry of the nature of the Four Elements, declaring many proper points of philosophy natural and of divers strange lands and of divers strange effects and causes . . .*) denounces with vigour the cowardice and backwardness of English sailors towards enterprises of discovery.

In this play one character, named Experience, whom some have supposed wildly enough to represent Sebastian Cabot himself, describes some of the adventures of an ancient mariner of the time :

> *Right far, sir, I have ridden and gone,*
> *And seen strange things many one*
> *In Afric, Europe, and Inde ;*
> *Both East and West I have been far,*
> *North also, and seen the South Star,*
> *Both by sea and land.*

Then, as if he had a map before him, and were pointing his listener to it, he continues :

> *There lieth Iceland, where men do fish ;*
> *But beyond that so cold it is*
> *No man may there abide.*
> *This sea is called the Great Ocean,*
> *So great it is that never man*
> *Could tell it sith the world began,*
> *Till now, within this twenty year,*
> *Westward we found new lands*

That we never heard tell of before this,
By writing nor other means.
Yet many now have been there,
And that country is so large of room—
Much larger than all Christendom—
Without fable or guile ;
For divers mariners have it tried,
And sailed straight by the coast side
Above five thousand mile.
But what commodities be within
No man can tell, nor well imagine ;
But yet not long ago,
Some men of this country went,
By the King's noble consent,
It for to search to that intent,
And could not be brought thereto ;
But they that were the venturers
Have cause to curse their mariners,
False of promise, and dissemblers,
That falsely them betrayed ;
Which would take no pain to sail further
Than their own lust and pleasure,
Wherefore that voyage and divers others
Such caitiffs have destroyed.
O what a thing had been then,
If that they that be Englishmen
Might have been first of all ;
That they should have taken possession,
And made first building and habitation

A memory perpetual;
And also what an honourable thing,
Both to the Realm and to the King,
To have had his dominion extending
There, into so far a ground,
Which the noble King of late memory,
The most wise Prince, the VIIth Harry,
Caused first to be found.[1]

The date of this most curious passage has been by some fixed at about 1510–11, because of the allusion, ' Within this twenty year, westward we found new lands.'

But, on the other hand, it has been pointed out that Columbus is not named in the whole play, and that the finding of the new lands westward ' within this twenty year ' is distinctly ascribed to Amerigo Vespucci, whose earliest pretended voyage was made in 1497.   Thus the Interlude elsewhere :

> *But these new lands found lately*
> *Be called America, because only*
> *Americus did first them find.*

This would bring the time of composition to about 1516–17, and the date is absolutely fixed to the year 1519–20 by an additional piece of evidence, if this may be accepted.   The only existing copy of the Interlude is in the British Museum ; it was once the

[1] See for more about the Interlude, Appendix, pp. 279–82.

property of David Garrick, the actor ; the colophon is now missing, but Garrick has presumably supplied its place with a manuscript note, 'First impression dated 25th Oct., 11 Henry VIII.' On the first blush we might well suppose that the passage quoted refers to the abortive venture of 1516–17, as described by Eden and Hakluyt. The most suspicious critics have admitted the possibility of an English expedition to the West at the time aforesaid, and of Sebastian Cabot as a sharer in the command. Ferdinand of Aragon, as we have said, died at the beginning of A.D. 1516 ; it appears beyond question that the voyage mentioned by Martyr as projected by the old king for that year under Sebastian's leadership did not take place, and Cabot may have returned to England to pick up any good offer in the uncertain interval between the death of his older patron and his appointment as Pilot-Major by Charles V. on February 3, 1518. It may also be worth considering whether the legacy (four shillings and fourpence) of the Reverend William Mychell to Sebastian's daughter, under date of May 7, 1516, is not another evidence of Cabot's alleged visit to England at this time. As a downward limit for the expedition recorded by Eden we may also notice that Thomas Spert, on 10th of July, 1517, collected his charges for ballasting his ship the *Mary Rose* in the Thames ; so the venture spoiled by his 'faint heart' (if it be the same man) must have taken place before this. Indeed, if it is to be strictly in accord with the date given, 'the eighth year of Henry VIII.' it must have been between April 15, 1516, and April 15, 1517.

One other point remains to be noticed about this alleged expedition. If Eden, as quoted above, gives us a true statement, there were plans of treasure-hunting, if not of buccaneering, as well as of discovery. For 'if,' says our author, 'such manly courage whereof we have spoken had not at that time been wanting, it might haply have come to pass that that rich treasury called Perularia (which is now in Spain in the City of Seville, and so named for that in it is kept the infinite riches brought thither from the new found land of Peru) might long since have been in the town of London."

But whether Sebastian Cabot did or did not take part in the alleged voyage of 1517, it seems pretty certain that he was thought of by Henry VIII. and Cardinal Wolsey as a fit person to command an English expedition intended for the year 1521.

In February of that year the King of England, through Sir Robert Wynkfeld and Sir Wolston Brown, made the following demands upon the twelve great Livery Companies of London :—' To furnish five ships after this manner. The King's Grace to prepare them in tackle, ordnance, and all other necessaries at his charge. And also the King to bear the adventure of the said ships. And the merchants and companies to be at the charge of the victualling and men's wage

of the same ships for one whole year, and the ships
not to be above VI^{xx} tons apiece. And that this City
of London shall be as head rulers for all the whole
realm for as many cities and towns as be minded to
prepare any ships forwards for the same purpose and
voyage, as the town of Bristol hath sent up their
knowledge that they will prepare two ships.' These
vessels were required ' for a voyage into the new found
Island,' and the command was to be given, as we learn
from the Liveries' reply to 'one man, called Sebastian,'
viz., Sebastian Cabot.

To secure the compliance of the Companies, they
were offered the following privileges : Firstly, ' That
ten years after there shall no nation have the trade
but ' the Companies ; secondly, ' And to have respite
for their custom XV. months and XV. months.'

Thus the bait was made as attractive as possible,
but the Companies were not satisfied, and they returned
an answer full of objections, as follows :—

'The answer of the Wardens of Drapers of London
with the assent and consent of the most part of all
their Company, unto a bill lately sent unto them by
the Wardens of the Mercers of London containing
the appointment of five ships to be prepared towards
the New-Found-Land.

' First the foresaid Wardens and Company of Drapers
suppose and say that if our Sovereign Lord the King's
Highness, the Cardinal's Grace, and the King's most
honourable Council, were duly and substantially

informed in such manner as perfect knowledge might
be had by credible report of masters and mariners
naturally born within this realm of England, having
experience and exercised in and about the foresaid
island, as well in knowledge of the land, the due
courses of the sea thitherward and homeward, as in
knowledge of the havens, roads, ports, creeks, dangers,
and shoals there upon that coast and thereabouts being,
that then it were the less jeopardy to adventure
thither, than it is now, although it be further hence
than few English mariners can tell.   And we think it
were too sore adventure to jeopard five ships with men
and goods into the said Island upon the singular trust
of one man called as we understand Sebastian, *which
Sebastian, as we hear say, was never in that land himself,
all if he makes report of many things as he hath heard
his father and other men speak in times past.* And
also we say that if the said Sebastian had been there,
and were as cunning a man in and for those parts as
any man might be, having none other assistance of
masters and mariners of England (exercised and
laboured in the same parts for to guide their ships and
other charges) than we know of, but only trusting to
the said Sebastian, we suppose it were no wisdom
to adventure lives and goods thither in such manner.
What for fear of sickness or death of the said Sebastian
or for dissevering of the said five ships by night or by day,
by force of tempests or otherwise one from another out
of sight, for then it should be greatly to doubt whether

ever these five ships should meet again in company or nay, for the said Sebastian cannot be but in one ship, then the other four ships and men stand in great peril for lack of cunning mariners in knowledge of those parts and to order and guide them ; and so the victual and men's wages shall be spent in vain . . . for it is said among mariners in old proverb " He sails not surely that sails by another man's compass." Also we say that it is not possible for the said five ships besides their ballast may receive the victuals to suffice so many men for one whole year. So that we think verily that in this adventure can[not] be perceived any advantage or profit to grow unto any man . . . '

Finally, the Royal Commissioners appointed to sound the Companies obtained the following reply ' from the Wardens of XI Companies.' ' That their Companies be willing to accomplish the King's desire and pleasure in furnishing of two ships accordingly, and they suppose to furnish the third, so that one may bear with another indifferently of XI Fellowships assembled with the Aldermen of the same. . . . And the said Wardens desire to have longer respite for a full answer therein to be given.'

To all which 'the said Commissioners brought answer from my Lord Cardinal that the King would have the promises to go forth and to take effect. And thereupon my Lord the Mayor was sent for to speak with the King for the same matter. So that his Grace would have no nay therein, but spake sharply to the Mayor

to see it put in execution to the best of his power.'
The Mayor accordingly convened the Drapers in the
hall of the Fraternity ' where was with great labour
and diligence and many divers warning[s] granted
first and last two hundred marks ' on the 26th of March,
1521. This grant was formally stated to be ' towards
mariners' wages and victualling of certain ships for one
voyage to be made . . . unto the new found island.'
The Mayor himself, Sir John Brugge, headed the list
with £8 ; seventy-eight of the ' Masters and Livery '
contribute in a first list of more honourable names ; a
second roll follows, of Bachelors, who give smaller
sums, tailing down to contributions of twelve pence
or about twelve shillings in money of our value.

Sir Thomas Lovell, K.G., Steward and Marshal of
Henry VIII., apparently had charge of the personal
conveyance of Cabot from Spain to England at this
time ; and he employed the services of one John
Goderyk of Fowey in this matter of trans-shipment.
Among the debts acknowledged in Lovell's will
(February 18, 1523) is one of £2 4s. 3d. to the said
John Goderyk, ' in satisfaction and recompense of his
charge, costs, and labour in conducting of Sebastian
Cabot, Master of the pilots in Spain, to London,
at the request of the testator.'

On the other hand, Cabot himself told Gaspar
Contarini (in 1522) that three years before, viz.,
in 1519, Cardinal Wolsey had asked him to take
charge of an expedition across the Atlantic in the

English service, but that he had rejected the offer, saying that his obedience was due to the King of Spain and that he could not put himself at the disposal of any other monarch without the permission of Charles. Further, he wrote to the latter, according to his own account, declining beforehand any offer the King of England might make to him. The offer here referred to is almost certainly the same which led to the protest of the London Livery Companies; but in spite of Sebastian's visit, and the subscription so grudgingly commenced, nothing seems to have come of the project, and Cabot returned to Spain—not to leave it again till after the accession of Edward Tudor.

CHAPTER IX

THE VENETIAN INTRIGUE OF 1522—THE LA PLATA
VOYAGE OF 1526–30—THE LAWSUIT OF 1535
—ACTS OF SEBASTIAN IN SPAIN 1540–47

ON the collapse of the plan of 1521, Sebastian does not appear to have been connected with England in any way for many years. True in 1538 he seems to have endeavoured to re-establish himself in this country, but the scheme did not apparently go beyond a conversation with Henry VIII.'s ambassador in Spain, and it was not till 1547 that the project was seriously resumed.

The career of Sebastian Cabot in the Spanish service is the best known and in some respects the most important part of his life, but we are obliged here to pass over it somewhat briefly, as our main attention must be given to his connection with England. In general, we may notice that in this time he gained considerable reputation as a cartographer and a learned geographer, but failed miserably as a practical explorer and com-

mander of naval expeditions. As 'Pilot-Major,
'Pilot of His Majesty,' 'Naval Captain,' and 'Fleet
Captain,' his primary duties, taking one time with
another, were to examine and license pilots, to teach
cosmography, to keep maps and instruments up to
date by incorporating all new knowledge which had
been sufficiently tested, to register all geographical
discoveries in the official chart kept by the Spanish
Government—in a word, his work was scientific, and as
such seems to have given full satisfaction. It is equally
certain that the only practical exploring enterprise
undertaken by him in these years—the only one, at
least, of which we have any account, viz., that to the
La Plata—gave as great dissatisfaction and was pretty
nearly ruining his career.

The first incident of this period to which we may
devote some attention is the negotiation or intrigue of
Sebastian with Venice in 1522. In this some have
perceived an 'element of conscious insincerity,' but
we must briefly recount the facts, as they are given
us by contemporary evidence, before we try to decide
upon their value.

First of all, on September 27, 1522, the chiefs of
the Council of Ten at Venice write to Gaspar Contarini, Venetian Ambassador in Spain, to the following
effect : 'There arrived here (in Venice) the other
day one Hieronimo de Marin de Busignolo, a native
of Ragusa, who before the chiefs of the Ten declared
that he had been sent by one Sebastian Cabotto, who

says that he is a Venetian, and now resident in Seville,
where he receives a salary from the Emperor as his Pilot-
Major in voyages of discovery.   On behalf of this man
the Ragusan made the enclosed statement.[1]   Although
it is perhaps not worthy of much credit, yet because
of its [seeming] import we did not think well to
decline Sebastian's offer to come here and explain his
scheme.   We have allowed Hieronymo to answer
him, as you will see by the accompanying letter.
Contrive to find out if Sebastian is at the Imperial
Court or is expected there shortly.[2] . . . Discover as
much as you are able about this plan of his, and
persuade him to come here if his projects seem well
founded and attainable.'

The second stage in this negotiation is marked by
Contarini's answer to the Council of Ten at the end
of this year, and owing to the peculiar interest of this
letter we transcribe it in full : —Valladolid, December
31, 1522 : 'According to your letter of the 27th of
September, I ascertained that Sebastian Cabot was at

[1] Sent herewith to Contarini but now lost.

[2] Cabot was now receiving from Charles a salary of 125,000 maravedis, or 300 ducats, a much better payment than Vespucci or
De Solis had had during their tenure of the same office (Vespucci
70,000 maravedis, De Solis 50,000).   Yet he would seem to have
acted meanly towards Vespucci's widow, to whom, as Vespucci's successor in office, he was bound to pay 10,000 maravedis a year.   De Solis,
Vespucci's first successor, had paid this charge regularly ; but Cabot
stopped payment, and on November 26, 1523, Charles V. ordered the
'Contractation House' in Seville to discharge the widow's arrears out
of the Pilot's salary, and to continue to remit the due amount year by
year till her death (which happened on December 26, 1524).

the Court, and where he dwelt. I sent to say that my Secretary had a letter for him from a friend of his, and that if he chose he might come to my residence. He told my servant he would come. He made his appearance on Christmas Eve. At dinner-time I withdrew with him and delivered the letter, which he read, his colour changing completely during its perusal. Having finished reading it, he remained a short while without saying anything, as if alarmed and doubtful. I told him that if he chose to answer the letter, or wished me to make any communication in the quarter from whence I had received it, I was ready to execute his commission safely. Upon this he took courage and said to me, "Out of the love I bear my country, I spoke heretofore to the ambassadors of the most illustrious Seigniory in England [1] concerning these newly-discovered countries, through which I have the means of greatly benefiting Venice. The letter in question concerned this matter, as you likewise are aware ; but I most earnestly beseech you to keep the thing secret, as it would cost me my life." I then told him I was thoroughly acquainted with the whole affair, and mentioned how Hieronimo the Ragusan had presented himself before the tribunal of their Excellencies the chiefs, and that the most secret magistracy had acquainted me with everything and forwarded that letter to me. I added, that as some noblemen were dining with me, it would be very inconvenient for us to talk

[1] No documentary evidence of this has yet been found.

together then, but that should he choose to return late in the evening we might more conveniently discuss the subject together at full length.   So he then departed, and returned at about 5 p.m., when being closeted alone in my chamber, he said to me :

'" My Lord Ambassador, to tell you the whole truth, I was born in Venice, but brought up in England, and then entered the service of their Catholic Majesties of Spain, and King Ferdinand made me captain with a salary of 50,000 maravedis.   Subsequently his present Majesty gave me the office of Pilot-Major, with an additional salary of 50,000 maravedis, and 25,000 maravedis besides as a gratuity, forming a total of 125,000 maravedis, equal to about 300 ducats.   Now it so happened that when in England some three years ago, if I mistake not, Cardinal Wolsey offered me high terms if I would sail with an armada of his on a voyage of discovery.   The vessels were almost ready, and they had got together 30,000 ducats for their outfit. I answered him that being in the service of the King of Spain I could not go without his leave, but if free permission were given me from hence, I would serve him. At that period, in the course of conversation one day with a certain friar, a Venetian named Sebastian Collona, with whom I was on a very friendly footing, he said to me, ' Master Sebastian, you take such great pains to benefit foreigners, and forget your native land ; would it not be possible for Venice likewise to derive some advantage from you ? '   At this my heart

K

smote me, and I told him I would think about it. So, on returning to him the next day, I said I had the means of rendering Venice a partner in this navigation, and of showing her a passage whereby she would obtain great profit; which is the truth, for I have discovered it. In consequence of this, as by serving the King of England I could no longer benefit our country, I wrote to the Emperor not to give me leave to serve the King of England, as he would injure himself extremely, and thus to recall me forthwith. Being recalled accordingly, and on my return residing at Seville, I contracted a close friendship with this Ragusan who wrote the letter you delivered to me ; and as he told me he was going to Venice, I unbosomed myself to him, charging him to mention this thing to none but the chiefs of the Ten ; and he swore to me a sacred oath to this effect."

'I bestowed great praise on his patriotism,' continues Contarini, 'and informed him I was commissioned to confer with him and hear his project, which I was to notify to the chiefs, to whom he might afterwards resort in person. He replied that he did not intend to manifest his plan to any but the chiefs of the Ten, and that he would go to Venice after requesting the Emperor's permission, on the plea of recovering his mother's dowry, concerning which he said he would contrive that I should be spoken to by the Bishop of Burgos and the Grand Chancellor, who are to urge me to write in his favour to your Serenity.

' I approved of this, but said I felt doubtful as to the possibility of his project, as I had applied myself a little to geography, and bearing in mind the position of Venice, I did not see any way of effecting this navigation, as the voyage must be performed either by ships built in Venice, or else by vessels which it would be requisite to construct elsewhere. Venetian-built craft must of needs pass the Gut of Gibraltar to get into the Ocean ; and as the King of Portugal and the King of Spain would oppose the project, it never could succeed. The construction of vessels out of Venice could only be effected on the southern shores of the Ocean or in the Red Sea, to which there were endless objections. First of all, it would be requisite to have a good understanding with the Great Turk. Secondly, the scarcity of timber rendered shipbuilding impossible there. Then, again, even if vessels were built, the fortresses and fleets of Portugal would prevent the trade from being carried on. I also observed to him that I did not see how vessels could be built on the northern shores of the Ocean, that is to say, from Spain to Denmark, or even beyond, especially as the whole of Germany depended on the Emperor ; nor could I perceive any way at all for conveying merchandise from Venice to these ships, or for conveying spices and other produce from the ships to Venice. Nevertheless, as he was skilled in this matter, I said I deferred to him.

' He answered me, " You have spoken ably, and in

truth neither with ships built at Venice, nor yet by the way of the Red Sea, do I perceive any means whatso-ever. But there are other means, not merely possible, but easy, both for building ships and conveying wares from Venice to the harbour, as also spices, gold, and other produce from the harbour to Venice, as I know, for I have sailed to all those countries, and am well acquainted with the whole. Indeed, I assure you that I refused the offer of the King of England for the sake of benefiting my country, for had I listened to that proposal, there would no longer have been any course for Venice."

'I shrugged my shoulders, and although the thing seems to me impossible, I nevertheless would not dissuade him from coming to the feet of your Highness (without, however, recommending him), because possibility is much more unlimited than man often supposes. Added to which this individual is in great repute here. He then left me. Subsequently, on the evening of St. John's Day,[1] he came to me in order that I might modify certain expressions in the Ragusan's letter, which he was apprehensive would make the Spaniards suspicious. It was therefore remodelled and written out again by a Veronese, an intimate of mine.

'When discussing a variety of geographical topics with me, he mentioned among other things a very clever method observed by him,[2] which had never been previously discovered by any one, for ascertaining by

[1] December 27th.   [2] See chapter xv., pages 255–6.

the needle the distance between two places from East to West, as your Serenity will hear from him if he comes. After this, continuing my conversation with him concerning our chief matter, and recapitulating the difficulties, he said to me : " I assure you the way and the means are easy. I will go to Venice at my own cost. They will hear me ; and if they disapprove of the project devised by me, I will return in like manner at my own cost." '

So much for the end of A.D. 1522.

On March 7, 1523, another despatch of Contarini's shows us the same negotiation at a more advanced stage in time, but less hopeful in circumstance :—
' Sebastian Cabot,' says the Ambassador, ' with whom you willed me to converse on matters of the spice trade, has since [1] been to see me several times, always telling me how much disposed he is to come to Venice for the purpose of carrying out his schemes for the benefit of the Seigniory. To-day he informed me that he could not ask leave at present, lest they should suspect him of a purpose of going to England.' He hoped, however, ends the despatch, to be able to resume his project in three months, and for that end asked for a second letter from the Ten bidding him come to Venice for the dispatch of his affairs. In exact agreement with this we find, little more than three months later, namely, at the end of July, 1523, that Sebastian Cabot has resumed the negotiation, as described in

[1] Namely, since the interview on Christmas Eve, 1522.

another despatch of Contarini's (July 26, 1523) to the Council of Ten. 'The aforesaid Sebastian, he remarks, has been residing at Seville, but he has now returned hither (Valladolid) on his way to Venice. He is endeavouring to obtain leave from the Imperial Councillors to return to Venice and to induce them to speak to me in his favour.'

But, as with so many of Sebastian's projects, this Venetian journey seems never to have been realised. Contarini says no more about it in his despatches, though he resided in Spain till 1525 ; and Cabot was soon busily engaged in the Molucca controversy of 1523–24, which led to his La Plata voyage of 1526–30, and which itself resulted from the *Victoria's* circumnavigation of the globe.

What are we to think of the Contarini narratives ? Their importance, on the one hand, must not be exaggerated. It is not difficult to find parallels in the sixteenth century to Sebastian's 'double-stringed playing,' and the feeling of patriotism he puts forward as his excuse may not have been altogether absent. But that the matter was serious and no mere farce cannot be doubted : Sebastian's fear of discovery, the time and place of the conferences, the language of the despatches, all go to prove this. He insists that he is telling the whole truth, he warns the Ambassador that discovery may cost him his life, he refers to a suspicion already attaching to him—of English preferences against Spanish. His plan for helping Venice, as far as it is explained, is of course preposterous, and so it appeared to Contarini ; but there were not a few men in authority at that time who would have risked something for a famous man, and committed ships and men to his charge on no more certain assurance than Sebastian could give for his mysterious scheme—that ' it was not only possible but easy.'   We shall find him renewing his overtures to the Ten, and once again meeting with encouragement twenty-nine years later (1551), when he had returned to the English service.

On the other hand, the specific excuse both then and now alleged for his projected Venetian journey— the dowry of his ' mother ' and his 'aunt '—has been supposed by some to be a mere concoction of Cabot and Contarini together.   Certainly it was used as a blind for matters of a very different kind—and on both sides the pretext was transparent enough. This is practically avowed in Contarini's letters of March 7, 1523, and December 31, 1522 ; but something more than a legal fiction is implied by Cabot's agent in Venice, Hieronymo the Ragusan, on April 28, 1523: 'Some months ago, on arriving here in Venice, I wrote to you what I had done to discover where your property was.   I received fair promises from all quarters, and was given good hope of recovering the dower of your mother and aunt, so that I have no doubt, had you come hither, you would already have attained your object.   I therefore exhort you not to sacrifice your interests, but betake yourself here to Venice. Do not delay coming, as your aunt is very old.' In the same way, in 1551, Cabot's claims to 'credits and recovery of property' in Venice seem to have had this much of truth at the bottom of them—that relatives of his had lived and died within the territories of the Republic, and that there existed property left by them to which Sebastian may have had less claim than others in (or out of) possession, but which at any rate gave a decent pretext for him as a descendant of John Cabot to institute legal inquiries in his native place.

But to return. The next point of importance in Sebastian Cabot's Spanish period is his share in the 'Molucca' or 'La Plata Voyage' of 1526–1530. Magellan's voyage,[1] as we have hinted, upset or greatly modified the idea of a demarcation line between Spanish and Portuguese possessions in new discovered lands ; and especially it roused a controversy as to the ownership of the rich Spice Islands of the Moluccas in the East Indies. Spain claimed them as falling within her western division ; Portugal insisted that they were included in her eastern allotment. Among other measures taken for determining this point was a conference of experienced pilots and geographers to draw up a scientific report. On the 15th of April, 1524, Sebastian Cabot, who was one of this committee of experts, signed, with others, the report on the longitude of the partition line in the

---

[1] Completed by Sebastian del Cano in the *Victoria*.

Moluccas, and on the 25th of April a letter to the Emperor from Badajos, the place of meeting, telling him in effect that no agreement could be come to with the Portuguese representatives. In the same year a Spanish expedition was equipped for the Spice Islands, with Sebastian as chief pilot. He had declared that there were plenty of other spice islands near the Moluccas, to which he knew the way (one much shorter than Magellan's route), as he had been there himself before. So at least he was reported to have spoken, by some of his companions in the new 'spice island' voyage. Of this enterprise, which started on April 3, 1526, but never reached the Moluccas at all, resolving itself into a futile expedition in the La Plata estuary, we shall say little in this place, as it belongs exclusively to Spanish history. But we may summarise the chief events of the ill-starred venture in a few words.

While crossing the Atlantic, the fleet managed to make the most instead of the least of that 'zone of calms and baffling winds' near the line which all navigators strove to avoid, and this delayed their arrival on the South American continent till the end of June. Putting in at Pernambuco, Cabot punished certain of his officers, whom he accused of disaffection, and hearing great talk of mineral wealth in the estuary of the Rio de La Plata, he deferred altogether his journey to the Spice Islands, and made for Paraguay. But it was not till the last week of September that the fleet left

Pernambuco. On the 28th of October the chief ship was lost on the island of Santa Catalina, and the squadron did not cross the bar of the La Plata till about the 25th of March, 1527. Nearly three years were spent in most unprofitable attempts to explore, settle, and find gold in this region ; but after many disasters Cabot set out for Spain in November, 1529, and reached home in the summer of 1530 (July 22nd) ' without honour or profit.' This is not the place to discuss the intricate details of Cabot's seamanship and conduct which are connected with the La Plata voyage, but the event certainly justified Oviedo's saying, that a man of science might often be very incapable of managing an expedition.[1] At every point misfortune, whether deserved or undeserved, seems to have dogged his footsteps ; the Indians cut off many of his colonists ; no gold or silver was found to reward the departure from the original plan ; the chief associates in the command fell to wrangling among themselves, as so often happened in the exploring voyages of this time ; and on Cabot's reappearance

[1] Sebastian Cabot, says Oviedo (*Hist. Gen.* ii. 169–170), 'is competent in his cosmographical art, but he is quite ignorant of the science of Vegetius, who believes that it is . . . needful for a commander to . . . be thoroughly acquainted with all the . . . routes of the countries where he is to wage war. . . . Cabot is skilful in . . . constructing both plane and spherical plans of the . . . world. But there is a great difference between leading . . . men and handling an astrolabe or a quadrant.' So Diego Garcia, ' Sebastian Gavoto did not know how to stem those currents [that impeded him] because he was no seaman and possessed no nautical [=practical] science. . . . That navigation Gavoto could not make, with all his astrology.'

in Spain, he was arrested and prosecuted at the suit of four of his principal companions.   He was also arraigned on charges of disobeying his instructions, abusing his authority, committing violences against certain members of the squadron, and causing the loss of certain ships, partly by taking them away from their proper destination.   These proceedings opened on the 28th of July, 1530 ; he was heavily cast ; and after various appeals of his had been heard before the Council of the Indies, he was sentenced (February 1, 1532) to four years' banishment in the Spanish penal colony in Morocco, where he was also to perform military service against the Moors at his own cost.   His salaries were 'levied upon' in order to pay the fines also inflicted upon him, besides the costs of the suits that he had lost.

And now comes in another of the mysteries, or rather, perhaps, another example of the standing mystery of Cabot's life—his amazing influence over the most important men of his time. Very soon after the inferior authorities, up to the Queen Regent herself, had so decisively condemned all Cabot's excuses and appeals, Charles V. returned to Spain, and apparently pardoned Cabot for all his offences, restored him to his position of Pilot-Major (of which, indeed, he seems to have been only temporarily deprived in favour of Alonzo de Chaves), and employed him again in extensive Government works. The sentences against him, with the possible exception of some of the fines, cannot have been carried out ; almost certainly he was never deported to Morocco ; and in the spring of 1533 he was at work on a plani- sphere for the Council of the Indies. Yet another storm he seems to have surmounted at this time. On March 13, 1534, the King authorises an inquiry into Cabot's examination of pilots, and into the offences alleged to have been committed by him in this matter ; but on the 11th of December (in the same year) these charges must plainly have come to nought, as on that date Charles V., in authorising a thorough examina- tion of pilots for their own proper work, orders Cabot to direct the inquiry himself.

There is not much more that need be noticed here of Sebastian's career in Spain, although this lasted till 1548. He was employed in teaching the use of nautical instruments and scientific text books, in examining and granting licences to pilots, in rectifying charts and instruments used at sea, and especially in seeing after the correctness of the great Model Map, established by the Spanish Government, and called the Padron General. He was also bound to enter and tabulate in an official book of entries all descriptions of new found lands given him by pilots, who on their return from every transatlantic voyage were obliged to furnish a report to the Pilot-Major at Seville ; and once again he stamped the maps and instruments issued from the Sevillian 'hydrographical bureau' to navigators, kept a stock of the same in reserve in his own charge, and by a modification of the original contract with the Government, sold maps, which he had constructed, to any one desiring (and privileged) to purchase.

According to Ramusio, Cabot also professed to have made 'many other voyages' after his return from La Plata, but no trace can be found of any of these, unless we count as one his journey to England in 1548, when he quitted the Spanish service. We are on more certain ground when we come to his utterances, on certain geographical matters, delivered in the course of a lawsuit in A.D. 1535, when he was summoned as a witness. This matter arose out of an action of Luis Columbus, grandson of Christopher, to acquire, or rather to reclaim from the Crown of Spain various rights and privileges accruing to his grandfather by contract with Queen Isabella. Here Cabot was called upon as an expert in North-Western questions, and in answer to the inquiry, ' Do you know whether Christopher Columbus was the first to discover the Indies as well as the Islands and Continent or the Ocean, and that no one before him possessed any knowledge of the same ? ' he gave the following reply, mediæval in tone and evasive in character :—
' Solinus, an historical cosmographer, says that among (beyond ?) the Fortunate Islands called Canaries . . . there are isles called Hesperides, which he (Cabot) presumes to be identical with those that were found in the time of the Catholic Kings, and he has heard many

people in this city of Seville say that it was Christopher Columbus who discovered them.' Again, on the question, whether from Venezuela to the Cod Fish country there was continental land 'without any sea intervening,' and whether this was the only mainland discovered in the Ocean, he replied that in his opinion all the countries named as far as the river of the Holy Spirit (in Mexico [1]) were continental because he had seen it, and knew it also from reports of pilots and maritime charts ; but as to the countries beyond (that is, Florida and the Cod Fish Land), he could not assert whether they were a continent or not.

Again, as to the question (which several other pilots had answered in the affirmative) whether the lands mentioned (with others) were commonly set forth in pilots' charts, so as to represent a continuous coast line, Cabot entirely evaded the point at issue. 'All those lands, or most of them,' says he, 'are set forth in maritime charts, many of which differ from each other.' Yet Cabot posed before the world as the great authority on the Cod Fish Land and the North-West passage supposed to lie through them to Asia ; and he was believed by some to have coasted the whole Atlantic seaboard of North America from Newfoundland down to Florida. Now, perhaps, in order to help the Crown to resist the claims of the Columbus family, he throws doubt upon the best ascertained facts about that same seaboard.[2]

[1] This river was in twenty-one degrees north lat.
[2] See additional note at end of this chapter.

In apology for him it may be said that he was possibly influenced by the Verrazano map, or rather by a copy of a portion of the same, which not only showed a great Ocean (Mar de Verrazano) to the West of that strip of Eastern seaboard which was the whole of North America then known, but depicted this Western Ocean as communicating with the Atlantic by a narrow channel a little to the north of Florida. True the Verrazano map itself, in an inscription at this point, carefully stated that an isthmus of land six miles across separated the two seas, and thus left no doubt as to the ' continental ' and unbroken character of the North American Atlantic seaboard; but this inscription was omitted in the earliest copy we possess,[1] which also substituted a connecting strait for a dividing tongue of land. In many respects the Harleian map here referred to bears a striking resemblance to the Cabotian planisphere of 1544—quite as close a likeness, in fact, as is borne to that same planisphere by the Desliens map of 1541 ; and the probability is strong that Cabot was acquainted with both. But in any case, it may be said, the story of Sebastian's actual coasting of that seaboard as far as Florida would be disproved by this Apology, for then Sebastian would have known enough to contradict, from personal knowledge, the mistake suggested by his interrogator,

[1] See the portrayal of this feature (the isthmus) in the Harleian map of *circa* 1536 to 1540, which is the oldest existing known specimen of Dieppese cartography.

and writ large in the Verrazano copy. In answer to this, and as a further excuse for Cabot's evasion, we may perhaps admit that he found it difficult to decide about such great inlets as the mouths of the Chesapeake, the Delaware, or the still larger Pimlico Sound in North Carolina—and did not feel able to say confidently that one of these was not an arm of the Western Ocean on the other side of 'America' communicating here with the Atlantic.

There is not much more for us to notice in this brief review of Sebastian Cabot's career in Spain. Among the last acts recorded of him as Pilot-Major of Charles V., we may mention his official veto on one Diego Gutierrez (pronounced November 5, 1544), who as 'cosmographer royal' was constructing maps and nautical instruments in a way 'prejudicial to navigation.' Gutierrez seems to have appealed to the Council of the Indies, which confirmed Cabot's decision on February 22, 1545.

Again in October, 1545, we find Cabot giving his imprimatur to a book just published at Valladolid— Pedro de Medina's *Art of Navigation.*

And lastly, in the early part of the year 1547, before leaving for England to push his prospects at the Court of Edward VI., Cabot appointed Diego Gutierrez as his deputy in the office of Pilot-Major. This would be a strange measure, even among the many strange things attributed to Sebastian, if this were the same Gutierrez whom he had interdicted

a little more than two years previous ; but there were
two men of this name, both known to history, though
belonging to the same family, then resident in Spain—
one being the father and the other the son, and there
is no proof that both the above-quoted measures refer
to the same individual.   However this may be, the
claims of the new deputy were not admitted by the
Council of the Indies.   On September 22, 1549,
when it had become pretty clear that Cabot was
not intending to resume his duties in Spain, the
Council declared Gutierrez incompetent to fill the
post to which Sebastian had appointed him.

CHAPTER X

AND now the scene shifts back once more to our own
island, and we come to what we may call the 'Second
English Period' in the life of Sebastian Cabot. In
this, though difficulties and contradictions still await
us, we shall perhaps find them less entangling than
before; the 'Sphinx of the sixteenth century' is now
prepared with a plainer account of himself; and the
questions of historical inquiry are able to elicit a more
satisfactory account of the last ten years of his life
than of any other period.

As early as 1538 Sebastian is putting out feelers,
we may say, towards England. Thus Sir Thomas
Wyatt, English Ambassador in Spain at that time,
addresses a memorandum (November 28, 1538) to
Sir Philip Hoby in the following terms : ' To

remember Sebastian Cabot. He hath here but 300
ducats a year, and is desirous, if he might not serve
the King (Henry VIII.), at least to see him, as his
old master. And I think therein. And that I may
have an answer in this.' Hoby was then just leaving
Spain for England, so that Cabot's request was given
with all the urgency possible. But nothing immediate
came of it ; and, indeed, with one very doubtful
exception, we have at present no evidence of any
result before the death of Henry VIII. The exception lies in a possible allusion of Chapuys, Charles
V.'s Ambassador in England, under the year 1541.
Writing from London to the Queen Regent of the
Netherlands (the Queen of Hungary) on May 26th,
Chapuys speaks of the English monarch as disinclined
to enter upon war with the Emperor, though 'if he
knew of any other country where his subjects could
barter their merchandise, except the Emperor's
dominions, he would willingly send them thither to
sell their goods, even if his own revenue were
diminished by it ; he would find other marts where
his people could take their goods rather than suffer
the retaliations to which the English merchants trading
with the Emperor's dominions must and will be
subjected. As a proof of this statement, about two
months ago, there was a deliberation in the Privy
Council as to the expediency of sending two ships
to the Northern Seas for the purpose of discovering
a passage between Islandt (Iceland) and Engroneland

(Greenland) for the Northern regions, where it was thought that, owing to the extreme cold, English woollen cloths would be very acceptable, and sell for a good price. To this end the King has retained here for some time a pilot from Civille (Seville) well versed in affairs of the sea, though in the end the undertaking has been abandoned, all owing to the King not choosing to agree to the pilot's terms, so that for the present, at least, the city of Antwerp is sure of not losing the commerce of woollen cloth of English manufacture.'

Was this pilot from Seville no other than Sebastian Cabot? It is hard of belief. Chapuys would surely have written very differently if the pilot he mentions had been, to his knowledge, the ' Pilot-Major ' of his master's naval service ; and yet nothing in the tenor of his despatch indicates that the name of the stranger ' well versed in affairs of the sea ' was in any way kept secret from the Ambassador's informant. If he was so well informed about so secret a meeting of the Privy Council, he is likely also to have been informed of the identity of their foreign adviser. Now in 1541 Sebastian Cabot was deeply engaged in work for the Spanish Crown. How could he have returned to Spain, taken up his offices, and enjoyed the favour of Charles V. till his final departure in 1548, if in 1541 he was advising—and was known to be advising —the King of England in schemes which might prove highly prejudicial to Spanish interests over-sea?

Strange as are the fluctuations of his life, marvellous as is the good fortune of his career, and apparently inexhaustible as is the influence he exerted over men of the highest position and authority, yet the assumption here required is too hard a saying for us. And besides its abstract difficulties, there is, in the concrete, no sufficient warrant for it. Chapuys' language is far too indefinite, and no sufficient proof exists that his 'pilot from Seville' is Sebastian Cabot. The merely negative argument is not sufficient,—that since the death of Estevam Gomez, who cannot be traced later than 1537 by our present lights, Cabot was the only mariner in Spain who had or pretended to have a knowledge of the seas between Iceland and Greenland; and that consequently he must be the person mentioned by Chapuys. This is surely applying the exhaustive method with rather too off-hand a touch.

Sebastian Cabot could not well complain of Spanish ingratitude. As Pilot-Major he had long been drawing from the Treasury of Charles V. more than twice the income which De Solis, nearly twice the salary which Vespucci, had enjoyed; in 1525 he had been allowed to transfer to his wife, for her lifetime, a gratuity of 25,000 maravedis which had been conferred on him; the sovereign had stood between him and his enemies, had saved him from most of the penalties of his misfortunes on the La Plata voyage, and had kept him in office as the chief geographical adviser of the Government in spite of laws (of 1527 and 1534) which debarred foreigners from holding the position of pilot in Spain. Yet Cabot, as we have seen, had entertained the idea of returning to the English service as early as 1538 ; when he furnished material for his famous surviving planisphere in 1544 he at any rate was ready to credit the English discovering claim in North America with a far more southerly landfall than was generally conceded at that time in Spanish maps ; and on the accession of Edward VI., in 1547, he renewed his application to the English Government with success. He may be fairly supposed to have conveyed a definite offer in the summer of 1547 ; on the 29th of September of that year his offer was accepted by the Privy Council ; and on the 9th of October order was given to Sir Edward Peckham, High Treasurer of the Mints, to supply the money necessary for Cabot's conveyance to this country—or as the memorandum expressed it : 'Mr. Peckham had warrant for £100 for the transporting of one Shabot, a pilot, to come out of Hispain to serve and inhabit in England.'[1] By January of the year 1548 Cabot had returned to his 'old employment' ; and on the Feast of the Epiphany (6th of January) of that year Edward VI. granted him an annuity of £166 13s. 4d. in the following terms :—

'The King to all to whom these presents shall

---

[1] This is signed by E. Somerset (the Lord Protector) ; T. Cantuarien (Cranmer), and four others.

come, greeting :—Know ye that we, in consideration
of the good and acceptable services done *and to be done*
unto us by our beloved servant Sebastian Caboto,[1] of
our special grace, certain knowledge, mere motion,
and by the advice and counsel of our most honourable
uncle Edward Duke of Somerset, Governor of our
person, and Protector of our kingdom, dominions, and
subjects, and of the rest of our Council, have given and
granted, and by these presents do give and grant, to
the said Sebastian Caboto, a certain annuity or yearly
revenue of one hundred threescore and six pounds,
thirteen shillings, and four pence, sterling, to have,
enjoy, and yearly receive the foresaid annuity or yearly
revenue ; to the foresaid Sebastian Caboto during his
natural life, out of our Treasury at the receipt of
our Exchequer at Westminster at the hands of our
Treasurers and paymasters, there remaining for the
time being ; at the Feasts of the Annunciation of the
blessed Virgin Mary, the Nativity of St. John Baptist,
St. Michael the Archangel, and the Nativity of Our
Lord, to be paid by equal portions. And further, of
our more special grace, and by the advice and consent
aforesaid, we do give, and by these presents do grant,
unto the aforesaid Sebastian Caboto, so many and so
great sums of money as the said annuity or yearly
revenue of an hundred threescore and six pounds,
thirteen shillings, four pence, doth amount and rise
unto from the Feast of St. Michael the Archangel

[1] Not Cabot*a*, as Harrisse reads.

last past unto this present time, to be had and received by the aforesaid Sebastian Caboto, and his assigns, out of our aforesaid Treasury, at the hands of our aforesaid Treasurers and officers of our Exchequer, of our free gift, without account, or anything else therefore to be yielded, paid, or made, to us our heirs or successors, forasmuch as herein express mention is made to the contrary.

'In witness whereof we have caused these our Letters to be made patents : Witness the King at Westminster the Sixth day of January in the second year of his reign. The year of our Lord 1548.'

From the terms of this document, as well as from the other official papers relating to Cabot's second sojourn in this country, it does not appear that any particular office was created for Cabot in England, or that Hakluyt is *technically* correct when he says that 'King Edward VI. advanced the worthy and excellent Sebastian Cabota to be Grand Pilot of England.' On the contrary, a paper of Queen Elizabeth's time, still preserved among the Lansdowne manuscripts, offers a presumption to the contrary. This is a 'copy of the appointment of Stephen Burrough [Borowghe] to the office of Chief Pilot of England, with his own reasons for the necessity of such an office, 1563.' The whole tenor of this memorial, which discusses ' three especial causes and considerations amongst others, wherefore the office of Pilot-Major is allowed and esteemed in Spain, Portugal, and other places where navigation flourisheth,' is adverse to any theory of Cabot's previous tenure of such office—no word is dropped which could imply a precedent—and Burrough discusses the duties of a Chief Pilot as one would discuss the working of a new venture. So if Sebastian really discharged the aforesaid duties (*e.g.*, from 1549 to 1553, or 'before he entered into the Northern Discovery' as Hakluyt puts it) he must have done so in a very undefined and general way. Certainly he does not appear to have been charged in England, as in Spain, with the official 'examination and appointing of all such mariners as shall from this time forward take the charge of a pilot or master upon him in any ship within this realm.' But, nevertheless, as we shall see presently by particular proofs, Cabot seems to have enjoyed considerable authority in naval matters during the reigns of Edward VI. and Mary. He was, in all probability, what may be called 'nautical adviser' to the English Government.

Peckham had warrant, as just above related, on the 9th of October, 1547, to pay the expenses of Sebastian's trans-shipment from Spain to England ; and the official notices of this business (which appears to have been transacted between October, 1547, and January, 1548) are completed by another memorandum of the Privy Council, under date of the 2nd of September, 1549—'The Exchequer had warrant for £100 to Henry Oystryge, by him taken up by exchange for conducting of Sebastian Sabott [Cabot].' But already, by the time of this last settlement, difficulties had arisen (or were very shortly to arise) about the various claims on Sebastian's services. He was now definitely committed, as he had never been before, to the allegiance of the Crown of England. Yet he had only left Spain on a leave of absence, and had resigned neither the office nor the pay which he received from Charles V. Accordingly the Emperor demands his return on the 25th of November, 1549, in a despatch to the Privy Council : 'Whereas one Sebastian Cabot, General Pilot of the Emperor's Indies, is presently in England, forasmuch as he cannot stand the King your master in any great [stead], seeing he hath small practice in these seas, and is a very necessary man for the Emperor, whose servant he is [and] hath a pension of him, his majesty desireth some order to be taken for his sending over in such sort as his Ambassador shall at better length declare unto the King your Master's Council.' To add another small mystery to the greater ones we have already puzzled over, it seems extraordinary that for nearly two years Cabot should have drawn his new English salary, and enjoyed his new English office, without being brought to any definite renunciation of his Spanish one, and that Charles should appear to be entirely ignorant that 'his servant' had accepted any other appointment.

The Privy Council replied to the Emperor on April 21, 1550, that 'Cabot was not detained in England by them, but that he of himself refused to go either into Spain or to the Emperor, and that he being of that mind and the King's subject[1] (*i.e.*, an Englishman) no reason nor equity would that he should be forced to go against his will.'

The correspondence did not stop here, but was briskly continued on the Emperor's side by his envoy in England : 'Upon the which answer,' ran the report of the English Privy Council, ' the said Ambassador said that if this were Cabot's answer, then he required that the said Cabot, in the presence of some one whom we could appoint, might speak with the said Ambassador, and declare unto him this to be his mind and answer. Whereunto we condescended, and at the last sent the said Cabot with Richard Shelley to the Ambassador. Who, as the said Shelley hath made report to us, affirmed to the said Ambassador that he was not minded to go neither into Spain nor to the Emperor. Nevertheless, having knowledge of certain things very necessary for the Emperor's knowledge, he was well contented, for the good will he bore the Emperor, to write his mind unto him,[2] or declare the same here to any such as should be appointed to hear him. Whereunto the said Ambassador asked the said Cabot, in case the King's Majesty or we should command him to go to the Emperor, whether then he would not do it ? Whereunto Cabot made answer

---

[1] Does this mean that he had been naturalised between 1548 and 1550 ? This is the only document known where Sebastian is explicitly called a subject of the King of England.

[2] As he does in 1553. See p. 197, &c.

as Shelley reporteth, that if the King's Highness or we did command him so to do, then he knew well enough what he had to do. But it seemeth that the Ambassador took this answer of Cabot to sound as though Cabot had answered that, being commanded by the King's Highness or us, then he would be contented to go to the Emperor, wherein we reckon the said Ambassador to be deceived, for that the said Cabot had divers times before declared unto us that he was fully determined not to go hence at all.'

Sebastian accordingly stayed in England ; established himself once more in Bristol ; and petitioned successfully for a copy of the letters patent granted to his father, his brothers, and himself, on March 5, 1496. 'We have ascertained,' declares the patent copy, 'by an inspection of the records of our Chancery that the Lord Henry VII., formerly King of England, has issued letters patent, the tenor of which is as follows.' The original patent of 1496 is then recited, with a mistake as to the date of issue, which is given as April 5th (for March 5th) ; and the document concludes with this explanation : 'Whereas the aforesaid letters have been lost by accident, as the said Sebastian has declared, saying that should they be found again he will return them to our Chancery to be put on record :—Now we, by these presents, at the request of the said Sebastian, have thought fit to cause the tenor of the said letters to be copied.'

The English Government, like the Spanish, seemed

eager to heap upon Cabot rewards and privileges. And among these we have in 1550, 'An acquittance to the Treasurer and Barons of the Exchequer for the payment of diver sums of money by the Council's warrant from the Feast of Easter in the fourth year of Edward VI. until Michaelmas following. To Sebastian Cabot ICI ħ [£200] by way of the K[ing's] M[ajesty's] reward.' Again, on June 26, 1550, there is a similar warrant to the Exchequer to pay unto Sebastian Cabot £200 by way of the King's Majesty's reward. And once more, but of doubtful authenticity, resting only on the word of Strype, another grant of equal amount was bestowed on 'Sebastian Cabot the great seaman' in March, 1551. This last is probably only a confused and wrongly dated version of the present of June 1550, while even the first quoted and dateless 'acquittance' has been conjectured to be a variant of the same warrant. In any case Sebastian received in 1550–51, at least one gratuity of £200, [= £2,400 in our money] from Edward VI., altogether independent of his pension.

Yet at this very time the 'great seaman' was re-opening his old intrigues with Venice, through Giacomo Sorenzo, the Venetian Ambassador in London. To Sorenzo he seems to have repeated the statements he had made to Contarini, of his Venetian origin, of his zeal to serve the Republic, of the secrets which he could reveal. His overtures were again received with favour : the Council of Ten were 'much pleased' with what they had just heard 'about their most faithful Sebastian Cabot,' and Sorenzo was directed to 'endeavour to obtain from Cabot as many particulars as possible about his design respecting *this navigation*,' —probably the old idea of a North-Western passage to Asia, answering to the South-Western way found by Magellan.

While this was being so favourably discussed from the Venetian side, the services of the Reverend Peter Vannes, the English Ambassador to the Republic, were also enlisted in aid of Cabot's alleged property rights in Venice. 'Cabot's matter' to Vannes meant the recovery of a claim based on an estate in Venetian territory once belonging to Sebastian's mother and aunt. It was the same excuse apparently which had served in the negotiations with Contarini in 1523, and the 'matter,' as Vannes wrote to the English Council, was now about fifty years old. The Seigniory, in their letter to Sorenzo of the 12th of September, 1551, urge Cabot to appear personally in Venice and identify himself, as 'no one there knows him familiarly, and his affair is of very ancient date.' Meantime, however, as Vannes informs the English Council, the Ten had ordered 'Baptista Ramusio, one of their secretaries,' to make inquiries; Vannes had delivered to Ramusio, in the presence of the Seigniory, such evidence as had come into his hands; and the said Ramusio, being 'put in trust' of the matter by Cabot, would 'ensearch with diligence any

way and knowledge possible' that might 'stand to
the said Sebastian's profit and obtaining of right,'
though 'by the death of men, decaying of houses, and
perishing of writings . . . it were hard to come to
any assured knowledge thereof.'   Here, nevertheless,
the matter ends ; Sebastian appears not to have gone
to Venice either to prosecute his claim or to concert
measures with the Seigniory for an exploring venture ;
on the contrary, he stayed comfortably in ¦England,
enjoying the very solid advantages of a good position ;
nor is there any evidence of his visiting Venice in
later life.   We may believe, if we like, what he said
to Eden about his infantile travels—how at four years
old he was taken to Venice by his father, and 'so
returned again [to England] after certain years'—
nothing warrants us in supposing that he ever quitted
England for Italy after he finally came to live among
us in 1547.

CHAPTER XI

CABOT'S EXACT EMPLOYMENT IN ENGLAND AT THIS TIME—HIS SUPPOSED CHAMPIONSHIP OF ENGLISH MERCHANTS AGAINST THE EASTERLINGS—HIS SHARE IN THE NORTH-EAST VENTURE OF 1553

SEBASTIAN CABOT'S employment in England, as we have hinted already, seems not to have been so definite as in Spain. There he was the Royal Chief Pilot; here he enjoyed an increased salary; but as to his duties, it is difficult to describe them more precisely than in Biddle's words, 'he would seem to have exercised a general supervision over the maritime concerns of the country, under the eye of the King and Council, and to have been called upon whenever there was occasion for nautical skill and experience.' His work also included, as in Spain, a supervision of pilots and ship-masters. Thus Hakluyt gives us the case of one John Alday, who was 'letted [from going to the Levant] by the Prince's letters, which my master Sebastian Cabot had obtained . . . to my great grief.' The

same great collector has inserted a notice of Cabot's
being present at the examination (in England) of a
French pilot, well acquainted with the coast of Brazil.
But the most important of Cabot's enterprises, in this
last period of his life, was his promotion of the North-
East venture of 1553, and possibly of other new movements, through his connection with the Company
of Merchant Adventurers, of which he was Governor.
Hakluyt has preserved the instructions drawn up by
Cabot for the use of the mariners on this voyage, and
his share in the whole scheme is borne out by many
evidences. For instance, when the Company ('of
Merchant Adventurers' or 'of Muscovy') was
formally incorporated on February 6, 1555, it is
with this proviso : 'In consideration that Sebastian
Cabot hath been the chief setter-forth of this
journey : [1] therefore we make, ordain, and constitute
the said Sebastian to be the first and present Governor
of the same fellowship and commonalty. . . . To
have and enjoy the said office of Governor, to him
the said Sebastian Cabota, during his natural life,
without amoving or dismissing from the same
room.'

But before coming to the voyage of 1553, we have
to notice Cabot's alleged leadership of the Merchant
Adventurers in their struggle with the Easterlings of
the Hanse towns. This story, in its connection with
Sebastian, appears first to be found in Campbell's *Lives*

[1] Namely, the journey of Chancellor and Willoughby, A.D. 1553.

M

of the British Admirals, written in 1742, in the following shape :—

'At last the Company of Merchant Adventurers,
at *the head of which was our Sebastian Cabot,* on
the 29th of December, 1551, exhibited to the Council
an Information against the Merchants of the Steelyard,[1] to which they were directed to put in their
answer. They did so, and after several hearings and
a reference to the King's Solicitor-General, his Counsel
learned in the law and the Recorder of London, a
decree passed on the 24th of February, whereby these
Merchants of the Steelyard were declared to be no
legal corporation.'

The Merchant Adventurers, known in mediæval
times (at least, from 1399) as the 'Brotherhood of St.
Thomas of Canterbury,' had gained their later title in
1513 as the 'Company of Merchant Adventurers of
England,' and successfully routed their Easterling
rivals of the Steelyard in 1551, as above stated. But
no official document, Government record, or chronicle
of the time, mentions the name of Cabot in connection
with this commercial struggle. The grant of Edward
VI. to Cabot in March, 1551, as given by Strype—
'To Sebastian Cabot (the great seaman), £200, by
way of the King's Majesty's reward'—has been
supposed by Biddle and others to be an acknowledg-
ment of his services on this occasion, but there is no
positive proof of this. John Wheeler, in his account

[1] The London House of the Hanse Merchants.

of the Company, written by him as Secretary of the same in 1601, does not refer to Cabot's supposed championship, and the same is true of all other contemporary evidence. Records were not, however, then so exhaustive and so careful that their omission of a circumstance need absolutely preclude all possibility of it ; and if we could prove that Sebastian had as early as December, 1551, become, as Campbell says, head of the Company of Merchant Adventurers, it would then be not merely possible, but probable, that he took a prominent part in the contest with the Easterlings. But the earliest documentary evidence of Sebastian's Governorship is of the 9th of May, 1553, when in the instructions given to the expedition of Chancellor and Willoughby, it is stated that these same instructions were ' compiled, made, and delivered by the right reverend Sebastian Cabota, Governor of the Mystery and Company of the Merchant Adventurers,' and his signature is appended in a corresponding form, ' I, Sebastian Cabota, Governor.'   But in March, 1551–52, viz., after the conclusion of the Steelyard contest, William Dansell was still Governor of the Company, as John Sturgeon had been in 1549.   Cabot therefore can only be assumed to have been Governor of the Merchant Adventurers in the spring of 1553, before the incorporation of the Company in 1555, but not (in that case) before the battle of the Company with the Easterlings.

And now we come to the North-East venture of
1553, the real beginning of English exploring activity,
of our wider commercial ambitions, and of national
interest in schemes of discovery, leading to trade.
With this Sebastian Cabot was, beyond all cavil,
intimately associated ; and it is curious that the same
family should have had such a share in furthering
English enterprise both to the North-West and the
North-East. Up to this time all our efforts had been
turned Westwards ; the Portuguese voyage to Novaia
Zemlya[1] in search of the North-East waterway to
Cathay (in 1484) had not drawn many imitators in
its track ; and only the repeated failure of all attempts
to the North-West[2] drove the English adventurers
to consider seriously the other alternative.

It was time something fresh was done, for the
prosperity of English commerce was now at a very
low ebb, and the outlook sufficiently dreary, as
Hakluyt tells us : ‘At what time our merchants
perceived the commodities and goods of England to
be in small request with the countries and people
about us and near to us ; and that those merchandises
which strangers did earnestly desire were now
neglected and the price thereof abated, though by us
carried to their own ports, and all foreign merchandises
in great account, certain grave citizens of London

[1] Under King John II.
[2] And the increased knowledge of the length and difficulties of this
enterprise, after the discoveries of Balboa, Magellan, Cartier, and others.

began to think how this mischief might be remedied. Neither was there a remedy wanting—for as the wealth of the Spaniards and Portuguese, by the discovery and search of new trades and countries, was marvellously increased ; supposing the same to be a means for them to obtain the like, they thereupon resolved upon a new and strange navigation.'

The first suggestion of a North-*East* attempt to reach Cathay, in the English service, seems to have been made in 1525 by Paulo Centurioni to Henry VIII. His plan was exactly the same as that of the Adventurers of 1553—'to bring the merchandise of Calicut to the north part of Europe by way of Muscovy.' Centurioni's premature death postponed his enterprise, which had found great favour with Henry VIII. ; but, after Cabot's first departure from England, the voyage of John Rut in 1527, of Grube and an unnamed adventurer in the same year, and of Hore in 1536 (all, however, to the North-*West*), as well as the plan already noticed in 1541 for finding a passage between Iceland and Greenland, and the letter of Robert Thorne from Seville in 1527, bore witness to the interest still taken, so many years after the Cabots had first essayed it, in the plan of a northern passage to Asia.

It was, however, with the enterprise of 1553 that the English nation, as a whole, woke up to their opportunities and their mission in exploration, trade, and colonisation. The half-century that had elapsed between the first voyage of John Cabot and the present year (1553) had been singularly barren of discovering enterprises on the part of Englishmen ; but from this time, at the close of the reign of Edward VI., and still more from the beginning of that of Elizabeth, England fairly entered into competition with the other exploring nations ; and Sebastian Cabot, as one of the leading figures, at any rate, among the English Merchant Adventurers, was here certainly engaged in the work of building up Greater Britain. It is childish and unfair to detract from his credit by the argument that his object was only an expedition to Cathay, that he had no idea of the Muscovy trade, and that the real success of the expedition was unintended and unexpected by him. The same is true both of Willoughby and of Chancellor, who actually made so much of the incidental success. It is also true, of course, in the case of the discovery of America by Columbus.

The voyage of 1553, which discovered Russia to English politics and trade, is in one sense the most important of all our commercial ventures. For in this we have the start of Greater Britain, and the first step in such a movement must always have a place of its own. John Cabot's success in 1497 and 1498 had not really aroused the nation ; our destiny had to wait another half-century before its fulfilment began ; and it is only in 1553 that continuous English enterprise begins. The first half of the six-

teenth century, though it cannot be included in our
mediæval period, is still less a part of modern exploration.   It is essentially a time of change and preparation, when foreign mariners and their disciples from
amongst ourselves drilled into the English mind
some understanding of that expansion of Europe
which men saw going on all around them.   By the
time of this new 'trial' of the Russian trade and
North-East passage, native English feeling was ready
to work in its own interest for its own gains, and
with this voyage we have fairly entered upon the age
of the adventurers and discoverers who founded our
colonies and our modern commerce.

Sebastian Cabot himself took no part in the actual
voyage of 1553.   He was now an old man—seventy-
eight, at least—and his office as Governor of the
Adventurers' Company required of him rather the
stay-at-home work of general supervision than the
duties of pioneer enterprise.   But one task obviously
fell to his share—the issuing of general instructions ;
and as these instructions have especial interest from
various points of view, we give the substance of all
the three and thirty articles now composed for the
fleet.   For they are the only writings that have come
down to us (with the possible exception of some
of the 'Legends' on the map of 1544) from either
John or Sebastian Cabot ; they are interesting in
themselves, and full of shrewdness and experienced
wisdom—of devoutness, too, as became one who

was a servant of a Puritan *régime*. In the thirty-second article we have a clear reference to opponents and their arguments—so excellent against the North-East passage in itself, so happily ineffective against the spirit of enterprise, which even in its failures brought to England so much incidental gain. Taking Cabot's thirty-three articles together, they make up a sort of Whole Duty of Man, as seaman, as Protestant, and as trader; it is curious to see how far their tone has been preserved in the expansion of England from that day onward; in the light of such counsels we may understand something of our success. They are a good charter for the men who were beginning to work at the creation of an English empire. The first four enjoin loyalty and obedience, and warn against dissensions; the seventh prescribes the keeping of a log and journal—a very early case of systematic attention to such matters; the ninth orders weekly accounts of expense; the twelfth and thirteenth are concerned with religious matters—prayers are to be read on board twice a day; but by the twenty-second there was to be no religious controversy and no preaching or proselytising in foreign ports; where necessary, the mariner's religion was to be 'dissembled.' Articles 20 and 21 forbid all private bargaining— every one is to remember that he belongs to a Company and Mystery; by the twenty-third, information is to be got by all means possible from the natives of new countries; 'and if the person taken,' suggests Article 24, 'may be made drunk with your beer or wine, you shall know the secrets of his heart.' Moreover, the crews are never to go far inland ; and are never to enrage foreigners by laughing at their customs, however odd they may seem ; descriptions of all new lands are to be written down ; and natives must be allured to the ships by a brave show and noise. If any go to entertainments on shore, it must be armed, and in a strong party ; watch is always to be kept on board, and the London merchants are to be well advertised of everything that is being done.

CHAPTER XII

THE full text of Sebastian's instructions to the fleet of Willoughby and Chancellor is, with some unimportant omissions, as follows :—

'Ordinances, Instructions, and Advertisements of and for the direction of the intended voyage for Cathay, compiled, made, and delivered by the right worshipful M. Sebastian Cabota, Esquire, Governor of the Mystery and Company of the Merchant Adventurers, for the discovery of Regions, Dominions, Islands, and places unknown . . . the ninth of May in the year . . . 1553 and in the seventh year of the reign of . . . Edward VI.

'First, the Captain-General, with the pilot-major, the masters, merchants, and other officers, to be so knit and accorded in unity, love, conformity, and obedience in every degree on all sides, that no dissension, variance, or contention may rise or spring betwixt them and the mariners of this Company, to the damage or hindrance of the voyage ; for that dissension, by many experiences, hath overthrown many notable, intended, and likely enterprises and exploits.

‘ 2. Item, forasmuch as every person hath given an oath to be true, faithful, and loyal subjects and liege men . . . it behoveth every person . . . to remember his said charge . . . [of loyalty to the English service].

‘ 3. Item, where furthermore every mariner or passenger in his ship hath given like oath to be obedient to the Captain-General and to every Captain and master in his ship, for the observation of these present orders contained in this book and all other which hereafter shall be made by the 12 Counsellors in the present book named . . . therefore it is convenient that this present book shall once every week (by the discretion of the Captain) be read to the said Company, to the intent that every man may the better remember his oath, conscience, duty, and charge.

‘ 4. Item, every person, by virtue of his oath, to do effectually, . . . as shall be . . . commanded by the Captain-General . . .

‘ 5. Item, all courses in Navigation to be set by the . . . Captain, Pilot-Major, Masters, and Master Mates, with the assent of the Counsellors . . . so that the Captain-General shall in all Councils and assemblies have a double voice.

'6. Item, that the fleet shall keep together and not separate . . . as much as by wind and weather may be . . . permitted, and that the Captains, Pilots, and Masters shall speedily come aboard the Admiral, when and as often as he shall seem to have just cause to assemble them for consultation. . . .

'7. Item, that the Merchants and other skilful persons in writing shall daily . . . describe . . . the Navigation of every day and night, with the points and observations of the lands, tides, elements, altitude of the Sun, course of the Moon and Stars—and the same so noted by the order of the Master and Pilot of every ship to be put in writing—the Captain-General assembling the Masters together once every week (if wind and weather shall serve) to confer all the observations and notes of the said ships, to the intent it may appear wherein the notes do agree, and wherein they dissent ; and upon good debatement . . . to put the same into a common ledger, to remain of record for the Company ; the like order to be kept in proportioning of the Cards, Astrolabes, and other instruments prepared for the Voyage, at the charge of the Company.

'8. Item, that all enterprises . . . of discovering or landing to search Isles . . . and such like . . . to be determined advisedly. And that in all enterprises, notable ambassages or presents to Princes to be done and executed by the Captain-General in person or by such other as he by common assent shall appoint. . . .

'9. Item, the Steward and Cook of every ship and their associates, to give and render to the Captain and other head officers of their ship weekly (or oftener) . . . a just . . . account of expense . . . and so to order the same that no waste be made.

'10. Item, when any inferior . . . officer . . . shall be tried untrue, remisse, negligent, or unprofitable . . . then every such officer to be punished . . . at the discretion of the Captain and assistants. . . .

'11. Item, if any mariner or officer inferior shall be found not worthy the place that he is shipped for . . . such person may be unshipped . . . at any place within the King's Majesty's . . . dominion, and one more . . . worthy to be put in his place . . . and Order to be taken that the party dismissed shall be allowed proportionally the value of that he shall have deserved to the time of his . . . discharge.

'12. Item, that no blaspheming of God, or detestable swearing be used in any ship, nor communication of ribaldry, filthy tales, or ungodly talk to be suffered in the company of any ship, neither dicing, carding, tabling, nor other devilish games to be frequented, whereby ensueth not only poverty to the players, but also strife, variance, brawling, fighting, and oftentimes murder, to the . . . destruction of the parties and provoking of God's . . . just wrath. . . . These and all such-like pestilences and contagions of vices and sins to be eschewed, and the offenders once monished, and not reforming, to be punished at the discretion of the Captain and master. . . .

'13. Item, that morning and evening prayer, with other common services appointed by the King's Majesty and laws of this Realm to be . . . read in every ship daily by the minister in the Admiral and [by] the Merchant, or some other person learned in other ships, and the Bible or Paraphrases to be read devoutly and Christianly to God's honour, and for His Grace to be obtained by humble prayer of the Navigants accordingly.

'14. Item, that every officer is to be charged by inventory with the particulars of his charge, and to render an . . . account of the same, together with . . . temperate dispending of powder, shot, and use of all kind of artillery, which is to be . . . preserved for the necessary defence of the fleet, together with due keeping of all instruments of your Navigation. . . .

'15. Item, no liquor to be spilt on the ballast, or filthiness to be left within board ; the cook room and all other places to be kept clean for the better health of the company—the gromals and pages to be brought up according to the laudable orders . . . of the sea, as well in learning of Navigation as in exercising of that which to them appertaineth.

'16. Item, the liveries in apparel given to the mariners to be kept by the Merchants, and not to be worn, but by order of the Captain. . . .

'17. Item, when any mariner or passenger have need of any necessary furniture of apparel for his body and conservation of his health, the same shall be delivered him by the Merchant . . . without any gain to be exacted by the Merchant. . . .

'18. Item, the sick, diseased, weak . . . person aboard to be . . . holpen in the time of his infirmity, and every manner of person without respect to bear another's burden, and no man to refuse such labour as . . . be put to him for the . . . public wealth. . . .

'19. Item, if any person shall fortune to die, such . . . goods as he shall have at the time of his death . . . to be kept by order of the Captain and Master of the ship, and an Inventory to be made and conveyed to the use of his wife and children, or otherwise according to his . . . will . . . and the day of his death to be entered in the Merchants' . . . Books . . . to the intent it may be known what wages he shall have deserved to his death. . . .

'20. Item, that the Merchants appointed for this voyage shall not make any show or sale . . . or open their commodities to any . . . without the consent of the Captains, the Cape Merchants, and the assistants, or four of them . . . and all wares . . . trucked . . . to be booked by the Merchants . . . and inventory of all goods . . . so trucked . . . to be presented to the Governor, Consults, and Assistants in London . . . and no embezzlement shall be used, but the truth of the whole voyage to be opened, to the common benefit of the whole Company and mystery, as appertaineth without guile, fraud, or male engine.

'21. Item, no particular person to hinder or prejudicate the common stock of the Company in sale of his own . . . wares.

'22. Item, not to disclose to any nation the state of our Religion, but to pass it over in silence, seeming to bear with such rites as the place hath, where you shall arrive.

'23. Item, forasmuch as our people and ships may appear unto them strange . . . it is to be considered, how they may be used, learning much of their natures and disposition, by . . . such . . . as you may either allure or take . . . aboard . . . and there to learn as you may, without violence or force, and no woman to be tempted to dishonesty.

'24. Item, the person so taken to be well entertained, and be set on land . . . that he . . . may allure other to draw nigh . . . and if the person taken may be made drunk with your beer or wine, you shall know the secrets of his heart.

'25. Item, our people may not pass further into a land than that they may be able to recover their pinnaces or ships, and not to credit the fair words of the strange people, which be many times tried subtle and false, nor to be drawn into peril of loss, for the desire of . . . riches . . . ; and esteem your own commodities above all other, and in countenance show not much to desire the foreign commodities; nevertheless, take them as for friendship or by way of permutation.

' 26. Item, every nation and region is to be considered advisedly, and not to provoke them by any disdain, contempt, or such like, but to use them with prudent circumspection, with all gentleness and courtesy, and not to tarry long in one place, until you shall have attained the most worthy place that may be found. . . .

' 27. Item, the names of every people of every Island are to be taken in writing with the commodities . . . of the same, their natures, qualities . . . the site of the same, what . . . they will most willingly depart with [export], and what metals they have.

' 28. Item, if people shall appear gathering of stones, gold, or other like on the sand, your pinnaces may draw nigh, marking what . . . they gather, playing upon the drum or other such . . . as may allure them to harkening, to fantasy . . . but keep you out of danger and show to them no sign of hostility.

' 29. Item, if you shall be invited into any Ruler's house, to dinner or other parliance, go in such order of strength, that you may be stronger than they; and be wary of woods and ambushes, and that your weapons be not out of your possessions.

' 30. Item, if you shall see them wear Lions' and Bears' skins, . . . be not afraid . . .

' 31. Item, there are people that can swim in the sea, havens, and rivers, naked, having bows, coveting

N

to draw nigh your ships, which if they find not well watched . . . they will assault ; if you resist, they dive . . . therefore diligent watch is to be kept both day and night in some islands.

'32. Item, if occasion serve, that you give advertisements of your proceedings in such things as may correspond to the expectation of the Company . . . passing such impediments which by divers writers have ministered . . . suspicion in some heads that this voyage could not succeed for the extremity of the North Pole, lack of passage, and such like ; which have caused wavering minds and doubtful heads not only to withdraw themselves from the adventure of this voyage, but also dissuaded others from the same ; . . . for declaration of the Truth . . . you may by common consent of Counsel send either by land or other ways, such two or one person to bring the same by credit, as you shall think may pass, for that you be not ignorant how many desire to know . . . your welfare, and in what likelihood you be to obtain this notable enterprise, which is hoped no less to succeed to you than the Orient or Occident Indies have to the benefit of the Emperor and Kings of Portugal.

'33. Item, that no conspiracies be suffered . . . but always obedience to be used by all, not only for conscience' sake towards God, under whose merciful hand navigants, above all other creatures, naturally be most high and vicine, but also for prudence and worldly policy. . . .

'In witness whereof I, Sebastian Gabota, Governor aforesaid, to these present Ordinances have subscribed my name and put my Seal, the day and year above written.'

As Sebastian himself did not sail with the expedition, it will be sufficient for the present purpose to say that Chancellor and Willoughby started from the Thames on the 20th of May, were separated off the Norway coast, and never met again—Willoughby and his crew being frozen to death near Kola in Lapland (1554), while Chancellor successfully rounded the North Cape, entered the White Sea and by a daring journey from the Dwina to Moscow, opened communication with the Russia of Ivan the Terrible. Before the close of 1554 Chancellor returned to England, with letters from the Czar to Edward VI., offering entertainment to Willoughby 'when he shall arrive,' and declaring that Russia was 'willing that you send to us ships and vessels. And if you send one of your Majesty's Council to treat with us . . . your merchants may, with all kinds of wares and where they will, make their market . . . with all liberties throughout my dominions, to come and go at their pleasure.'

But when Chancellor returned, Queen Mary was already on the throne, Cabot however apparently retaining for some years both his pension from the Crown and his Governorship of the Merchant Adventurers. At the beginning of her reign the old ques-

tion of the Spanish claim on his services reappears.
Charles had waited till July 11, 1552, before filling up
his place in Cosmography at the 'Contractation
House' of Seville; he did not even then appoint any
successor to him as Pilot-Major; and we find Alonzo
de Santa Cruz, in the very last years of Sebastian's
life, alluding to him as the 'Pilot-Major of His
Majesty, [now] in England.' Further, soon after the
accession of Queen Mary, who (both as a staunch
Catholic and as a possible daughter-in-law of his own),
might be supposed far more amenable to his influence
than Edward VI., the Emperor made another effort
(September 9, 1553) to recover 'his share in' Cabot,
couching his request[1] to the Queen of England under
forms of studied moderation: 'Most high, most excellent and most powerful Princess, our very dear and beloved kind sister and cousin; As I desire to *confer about
certain matters* relative to the safety of the navigation
of my kingdoms and dominions with Captain Cabote,
previously pilot of my Spanish realms, and *who with
my assent and consent* went to England several years
ago, I very affectionately ask of you to grant leave to
the said Cabot, and allow him to come near me, so
that I may make to him the aforesaid communication.
And by so doing you will give me great pleasure, as I
have directed my Ambassador at your Court to state
particularly to you.' To this Sebastian replied, after the
lapse of more than a month, with a somewhat elaborate

[1] Forwarded from Mons in Hainault.

letter of excuse (November 15, 1553), accompanied by pretended disclosures of English plots against Spain, as follows : ' I was almost ready to start on my journey to kiss the hand of your Majesty and give explanations of the affair which Francisco de Urista has related [to you] on my behalf, when I was seized with a quotidian fever, and according to the severity (or otherwise) of this illness, it depends whether I shall be able to undertake this journey, or no, being as I am, very weak and feeling sure that I shall die before reaching my destination . . . but before I arrive at such an end I wish to declare unto your Majesty the secret which I possess.   And because I cannot come in person for the reasons I have stated, and also because by putting it off harm would result, I have determined to say it to your Majesty by writing, and to send it to you by the hands of the aforesaid Francisco de Urista.   For the fact of the matter is that the French Ambassador Boisdauphin has asked me several times—and so has the Duke of Northumberland—as to the land of Peru, what sort of country it was, and what force your Majesty had there, and whether that land was as rich as it was said to be. And I said your Majesty had a very good force of Spaniards in those parts, very well equipped with all necessaries, both in the matter of arms and horses, and I added that the country abounded in mines of silver and gold.   And I would have your Majesty know that I ascertained from both my questioners that

they were seeking to make ready an expedition to go
to the river of the Amazons, and that the expedition
in question was to be made ready in France, and that
in the said fleet were to go 4,000 soldiers, besides the
crews, and that they were to take with them ten
pinnaces. Also that at the mouth of the said river of
the Amazons they were to build a fortress and [then]
to ascend the river with the ten pinnaces, there to
destroy and slay all the Spaniards and to take possession
of the land. And seeing that in the said river they
might very easily catch the Spaniards unprepared or
dispersed throughout the land, they have a chance of
succeeding with their evil plan, from which your
Majesty would receive the greatest injury. Against
this then let your Majesty order measures to be quickly
taken as your Majesty shall think best, for this which
I write to your Majesty is very certain and true. Also
as I ascertained and was given to understand the said
Boisdauphin when he left here [England] carried with
him 2,000 pounds which the Duke [of Northumber-
land] gave him for the purpose I have described, and
especially to make a beginning with the said expedition.

'And as regards the situation [?] of the coast of
Guinea, conformably to the variation of the mariner's
needle from the Pole, if the King of Portugal should
guess at it [the position on the map] your Majesty
knows from what I have said how to meet him.
Moreover, the said Francisco de Urista carries with

him (for your Majesty to see) certain plans, one of
which is a *mappemonde* plotted out to show the
equinox by which your Majesty may see the causes of
the variation of the mariner's needle from the Pole,
and the causes why at other times it [the needle] turns
directly to the Arctic or Antarctic poles; and the other
plan is to show the longitude under any parallel [?] in
which a man may be. And these two plans the said
Francisco de Urista will explain to your Majesty and
demonstrate the use of them, since I have completely
instructed him in all this ; and, being a man conversant
with maritime art [in general], he thoroughly under-
stands this particular matter. And as to the maritime
chart which the said Francisco de Urista has charge of,
I have written to your Majesty some time since about
it and have shown how important it is for your service ;
also I gave an account [of it] backed by my own
name and handwriting to Juan Esquete, your Majesty's
Ambassador, which he was to forward to your Majesty.
And as I am informed this account is now in the
possession of Secretary Eraso ; and to this I would
refer you and say that the aforesaid communication [a
map] is of very great service to your Majesty in the
matter of determining the line of partition made
between the Crown Royal of Spain and that of Portugal, for the reasons I have stated in the said communication. I beg your Majesty to accept the assurance of
my good will, and of the desire which (by the grace of
God and of His most holy mother) I always have and

shall have to serve your Majesty. And on this you may rely; for if it were not for my indisposition, I would come to kiss your Majesty's hand and give my relation in person concerning all that I have said rather than send it in writing [but my illness hinders me]. May God grant your Majesty, &c. From London, the 15 November, 1553. SEBASTIAN CABOT.'

Nor was this communication without effect: for on the 16th of February, 1554, Charles V. refers his son Philip to Cabot's warning: 'Herewith is enclosed a copy of a letter which Sebastian Cabot has written me, whereby you will see what he says about the expedition which the French are intending to make; you will give order that the necessary measures be taken in this matter.'

Three explanations seem possible here on general grounds. Either Cabot was betraying the English Government, while taking its pay; or, like Hawkins with Philip II. in after days, he was trying to draw valuable secrets from the Spanish authorities by a pretence of treachery; or, lastly, he was endeavouring to keep up his credit with his old master by the revelation of plots invented by himself to enhance his own value in view of a possible return to the Spanish service. As we might expect, the ordinary Cabotian difficulties crop up in this question as in others. Sebastian writes as if the Duke of Northumberland were still one of the directors of this Franco-English plot against Spain. But he had been beheaded in the previous summer—August 22, 1553. Since then Mary Tudor had become firmly established on the throne, and had shown a distinct welcome to the proposal of her marriage with Philip. Both from her religion, her politics, and her past and prospective connection with Charles V. himself, it was not inherently probable that England, under her rule, would enter into the scheme here described. Besides which, no other evidence of the alleged conspiracy is forthcoming. At a time when, as in 1553-4, the Spanish and English Governments were in agreement, the idea of simulated treachery lacks point altogether; and in view of Cabot's previous negotiations with Venice while in the service first of Charles V. and then of Edward VI., it is difficult to avoid the conclusion that the whole of his disclosures in the letter quoted above (as far as English statesmen are concerned) was a fabrication for his own safety against another change of fortune.

The last action recorded of Sebastian in the English service was his share in superintending another expedition to the North-East in 1556. This was the relieving fleet of Stephen Burrough, intended for a search after the missing ship and crew of Sir Hugh Willoughby; and Burrough himself describes how Cabot came down to Gravesend and attended to the final equipment of the new enterprise, joining in the parting festivities with surprising vigour :—On the 27th of April, 1556, 'being Monday, the right worshipful Sebastian Cabot came aboard our pinnace [the

Search-Thrift] at Gravesend accompanied by divers gentlemen and gentlewomen who, after they had viewed our pinnace . . . went on shore . . . and the good old gentleman, Master Cabota, gave to the poor most liberal alms, wishing them to pray for the good fortune of the *Search-Thrift*. And at the sign of *The Christopher* he and his friends banqueted and made me (Burrough) and them that were in the company great cheer, and for very joy that he had to see the towardness of our intended discovery, he entered into the dance himself with the rest of the young and lusty company ;—which being ended he and his friends departed, most gently commending us to the governance of Almighty God.'

Soon after this Cabot ceases to be active Governor of the Muscovy Company ; it appears probable that he was dismissed, in spite of the assurance of the grant in the Charter of Incorporation that his office was for life. Anthony Hussie appears as his successor on February 21, 1556–57. The pension conferred on Sebastian by Edward VI. is either re-granted, or a precisely similar though technically new pension is conferred, on the 27th of November, 1555 ; but on the 29th of May, 1557, he appears as having 'retroceded' or resigned the grant and a new grant is made to himself and William Worthington jointly —in a word his salary is halved,[1] and an additional

---

[1] Harrisse disputes this, but there cannot be any reasonable doubt of it.

provision is inserted, that on Cabot's death his whole
salary is to revert to Worthington.

'Know ye that by our Letters Patent, dated
Westminster, November 27th, the second and third
year of our reign, by virtue of our special grace . . .
and also in consideration of the good, true, and
acceptable service done and to be done unto us by
our beloved servant Sebastian Cabot, . . . we have
granted to the aforesaid Sebastian a . . . yearly
revenue of £166 13s. 4d. . . . The said Sebastian
and his assigns to enjoy the said annuity . . . from
the Feast of the Annunciation of the Blessed Virgin
Mary last past, for and during the life of the said
Sebastian, out of our Treasury and out of the Treasury
of our heirs and successors. . . . The same to be paid
annually by equal portions at the feasts of the
Nativity of St. John Baptist, St. Michael the
Archangel, the Nativity of our Lord, and the
Annunciation of the Blessed Virgin Mary, the first
payment to be made at the Feast of the Nativity of
St. John Baptist just past. . . . And whereas the
same Sebastian Cabot has returned and retroceded the
said Letters Patent to our Chancery to be recorded
. . . that we may . . . grant other Letters Patent
relative to the said annuity, to the said Sebastian
and to our beloved servant William Worthington
and the survivor of them :

Know ye therefore that we, in consideration of the
above . . . do grant for ourselves, our heirs, and

successors . . . to the said Sebastian, and William, and the survivor of them, the said annuity of £166 13s. 4d. The said Sebastian Cabot and William Worthington to enjoy . . . yearly the same annuity . . . they and the survivor of them, their assigns and the assigns of the survivor of them, from the feast day of the Annunciation of the Blessed Virgin Mary last past, for the terms of the lives of the said Sebastian and William and the survivor of them, payable annually by equal portions out of our Treasury.'

We may suppose that Cabot died shortly after this; on December 25th of the same year (1557) Worthington draws the quarterly pension alone [and in his own name], in other words, one fourth instead of one-eighth of the whole sum of £166 13s. 4d.; and we may fairly infer that the old pilot died somewhere between September 29th, the date of his last payment, and the Christmas day next following when he has disappeared from view. In a famous passage where he discusses the difficulties of finding the longitude at sea, Richard Eden probably gives us the last glimpse we have of Sebastian Cabot. The problem in question, he tells us, was supposed by some to be in the way of solution through some recent discoveries and inventions; in any case, it was 'a thing greatly to be desired and hitherto not certainly known, although Sebastian Cabot on his death-bed told me that he had the knowledge thereof by Divine revelation, yet so that he might not teach any man. But I think that the good old man in that extreme age somewhat doted, and had not yet, even in the article of death, utterly shaken off all worldly vainglory.' This was written in 1574–75, and probably refers to a year considerably preceding that in which Eden put down the recollection quoted ; but the context affords us no clue beyond a somewhat vague impression of 'a certain distance off.'

A more exact indication has been sought in the fact that Machyn's diary 'from 1550 to 1563' omits the name of Cabot among all the patrons or leaders of exploration who are mentioned as dying in these years. This worthy 'citizen and merchant-taylor' of London describes the obsequies, for instance, of Sir George Barnes, Sir John Gresham, and Anthony Hussie, who all appear in the Muscovy Company's Charter of 1555 as co-grantees along with Cabot. It is therefore suggested that Sebastian may have survived the disappearance of his name from the pension-grants of 1557, and that he did not die till after the year 1563, when the diary of Henry Machyn comes to an end. But if he had lived through the first few years of Elizabeth's reign we should probably have heard of him in connection with some of the exploring ventures now so vigorously taken up in England. The omission of his name by Machyn may be accidental, and is quite insufficient to ground any positive theory upon ; — taking one thing with another we cannot assume that he survived the re-arrangement of his pension more than a few months.

No will of Sebastian Cabot's has ever been found ; but in 1582 Hakluyt alludes to some of his literary remains, and alludes to them in a way that scarcely strengthens the theory of some critics as to Worthington's hostility to, and intrigues against, his old partner : 'Shortly, God willing, shall come out in print all his own maps and discoveries, drawn and written by himself, which are in the custody of the worshipful Master William Worthington, one of her Majesty's pensioners, who, because so worthy monuments should not be buried in perpetual oblivion, is very willing to suffer them to be overseen and published, in as good order as may be, to the encouragement and benefit of our countrymen.'

None of these, however, are now known to exist ; it is not certain from Hakluyt's language that he had personally inspected them ; but, in any case, his language is worth weighing by those who would deny Sebastian Cabot any real merit as a scientific geographer.

CHAPTER XIII

SEBASTIAN CABOT, it has been repeatedly said, left
only one map out of all the designs with which his
name was connected during his life or shortly afterwards ; and it is probable that even this one surviving
specimen of his work is only his in the same sense
that a painter of the school of Titian might ascribe
one of his own productions to his master. Yet, if only
from the fact that it, and it alone, bears his official
authorisation, it would deserve some notice in this
place ; and there is a further reason. Although it
is not probable that Sebastian himself either drew the
Planisphere of 1544, or wrote the Legends which
accompany it, it is almost certain that he supplied
material for its inscriptions and commentary ; he was
probably well aware that in one of the Legends the

authorship was distinctly attributed to himself; and as such, the design in question was copied and reproduced in England, whose claim on a good share of the North-West regions here received a more ample recognition than in any chart since the issue of La Cosa's in 1500.

In all, we possess seven separate references to lost maps of Sebastian Cabot—not necessarily to seven separate maps, however, as some two or more of these references are probably to the same original.

1. First of all there is the *mappemonde* ordered by Juan de Samano for the Council of the Indies in 1532 or 1533. This is described in the only remaining autograph letter of Sebastian's, addressed to Juan de Samano, as follows :—

'VERY NOBLE LORD,—On the day of the blessed St. John I received a letter from the Adelantado of Canary, by which it appears that he still wishes to undertake an expedition to the River Parana, which cost me so dear. A dependent of the said Adelantado gave me the letter and told me that he is going thither and is taking the letter of the said Adelantado to the Lords of the Council in the matter of the aforesaid enterprise. May it please our Lord God so to order everything that His holy Catholic Faith may be increased and the Emperor our Lord duly served. My Lord, the map which your Grace has ordered me to make is now quite finished and given to the Director of the Contractation House [at Seville] in order that he may for-

ward it to your Grace. I entreat your Grace to pardon
me for not having finished it sooner ; and, in truth, if
it had not been for the death of my daughter and the
affliction of my wife you would have received it many
days ago. Indeed, I intended to have brought the same
with me [from Seville] along with two others which
I have made for his Majesty. I trust that his Majesty
and the Council will be satisfied with these [especially]
as they can see [by means of them] how one may
navigate in all directions by the indications [of the
compass] as one does with a chart—and the reason
why the needle points to the North-East and North-
West, and why it cannot do otherwise—and to what
extent it points to the North-East and North-West
before pointing again [due] North, and through what
meridians. Hereby his Majesty will have a sure way
of finding the longitude.   My Lord, I beg your
Grace to write to my Lords the Officers of the Contractation House to help me by the grant of a third of
my salary, in order that I may be able to get rid of my
debts [which keep me in Seville] and come to kiss the
hands of your Grace and to speak with the Lords of the
Council, and to bring before them one of my servants
who was left on the coast of Brazil, the which servant
came with the Portuguese, who came from thence, in
order that he might give an account of all that the
Portuguese have done there.

'And I make bold to ask this of your Grace, besides
the many other favours which I have received of your

Grace. May God our Lord guard the noble person of your Grace and increase your estate as your Grace may desire and as your servants wish.

'I kiss the hand of my Lady Dona Juana.

'From Seville on the day of the blessed St. John, 1533.

'SEBASTIAN CABOT,

'Your most humble servant, kisses the hand of your Grace.'

To this we need only add that much of the geographical theory of the letter here transcribed, especially as to the use of the magnet, is revived in the inscriptions which accompany the 'Cabot' planisphere of 1544.

2. Next we have the allusion of the 'Mantuan gentleman' in Ramusio to a map which Sebastian himself had shown him while in Seville, some time before 1547. This was an example 'of large size, exhibiting particularly the navigations of the Portuguese and Spaniards.' It may have been identical with the map ordered by Samano (No. 1), with one of the two accompanying charts specially designed for the Emperor, as recorded in the preceding letter, or with another of the examples hereafter cited. We do not suppose, however, that it corresponds with the map of 1544 or with No. (4).

3. Thirdly, there is mention of a map in the Library of Juan de Ovando, some time President of the Council

of the Indies. This was executed by Cabot on parch-
ment and illuminated, but we know nothing more
about it, save that it was sold at Ovando's death in
1575. It is probably not identical with the plan of
1544.

4. In the fourth place, the letter of Cabot to
Charles V., under date of the 15th of November, 1553,
already quoted, refers to a map which he was
sending to his old master by the hand of Francisco
de Urista. · Sebastian, in the aforesaid letter, describes
this work as consisting of 'certain plans, one of which
is a mappemonde . . . by which your Majesty may
see the causes of the variation of the mariner's needle
from the Pole, and the causes why at other times it
turns directly to the Arctic or Antarctic poles ; and
the other plan is to show the longitude under any
parallel [?] in which a man may be.' [1]   In the same
letter, Cabot refers to a fuller account of this map,
which he had sent to Eraso, Secretary of the Council
of Charles V., but this is not discoverable at the present
day, any more than the original chart which it was
written to explain.

5. Once more, Guido Gianetti de Fano saw a map
in the possession of its designer, Sebastian Cabot, in

[1] M. Harrisse (*Cabot*, 1896, pp. 285–6) interprets this as 'meaning
that there was only one map, but in two sheets, one for the Northern,
the other for the Southern Hemisphere ;' and adds, 'The letter doubtless
set forth a magnetic point, or line with no variation, upon which' Cabot
'based his . . . pretension for finding the longitude at sea,'

London, in the reign of Edward VI.; and Livio
Sanuto tells us what he heard about this plan, viz.,
that it marked a meridian based upon a point of no
magnetic variation, one hundred and twenty miles
west of Flores in the Azores.[1]

6. In 1598 Andres de Cespedes, Cosmographer
Royal of Spain, wrote of a map of Cabot's, once
presented by the author to the King of Castille,
informing us that this design, ' like Jodocus Hondius,
placed 43 degrees of longitude between Goa and
Mozambique.'

7. Lastly, there are the plans mentioned by Hakluyt
in 1582 as then in the possession of William Worthington, Sebastian's co-grantee in the pension of
Philip and Mary, already mentioned. This allusion
of the *Divers Voyages* is fully transcribed on p. 206 ;
and it is highly probable, though now of course
unprovable, that among these charts was at least one
copy of the design of 1544, either in the original
edition or in the English re-issue of 1549.

And now, continuing this summary of Cabotian
cartography, and proceeding from the vanished to the
still existent, we should naturally come to the map
of 1544. But before dealing with this we must
briefly review our evidence along another line. We
have summarised all that is at present known of lost
maps whose authorship is attributed to Sebastian
Cabot ; we have seen reason to believe in the exis-

[1] See pp. 254–5.

tence of at least a fair number of separate and independent designs of the kind ; we must now look at the more important of existing maps of this period, by which we may better estimate the relative importance of the *mappemonde* of 1544. In other words, we must briefly examine, in chronological order, the chief cartographical documents which serve to illustrate the discoveries of the English in North America during the period of this survey (c. 1500–1550).

1. And first we come to the chart of Juan de la Cosa of A.D. 1500. Although this was discovered by Baron Walckenaer in 1832, it remains a disputed point among cartographers whether the coast-line in the north-west portion of the map represents the south shores of Labrador within the Gulf of St. Lawrence or the coast of the United States of America, including Nova Scotia and terminating at Cape Race, in Newfoundland. A comparison of the La Cosa map, with other Spanish and Italian charts of a slightly later date, which certainly indicate English discoveries, has given rise to the suggestion that the Legend of the ' Mar descubierta por Ingleses ' on the La Cosa plan is indicative of the Gulf of St. Lawrence, and not of the open Atlantic, otherwise designated by the same author as ' Mare Oceanus.' From this it would follow that the accompanying coast-line decorated with English flags [only], and terminating with Cavo de Ynglaterra, is no other than Southern Labrador. While, on the other hand, it has

been often and, in our opinion, rightly maintained that the aforesaid coast-line corresponds to the whole stretch of the North American shore, from Cape Race to Cape Hatteras.

2. Next we have the allusion in Johann Ruysch's Ptolemy, edited in 1508 under the title of *Universalior cogniti Orbis tabula*. Here we observe 'Terra Nova' joined on to the mainland of *Asia*, undoubtedly referring to Newfoundland with its south-eastern termination at Cape Race, here named 'C[avo] de Portogesi.' To assume, with some modern critics, that the Cavo de Ynglaterra of the La Cosa map is synonymous with the Cavo de Portogesi of Ruysch provides a convenient escape from various difficulties, but can hardly be treated as a certain solution of some of the most vexatious problems in the yet inexact science of comparative cartography. The special interest which attaches to this map is that Ruysch sailed from the southern part of England some years before the production of his Ptolemy and arrived on the eastern coast of Newfoundland soon after its first discovery. This voyage may or may not have been in the company of the Cabots; if so, it was probably made in 1498 ; but there is rather more evidence to establish the conjecture that Ruysch sailed with Nicholas, the father of Robert, Thorne.

3. Next we may take the anonymous Italian *portolano* of 1508, which as yet seems to have been unnoticed by cartographers. Thus the Vesconte di

Maggiola *portolano* of 1511 has been generally supposed to be the earliest example of map-work in this period which clearly shows the Continent of North America ; whereas it is decisively anticipated by the newly-acquired British Museum MS. (Egerton, No. 2803) here referred to.   On folio 1 of this we observe 'Terra de Labrados' and 'Terra de los Baccallaos' correctly located, together with the unnamed Gulf of St. Lawrence and Straits of Belle Isle, marked as an inland sea, and possibly answering to the Mar descubierta of the La Cosa chart.   On the general map of the then known world in this *portolano*, folio 1b, is to be seen a roughly painted outline of part of the shore of a North-Western continent, bearing three inscriptions—'Terra de Lebrados,' 'Terra de los bacalos' and 'Septem civitates.'

4. The Vesconte di Maggiola *portolano* of 1511 is noteworthy in this connection, because, as far as we know, it contains the earliest plain reference *by name* to Labrador as the 'land of the English'—or part of America discovered by them ('Terra de los Ingres'). Further, this reference is the earliest confirmation of the meaning assigned by the 'Labradorean' school to the 'English' coast-line on the La Cosa map of 1500.

5. Our fifth example is Robert Thorne's map of 1527. 'This . . . form of a map sent 1527 from Seville in Spain . . . to Doctor Ley, Ambassador for King Henry VIII. to Charles the Emperor' is found

in Hakluyt's *Divers Voyages* of 1582. Off the coast of Newfoundland (unnamed), and of the ' New Land called Labrador ' (Nova terra laboratorum dicta), we read : 'This land was first found by the English.' Our discoveries are here plainly referred to both regions—Newfoundland and Labrador.

6. Sixth comes the Verrazano map of 1529. M. Harrisse, in his *Discovery of North America*, pp. 575–7, by some oversight neglects to give the legend of this chart, which refers to the English discoveries, though he alludes to it in his latest work upon Cabot (*John Cabot . . . and Sebastian his son*, p. 79). The inscription, like the Maggiola *portolano*, attributes the discovery of Labrador, and of that only, to the English. 'The land of Labrador '—it runs—' this land was discovered by the English ' (Terra Laboratoris —Questa terra fu discoperta da Inghilesi).

7 and 8. In the same way the two Ribeiro maps of 1529 also ascribe the discovery of Labrador to our adventurers. But with a difference. On the earlier one, preserved at Weimar, we read : 'This land the English discovered. There is in it nothing profitable ' (Esta tierra descubrieron los Ingleses, no ay en ella cosa de provecho).[1] On the later copy, which is in the College of the Propaganda at Rome, appears an interesting variant, as follows : 'Land of Labrador, discovered by the English *of the town of Bristol*.'

---

[1] ' Labrador, the land allotted by God to Cain,' as Cartier called it.

9. After these we come to the map, executed about
A.D. 1530, known as Wolfenbüttel B. The portion
of this which is preserved seems to have been based
upon a copy of the Second Ribeiro chart (No. 8) just
noticed ; it has a legend about Labrador and the
English from Bristol of precisely similar tenor.

The united testimony of the Spanish and Italian
maps already described amounts to this—the English
discoveries are generally referred (except, on one interpretation, in the plan of La Cosa), to the Southern
part of Labrador, but there is no direct evidence of
Cabot cartography in these examples, and it is not
absolutely certain (as it has been sometimes assumed
from the language of contemporary letters) that a chart
of the discoveries of 1497 and 1498, drawn by John
Cabot himself, is embodied in La Cosa's map of 1500.

The only two remaining maps, which call for notice
prior to the appearance of the so-called Cabot *mappemonde* in 1544, are :

10. The Harleian (Descelier) *mappemonde* of 1536–
40, and

11. The map of 1541, executed by Nicholas Desliens, and rediscovered in our own day by Dr. Ruge,
in Dresden.

The special interest of these two Dieppese charts
arises from this circumstance. M. Harrisse, in his most
recent work on the Cabots, has charged Sebastian
with plagiarising portions of Desliens' chart of 1541
for his own delineation of the Gulf of St. Lawrence

and Newfoundland. A careful comparison of these two examples (Desliens of 1541 and 'Cabot' of 1544), and of the evidence brought forward in support of the charge, seems to show a certain weakness in the accusation. Finding that the comparative nomenclature of these regions fails to work out beyond seven names, out of a list of fourteen selected from the 'Cabot' map, the accuser invites us to compare these chosen Cabotian names with fifteen others, not derived from Desliens at all, but from another work, described as of 'Cartierean origin.' Again, on being unable to find the 'Lago di Golesme' of the Cabot map upon the Desliens example, M. Harrisse once more shifts his ground (to all appearance) and declares that Cabot's prototype was not, after all, the Desliens plan of 1541, but a derivative of some other Desliens map, constructed in 1542 or 1543.

Both Dr. Ruge and M. Harrisse seem to be quite mistaken in asserting that the Desliens map is the earliest of the Dieppese school. This position must be assigned to our 10th example, the Harleian chart of 1536–40 (anonymous Descelier ; Additional MSS., Brit. Mus. 5413), which will shortly be reproduced in natural size for private circulation.

The surviving 'Cabot' *mappemonde* of 1544, now preserved in the Geographical Cabinet of the Bibliothèque Nationale in Paris, was rediscovered in 1844, in the house of a priest in Bavaria, and purchased in the same year by the French Government for

4,000 francs. The projection is orthographic (according to the method devised by Apianus in 1524), on an ellipse with a longitudinal axis of 39 inches and a parallel axis of 44 inches, the whole engraved on copper and richly coloured. Besides the delineation of the world itself, this piece is accompanied by various ornaments and additional inscriptions, viz., (1) a large head of Eolus in each of the four corners of the map ; (2) an engraving of the Annunciation, with a Latin inscription of five lines on the upper part of the design, to the left of the reader ; (3) an apparently untranslateable legend, to the right, accompanying the engraved arms of the Empire, and reading as follows : ' Solas del solo en el mundo en servicio de las quales muriendo viven leales ' ; (4) cosmographical tables on each side, right and left, of the lower part of the map, within the frame ; and most important of all, (5) two tables of legends, forming a commentary upon the chart itself, pasted on to the right and left of the map— each table being 28 centimètres wide.

The map surface is composed of ' four separately-printed parts, each measuring 80 centimètres by 62,' all pasted together on pasteboard ; it ' contains indications of magnetic lines, with no variation (which Cabot transforms into meridians), and of starting points calculated, as he thought, to find the longitude at sea.'

The legends, twenty-two in number, seem to have been written first in Spanish by a certain Dr. Grajales, of the Puerto de Santa Maria in Andalusia, and then sent with the map itself to some place out of Spain,[1] but within the Emperor's dominions, where the design was engraved. This place was possibly Antwerp, then and long afterwards a centre of scientific printing and engraving and a home of cartographical study. Before being printed, the Spanish text of these legends [2] was also translated into Latin, and the version accompanied the original on the map as we have it, but it seems also to have been separately printed in pamphlet [3] form (without the Spanish) for separate use and for the elucidation of copies of the chart in its simple form, without pasted commentary.

These famous legends we now give at length, as the best and most complete account of the map itself, and as one of the fullest expositions now remaining of Sebastian Cabot's views on practical and scientific geography—only premising that the inscriptions may be placed at the following points, as indicated by numbers in our Paris example :—

The 1st lies between the Bermuda Islands and the West Indies, the 2nd north of Antigua, the 3rd opposite to the West Coast of Mexico, the 4th opposite to

[1] *E.g.*, the ñ was not much at the printer's disposal, so he usually doubles the letter to denote the Spanish sound, thus Sennor for Señor.

[2] Some of these are engraved in the body of the work, much corrupted by the copyist.

[3] A copy of this has been recently found in Germany, consisting of twenty-four unnumbered leaves or pages, with the title, 'Declaratio Chartæ Novæ Navigatoriæ Domini Almirantis,' as if the copyist thought the inscriptions accompanied a map by Christopher Columbus.

Magellan's Straits, the 5th at the Moluccas, the 6th
over against the coast of Peru, the 7th at the mouth
of the La Plata river, the 8th in Hudson's Bay, the
9th opposite Iceland, the 10th in the North of Russia,
the 11th in the North-East of Asia (where the
reference is incorrectly given to Table II., No. 2),
the 12th in the North of Asia, the 13th in Mid
Africa, the 14th in Hindostan (without numerical
reference, but indicated by a picture of Suttee), the
15th in the North of Japan, the 16th near Sumatra,
the 17th on the east side of the map, just south of
the Equator, the 18th running over some of the
North-East of Europe and North-West of Asia,
the 19th in the Indian Ocean, just south of India
itself, the 20th directly below the preceding (19th),
the 21st also in the Indian Ocean, south-west from
No. 19, the 22nd and last near Ceylon.

CHAPTER XIV

THE full text, in English, of these legends is as
follows :—

First Table.[1]   *Of the Admiral.*

No. 1. The Admiral Don Christoval Colon, a
Genoese by birth, offered to their Catholic Majesties
of glorious memory to discover the islands and mainland of the Indies [2] by the West, provided they gave
him for this purpose a sufficient fleet and favour ; [3]
and having obtained this, and having fitted out three
caravels in the year 1492, he proceeded to discover
them [the Indies] ; and from that time on many

[1] See the version in the Massachusetts Historical Society's Proceedings for 1890–91 (vol. vi.).   Important words found in the Spanish text,
and not in the Latin version, are in italics.   Important additions of the
Latin version (very few in number) are in footnotes.   At the beginning
all the additions of the same have been transcribed.

[2] 'Western Lands,' Lat.

[3] 'If they provided him sufficiently with the things needful for
him,' Lat.

other persons have continued the same discovery as is shown by the present description.

No. 2. In the island Española there is much virgin gold, *and very fine lapis lazuli*, and much sugar and cassia fistula, and an infinite number of cattle of all kinds. *The swine of this island they give to the sick, as here in our parts they give mutton.* The said island contains many harbours, *and very good ones*, and the chief of them is the city of Santo Domingo, which is a very good city, and of much trade, and all the others are places built and settled by the Spaniards. And in the island of Cuba and of San Juan, and in all the other islands, and on the mainland, virgin gold is found ; and in the city of Santo Domingo his Majesty has his royal chancery, and in all the other towns and provinces governors *and rulers* who govern *and rule* them with much justice ; and every day are discovered new lands and provinces, very rich, by means of which our Holy Catholic Faith is, and will be, much increased, and these kingdoms of Castille have become great with much and glorious fame and riches.

No. 3. This mainland which the Spaniards named New Spain, the most illustrious gentleman Don Fernando Cortez, Marquis dell' Valle de Guaxacon, conquered. There are in this land provinces and cities innumerable ; the chief of them is the city of Mexico,[1] which contains more than 50,000 inhabitants ; it is in a salt lake which extends over forty leagues. There

---

[1] ' Is called Mexico by the name of the Indians,' Lat.

is in the said city, and in all the other provinces, much
gold, virgin silver, and all kinds of precious stones ;
and there is produced in the said land and provinces
much very good silk and cotton, alum, orchil, dye-
wood, cochineal, and saffron, and sugar [1]—of all the
aforesaid great quantities, with which many ships come
loaded to these kingdoms of Spain.[2] The natives of
this land are very expert in all that relates to trade ;
instead of coins, they make use of certain kernels,
split in halves, which they call Cacao or Cacanghnate,
a barbarous expression. [3] They have much wheat and
barley and many other grains and vines, and many
fruits of different kinds. It is a land of many animals,
deer, mountain boars, lions, leopards, tigers, and much
other game, both birds and land animals. It is a people
very skilful in moulding any object after nature and in
painting pictures. The women usually adorn themselves with precious stones and valuable pearls. These
Indians use a certain kind of paper, on which they
draw what they want to express with figures [pictures]
instead of letters. They never had peace among
themselves ; on the contrary, some persecuted others
in continuous fights, in which the prisoners on either
side were sacrificed by their enemies to their gods, and
their bodies were given to the army, as public banquets.
They were idolaters and adored whatever took their
fancy. They were very fond of eating human flesh,

[1] ‘Or juice of the cane,’ Lat.   [2] ‘To Seville of Andalusia,’ Lat.
[3] ‘By the barbarous Indian name,’ Lat.

whereas now they have laid aside their fierce and cruel customs and have clad themselves in Jesus Christ, believing heartily in our holy Evangelical faith,[1] and obeying our most holy mother[2] Church, and its most holy precepts.

No. 4. This Strait of All Saints was discovered by Hernando de Magallanes, commander of an expedition which his Sacred Cæsarean Catholic Majesty, the Emperor and King Don Carlos our Lord, ordered to be made to discover the Maluco Islands. There are in this strait men of such great stature that they seem giants ; it is a very desolate land, and they dress themselves in the skins of animals.

No. 5. These islands of Maluco[3] were discovered by Fernando de Magallanes, commander of an expedition which his Majesty ordered to be made to discover the said islands, and by Juan Sebastian del Cano.[4] That is to say, the said Fernando de Magallanes discovered the Strait of All Saints, which is in 52½ degrees towards the Antarctic Pole ; *and after having passed the said strait* [not] without very great labour and difficulty, he continued his way towards the said islands ; after many days he arrived at certain islands, of which the southern one is situated in 12 degrees[5] ;

[1] 'And the religion of the Christians,' Lat.

[2] 'The orthodox Catholic Church,' Lat.

[3] 'Long closed to us,' Lat.

[4] 'Which said expedition set sail from the port of Seville, a famed city of the province of Andalusia,' Lat.

[5] 'North Latitude,' Lat.

P

and because the people were so turbulent, and because they stole from him the boats of one of his ships, they gave it the name of the isle of Ladrones (or Thieves). And thence continuing the journey, as has been said, they discovered an island which they called La Aguada, because they took in water there ; and from thence on they discovered another, which is called . . . Aceilani, and another which is called Cubu, in which island died the said Captain Hernando de Magallanes, in a skirmish which took place with the natives thereof; and the survivors of the said expedition chose Juan Sebastian del Cano as commander of it, who afterwards discovered the island of Bendanao, *in which there is much virgin gold and very fine cinnamon, and in the same way he discovered* the island of Poloan, and that of Brunay, and that of Gilolo, and the island of Tridore, and that of Terenati, and Motil, and many others in which there is much gold and cloves and nutmeg and other kinds of spices and drugs. The said Sebastian del Cano loaded two ships which ¹ remained to him out of five, from those they took with them, with cloves in the said island of Tidori, for in it, and in the said island of Terenati, the said cloves are said to grow and not in any other ; and in the same way he took much cinnamon and nutmeg ² ; and coming on through the Indian Ocean in the

¹ ' Which he had saved from shipwreck,' Lat.

² ' Much cinnamon and nutmeg is collected in Bendanao, of which likewise he took thence great quantities,' Lat.

direction of the Cape of Good Hope, one ship was forced to put back and return to the said island of Tidori, from which it had set out, on account of the great amount of water it was making, and the said Captain Juan Sebastian del Cano, with his ship called *Santa Maria de la Victoria*, came to these kingdoms of Castille, to the city of Seville, in the year 1522, by the Cape of Good Hope; whereby it clearly appears that the said Juan Sebastian del Cano [1] sailed round the whole universe,[2] because he proceeded only towards the West, although not on one parallel, through the East to the place in the West whence he set out.

No. 6. These provinces were discovered [3] by the honoured and valiant gentleman,[4] Francisco Pizarro, who [5] was governor of them during his life; in which there is infinite gold and virgin silver and mines of very fine emeralds. The bread which they have they make of maize,[6] and the wine likewise; they have much wheat and other grain. It is a war-like race; they use in their wars bows and slings and lances; their arms are of gold and silver. There are in the said provinces certain sheep of the form of small camels; they have very fine wool. They are an idolatrous people and of very subtle mind; and on all the sea-coast and for more than twenty miles inland

---

[1] Canno in text.   [2] 'In a circle,' Lat.   [3] 'And conquered,' Lat.

[4] 'Knights Francisco Pizarro and Almagro,' Lat.

[5] 'That is, Francisco Pizarro,' Lat.

[6] 'Very large corn, which in the language of the Indians is called maize,' Lat.

it never rains. *It is a very healthy land.* The Christians have made many settlements in it, and continually keep increasing them.

No. 7. The Indians call this great river the river Huruai, the Spaniards the Rio de la Plata (or River of Silver). They take this name from the river Huruai, which is a very mighty river [1] which runs into the great river Parana. Juan Diaz de Solis,[2] Pilot-Major of their Catholic Majesties,[3] *of glorious memory*, discovered it, and he explored it as far as an island, to which the said Juan Diaz gave the name of the island of Martin Garcia, because in it he buried a sailor who was called Martin Garcia, which said island is about thirty leagues above the mouth of this river, and the said discovery cost him very dear, for the Indians of the said land slew him and ate him ; and after many years had gone by it was again discovered by Sebastian Cabot, Captain and Pilot-Major [4] of *his Sacrea Cæsarean Catholic Majesty* the Emperor Don Carlos, fifth of the name, [who is] also the King our Lord, who was Commander of an expedition which his Majesty ordered should be made to discover Tarsis and Ophir and Oriental Cathay ; which said Captain Sebastian Cabot came to this river by chance, for the commander's ship in which he was was lost, and seeing that he could not continue his said voyage, he

---

[1] ' Into which runs,' Lat.   [2] ' Conquering and,' Lat.
[3] ' Ferdinand and Isabel,' Lat.
[4] ' Most skilful in the art of Navigation and of Astronomy,' Lat.

determined to explore with the people he had with him the said river, by reason of the very great account which the Indians of the land gave him of the very great wealth in gold and silver which there was in the land, and not without very great labour and hunger, and dangers both of his own person and of those who were with him.   And the said captain endeavoured to make near the said river certain settlements *of the people whom he brought from Spain.* This river is larger than any that is known up to the present time. Its breadth at the mouth where it enters the sea is thirty-five leagues and three hundred leagues above the said mouth it is two leagues in breadth.   The cause of its being so great and mighty is that there run into it many other and mighty rivers.   It is a river infinitely full of fish and of the best there is in the world.   The people on arriving in that land wished to learn if it were fertile and fit to plough and raise bread ; and they planted in the month of September fifty-two grains of wheat—for there was no more in the ships :—and they gathered soon in the month of December fifty-two thousand grains of wheat ; and this same fertility was found with all the other seeds. Those who live in that land say that not far from there, in the country inland, there are certain great mountain ranges from which they take infinite gold, and further on in the same mountains they take infinite silver.   There are in this land certain sheep as large as ordinary asses, of the shape of camels, except that the wool they bear is fine as silk, and other animals of different kinds. The people of the country differ very much ; for those who live on the slopes of the mountains are white like us, and those who are near to the banks of the river are dark. *Some say that in the said mountains* there are men who have faces like dogs and others are from the knee down like ostriches, and that these are great workers, and that they raise much maize, of which they make bread and wine. Many other things they say of that land, which are not put down here lest they be tedious.

No. 8. This land was discovered by John Cabot, a Venetian, and by Sebastian Cabot, his son, in the year of the birth of our Saviour Jesus Christ, 1494, on the 24th of June, in the morning, to which they gave the name of First Land seen (Prima Tierra Vista) ; and to a large island which is situated along the said land they gave the name San Juan, because it had been discovered the same day. The people of it are dressed in the skins of animals. They use in their wars bows and arrows, lances and darts and certain clubs of wood and slings. It is a very sterile land. There are in it many white bears and very large stags *like horses* and many other animals ; and likewise there is infinite fish —sturgeons, salmon, very large soles a yard in length, and many other kinds of fish—and the greatest quantity of them is called Baccallaos (codfish) ; likewise there are in the same land hawks black as crows,

eagles, partridges, *linnets*, and many other kinds of
birds of different species.

No. 9. In this same island of Iceland (Islanda)
there is a great quantity of fish. They take it in
winter and dry it by the means of the very great cold
which is there, because this said island is within the
Arctic circle ; and in summer men go there from many
parts and barter for this fish, thus dried, in exchange
for meal and beer ; and this said fish is so dry and
hard, that to eat it they beat it with certain hammers
of iron on certain stones hard as marble and then they
put it to soak for a day or two, and thus they eat it,
stewed with butter. And in all this Northern Sea
there is a very great quantity of fish, and many of
them large and of monstrous shape ; those who sail in
these seas have seen very large lampreys which re-
semble great serpents and attack ships in order to eat
the sailors. The natives of the said island most of
them build their houses underground and the walls of
fish bones. They have no wood except some extremely small trees, and of these very few and in few
places ; but the Provider of all things provides every
year that there comes to them by sea on the northern
parts of the said island a very great quantity of trees of
different kinds and sizes, as driftwood, borne by furious
north winds to the coast of the said island, with which
the natives provide themselves, and make use of it for
all that is needful to them. And they say that often
they hear spirits speak and call each other by name

and take the form of living persons and tell them who they are ; and in certain parts of the said island there rise up certain very dreadful fires, and other wonders the natives of the said island say there are in it.

No. 10. The men who dwell in this region are savages ; they are destitute of bread and wine, they tame deer and ride upon them, and they fight with another people which is situated further to the North, and which they call the Nocturnal people, for they go about in the night and perform their business as here [we do] in the day, and this because the days here from the 14th of September to the 10th of March are so short that there is not an hour of light. They are a very wicked people, quarrelsome, they rob all those who pass [through their country] *so that no ship dares to ride at anchor* near the coast for fear of these night people, because they slay and rob all who fall into their hands ; and a little beyond these night people towards the S.E. they say there are certain monsters which have bodies like those of human beings except the head, which is like that of a pig, and that they understand one another, grunting like pigs.

No. 11. Those who inhabit this region, some adore the sun, others the first thing they see in the morning, others adore a piece of coloured cloth which they place on a lance, and thus each worships what he prefers ; they are under the sway of the Great Khan, Emperor of the Tartars.

No. 12. Here there are monsters like unto men

who have ears so large that they cover the whole body, and they say that further on towards the East there are certain men who have no joints whatever at the knee nor in the feet; they are under the sway of the Great Khan. In the province of Balor, which is fifty days' journey in extent, there are wild men; they live in the mountains and forests.

No. 13. Here dwells that mighty King of Aziumba and Auxuma whom some call Prester John, to whom sixty kings yield obedience; he is very wealthy in all riches and there is no record that he was ever defeated in any battle; but often has he come back with glorious victory from the South from the Troglodyte people, a race naked and black, which people extend as far as the Cape of Good Hope. Among which people there is a race which does not speak, but they understand each other by whistling; and this is not Prester John, because Prester John had his Empire in Eastern and Southern India until Genghis Khan, first King of the Tartars, defeated and overcame him in a very cruel battle, in which he died, and the said Genghis took from him all his kingdoms and lordships, and allowed the Christians to live in their own faith and gave them a Christian king to rule and govern them, which king was called George, and from that time till now all the kings who succeed him are called George, as Marco Polo relates more at large in the 42nd and 48th chapters of his book.

No. 14. The king of this province and kingdom

of Bengal is a very mighty lord, and has under his rule many cities very large and of great trade. *There is in this kingdom and province* much cinnamon, cloves, ginger, pepper, sandalwood, lacquer, and silk in great quantities. They are wont in this province and kingdom to burn bodies after death, and when the husband dies before the wife the wife burns herself alive with her husband, saying that she is going to be happy with him in the other world. And it is done in this way, that the husband dying, the wife gives a great entertainment and dresses herself in the richest garments she has—to which entertainment come all her relatives and those of her husband ; and after having eaten, she goes with all the people to a place where a very great fire has been built, singing and dancing until she reaches the said fire, and then they throw in the dead body of the husband, and at once she bids farewell to her relatives and friends and leaps into the fire, and she who most nobly throws herself into the fire brings most honour upon her family ; but even now this custom is not observed as it used to be, since the Portuguese have traded with them and given them to understand that our Lord God is not served by such a practice.

No. 15. The Grand Khan of the Tartars is a very great lord and very mighty, he is called King of Kings and Lord of Lords ; he is wont to give garments to his liegemen thirteen times a year, at thirteen very great feasts which he holds each year ; and these garments are of greater or less value according to the quality of the person to whom they are given, and to each one is given a belt and leggings, a hat adorned with gold and pearls and precious stones according to the greatness of the personage ; and these garments which the said Grand Khan gives every year are 156,000 ; and this he does to give greatness and magnificence to his feasts, and when he dies they bear him to be buried to a mountain which is called Alcay, where are buried the Grand Khans, Emperors of the Tartars, and those who bear him to burial slay all those they find, saying to them : 'Go and serve our master in the other world' ; and in the same way they slay all his horses, camels, and baggage-mules which they have, thinking that they will go to serve their lord. When Mongui Khan, Emperor of the Tartars, died, there were slain 300,000 men, whom those who bore him to burial met on the way, as Marco Polo says in his book, chapter 42. Poggio, the Florentine Secretary of Pope Eugenius IV., *towards the end of* his second book, which he wrote on the variations and changes of fortune, does much to confirm what the said Marco Polo wrote in his book.

No. 16. There are various opinions as to what is Trapovana, since the Spaniards and Portuguese have navigated the Indian Ocean. How Ptolemy places it in degrees of latitude and longitude I think is well known to all. Some modern explorers hold that the island of Ceylon is Trapovana ; others hold that it is

the island of Sumatra. Pliny writes of Trapovana in
his sixth book, chapter 22, and says that there was
a time when the opinion was held that Trapovana
was another world, and that it was called Antichthon;
and that Alexander was the first to inform us that it
was an island; and that Onesicritus, Admiral of the
fleet, says that in the said island of Trapovana there
are larger and more warlike elephants than in India;
and that Magasæne gives as its length 7,000 stadia, and
as its width 5,000; that there is no walled city in it,
but 700 villages; and that in Claudius' reign ambassadors came from the said island to Rome. In this
way the freedman Damius Plocamius, who had bought
of the Republic the taxes of the Red Sea, and sailing
round Arabia was carried by the north wind in such
a way that on the 15th day he entered a port of the
said island called Hippius, and was very generously
received and treated by the King; and that after
having remained in the said island six months he
learned the language; and that one day talking with
the King he told him that the Romans and their
Emperor were incredibly just; and that the King,
seeing that the coins which the said Freedman had
were of equal weight, though the stamp showed they
were of different Emperors, moved by this, sent
ambassadors to Rome, the chief of whom was Rachia,
to make friendship with Claudius, from which ambassadors he heard that in the said island there were five
hundred cities; and that the said ambassadors were

astonished to see in these heavens of ours the North
Star and the Pleiades as something new and to them
unknown ; and that they said that in the said island
they only saw the moon above the earth from the
8th day to the 15th ; and they were especially
astonished that shadows turned towards our sky and
not towards theirs, and that the sun rose on the right
and set on the left ; from which aforesaid reasons it
seems that in the said island where the said freedman
made harbour the North Star is not seen, which is
seen in the island Trapovana ; whence it might be
said, considering whence the said freedman, Damius
Proclamius [sic], started, and the course he might have
made with a raging north wind, that the island where
he made harbour was the island of San Lorenzo and not
Trapubana [sic].   And that as king of the said island
an old and mild man without children is usually
elected, and if after being elected he should beget
any, they at once depose him ; and when they elect
him they give him thirty counsellors ; and that the said
King can condemn no one if the majority of his said
thirty counsellors are not agreed with him ; and that
afterwards the said condemned man can appeal to the
people, which thereupon elects seventy judges who
examine his case ; and if they find he was wrongly
sentenced they set him free and those counsellors who
agreed in condemning him are deprived of their offices
and are held infamous for ever after.

CHAPTER XV

THE LEGENDS OF THE MAP OF 1544, CONTINUED—
NOS. 17–33—REMARKS ON THE LEGENDS AND ON
THE WORKMANSHIP OF THE MAP—QUESTION OF
SEBASTIAN'S AUTHORSHIP — QUESTION OF THE
LANDFALL OF 1497 AS MARKED ON THIS MAP—
VARIOUS EDITIONS OF THE MAP—SEBASTIAN'S
CLAIMS OF NAUTICAL INVENTIONS.

No. 17. INSCRIPTION of the author with certain reasons
for the variation which the needle of the compass
makes with the Pole Star. Sebastian Cabot, Captain
and Pilot-Major of his Sacred Cæsarean Catholic
Majesty, the Emperor Don Carlos, fifth of the name, and
King, *our Lord*, made this figure projected on a plane
in the year of the Birth of our Saviour Jesus Christ,
1544, drawn by degrees of latitude and longitude with
its winds as a navigating chart, imitating in part
Ptolemy, and in part the modern discoverers, *both
Spanish and Portuguese*,[1] and partly discovered by

[1] ' And likewise the experience and labours of the long nautical life of
the most honest man John Cabot, a Venetian by birth ; and the knowledge of the stars and of the art of navigation of Sebastian, his most
learned son and my author, who discovered some part of the world
which had long been unknown to us,' Lat.

his father and himself, by which you may navigate as by a navigating chart, bearing in mind the variation which the needle of the compass makes with the Pole Star. For example, if you wish to get out from Cape St. Vincent in order to make Cape Finisterre, you will give orders to steer your ship to the North according to the needle of the compass, and you will strike within the said Cape ; but the real course which your ship made was to the North, a quarter North-East, because your compass-needle North-Easts you a quarter at the said Cape of St. Vincent ; so that, commanding your ship to be steered North by the compass-needle, your course will be North, quarter North-East ; and in the same way from Salmedina, which is a shoal, as you go out of San Lucar de Barrameda, to go to the point of Naga on the island of Teneriffe, you will give orders to steer S.W. by the needle, and you will make the said point of Naga because it is situated on the navigating chart.   But your course will not be to the south-west, inasmuch as your compass-needle north-easts you a wide quarter-point at Salmedina, but your course will be S.W., a wide quarter south.   So that you may say that sailing from St. Vincent to the North, your course will be North, quarter North-East ; and sailing from Salmedina to the South-West, your course will be South-West, quarter South.   And so consequently you will do in every other part of this universe, watching the variation which the said needle

of the compass makes with the North Star, for the
said needle does not turn or stay fixed to the North
in every place, as the vulgar think, since the magnet
stone, as it appears, has not the power to make it turn
to the North in every place, but, as is seen and
acquired by experience, it has only the power to make
it remain still and fixed in one place. Wherefore it
must point necessarily in a straight line whatever
wind you may have, and not in a curved line, and
this cause brings about the said variation. For if the
needle were to turn to the North always and in every
place there would be no variation, for then it would
follow a curved line, because you would always be on
one parallel, which cannot be when you go in a
straight line on a sphere. And you must notice that
the further you move from the meridian on which the
needle points directly North, towards the West or
East, so much the more will your compass move from
the North, that is from the Flower de Luce in it
which marks the North. Wherefore it clearly appears
that the said needle points along a straight line and not
along a curved line. And you must know that the
meridian where the Flower de Luce of the needle points
directly North is about thirty-five leagues from Flores,
the last island of the Azores towards the West,
according to the opinion of certain experts, because of
the great experience which they have of this, on
account of the daily navigation which is made towards
the West, to the Indies of the Ocean. The said

Sebastian Cabot, sailing towards the West, found himself in a place where North-East quarter North [of the compass] stood directly North, on account of which observations aforesaid it appears clearly that defects and variations which the said needle of the compass makes with the North Star really exist.

No. 18. Pliny, in the second book, chapter 79, writes that from Cadiz and the Columns of Hercules, sailing around Spain and Gaul, the whole West was sailed over. The greater part of the Northern Ocean was sailed over in the time of Augustus, passing by all Germany as far as the Cimbrian Cape and thence as far as Scythia. And from the East the fleet of Macedonia sailed along the Indian Ocean towards the North, until the Caspian Sea was to the South of them, in the time that Seleucus and Antiochus reigned, and they ordered that that region should be called Seleuchida and Antiochida. And to the North of the Caspian many parts have been sailed over, so that the Northern Sea has really been all traversed. And he likewise says in the same chapter that Cornelius Nepos writes, that to Quintus Metellus Celer, who had been consul with Apanius, and who was then proconsul in Gaul, there were sent certain Indians by the King of the Suevi, who, starting from the Indian Ocean, had without mischance been carried to Germany.

No. 19. In these Rocos Islands there are birds of such size, as they say, and strength, that they take

up an ox and bear it in their flight in order to eat
it ; and still more, they say, that they take a vessel,
no matter how great it may be, and raise it a great
height and then let it drop, and they eat the men.
Petrarch likewise says so in his books *of Prosperous
and Adverse Fortune.*

No. 20. There are in the island of the people
of Calenguan, lions, tigers, panthers, deer, and many
other different kinds of animals ; likewise there are
eagles and white parrots who speak, as clearly as
human beings, what is taught them, and many other
countless birds of various kinds. The people of the
island are idolaters ; they eat human flesh.

No. 21. A ship from Cambaya discovered this
island of Mamorare, and it is said there was so
much gold in it that they loaded it with nothing
else, according to what the Portuguese say.

No. 22. There are in this island of Ceylon native
cinnamon, and rubies, and hyacinths, and cats' eyes, and
other kinds of precious stones. Ciapangu is a large
island lying in the high seas, which island is fifteen
hundred miles distant from the mainland of the Grand
Khan towards the East. They are idolaters, and
a gentle and handsome race. It has an independent
king of its own, who is tributary to no one. It
contains much virgin gold, which is never taken
away from the said island, because ships never touch
there as it is so distant and out of the way. The
king of this island has a very great and wonderful

palace all made of gold in ingots of the thickness of two reals, and the windows and columns of the palace are all of gold.   It [the island] contains precious stones and pearls in great quantities.   The Grand Khan, having heard the fame of the riches of the said island, desired to conquer it, and sent to it a great fleet, and could never conquer it, as Marco Polo more amply relates and tells us in his book, the 106th chapter.'

Besides these twenty-two legends there are also some additional inscriptions, viz. : 1. In the S.W. quadrant of the map.   'In this figure, projected on a plane, are contained all the lands, islands, ports, rivers, waters, bays, which have been discovered down to the present day, and their names and who were the discoverers of them, as is made more manifest by the inscriptions [tables] of this said figure—together with all the rest that was known before and all that has been written by Ptolemy, such as provinces, regions, cities, mountains, rivers, climates, and parallels— according to their degrees of longitude and latitude, both of Europe, and of Asia, and of Africa.   And you must note that the land is situated according to the variation which the needle of the compass makes with the North Star, for the reason of which you may look in the second table, No. 17.'

2. In the S. E. quadrant of the map :—'Pliny writes in his ninth book, chapter 35, of a fish which is called Nichio, which he describes as being round, and says

that when it attaches itself to a ship it holds the same fast, even though it be under sail. And Petrarch, in the preface to the second book of his work on *Prosperous and Adverse Fortune*, says that the echenis or remora, a fish of half a foot in length, stops a ship, though it be very large and though wind and waves, oars and sails, aid its course. Alone, and with no other agency save its attachment to the planks of the ship, with no other force than its own nature, it overpowers the strength of the elements and of man. And this fish is like mud or mire, and if it be taken out of the water it loses its power. The aforesaid is found in very famous writings, which are not quoted here lest too much space should be taken up.'

So far the Legends. And to their text we may add the following remarks. (1) The Spanish original is so incorrect that as printed it is apparently not the work of a Spaniard; at any rate, if the manuscript was in good Spanish, the (Flemish?) copyist must have worked his will upon it pretty freely. (2) Further, Spaniards would not be likely to write (or to read without a smile) such explanations as that of Seville, 'a famous city in Andalusia,' added in the Latin version, whose readings, evidently designed for a people who were not fully in the swim of things American, are usually of the most simple and educational character, merely amplifying and explaining the words of the Spanish text. Nor would a Latin version have been inserted at all for a merely

Spanish public. (3) The said Latin version, once more, is as rough and ungrammatical as the Spanish it accompanies, and when Chytraeus transcribed it he apologises for the language, and excuses himself for his trouble on the score of the important matter contained in these barbarous paragraphs.   Both as to Spanish and Latin forms, in fact, the inscriptions show a hand fully as careless and under-educated as that of the draughtsman who executed the map itself. (4) The Legends, like many of the entries in the body of the map, abound with obvious mistakes, as well as with highly doubtful or improbable statements. As, for instance :—The Latin version of the eighth legend gives *July* 24, 1494, for the date of John Cabot's first landfall, while the Spanish text of the same legend supplies the elsewhere corroborated *June* 24.   The reference to Pliny in the eighteenth legend cites the wrong chapter.   The lake of St. Peter, called Lac d'Angoulesme, is rendered in Spanish as Laaga de Golesme.   In the seventh legend, where the Rio de la Plata is discussed, mention is made of the opinion of some people that in the mountains near that river are dog-faced and ostrich-legged [1] tribes ; also that on the banks of the said river, as a matter of fact, Cabot sowed fifty-two grains of wheat in September and reaped fifty-two thousand in December —the same story which Sebastian afterwards repeated to Eden.   In the ninth and tenth legends, dealing

[1] *I.e.*, ' From the knee down.'

with Iceland and other countries that border on the Northern Sea, are mentioned lampreys like serpents, which will attack ships,[1] ghosts in human form as well as ghosts invisible but audible (according to the native belief) and monstrous races with pigs' heads and grunting speech, or with flap ears (Legend 12) great enough to cover their whole body, or with jointless limbs. The thirteenth legend notes in the far South, among the Troglodytes, extending to the Cape of Good Hope, a people who only converse by whistling. Lastly, the spelling of the names, even for that time, is of unusual barbarity and contrariety— 'Tridore,' 'Trapobana,' 'Trapubana,' 'Aziumba,' 'Damius Proclamius,' and so forth, do not show a high standard of cartographical scholarship.

And, as already suggested, if such is the character of the legends, that of the map itself is not much better. It is in the closest relation to certain existing Portuguese and French examples, though it can hardly be assumed that it is copied bodily from any single one, as the Dieppese chart of 1541 emanating from Nicholas Desliens. But the works of Diego Homem and the charts of Jacques Cartier unquestionably form the basis of our planisphere of 1544, a planisphere which, compiled as it is by an inferior hand from a variety of well-known sources, without original information (certain exceptions allowed for) or even an average amount of accuracy and scholarship, was in

[1] This is in the Olaus Magnus Map of 1539, § B.

all probability neither drawn nor revised by Sebastian
Cabot. Yet the 'exceptions' we have alluded to
(especially in the 8th and 17th inscriptions) are
matters which at least show that the compiler had
original and fairly correct information about the first
voyage of John Cabot to North America, and make
it probable that Sebastian knew of the work in
question and supplied its author with some details,
allowing the whole to pass under his name, as the
17th legend, or 'inscription of the author,' inti-
mates. The main body of material here employed,
however, may be called rather Cartierean than
Cabotian ; most of Cartier's names reappear in the
Canadian portions of this map ; and the results of his
second voyage are detailed, with mistakes which can
mostly be corrected, as Mr. Dawson has pointed out,
by reference to other, and especially Dieppese, charts
of this period.

As examples of the slovenly workmanship of this
example we may notice : a reference in the right-hand
margin to 90 degrees where 80 should be read ; the
legend about the Cod Fish Country, really No. 8,
quoted as No. 3 ; a station called Brest, repeated
on the Labrador coast ; and various corruptions of
Cartier's (and other) names, as ' De Tronot ' and
' Y' de Tronot ' for ' Cap. Tiennot,' ' S. Quenain '
and ' Saqui ' for ' Saguenay, ' tuttonaer ' for ' Tude-
mans,' 'Loreme' for ' Laurent '—to go no further than
those North-West parts of which Sebastian claimed to

have peculiar and extensive knowledge. Once more : it is indeed surprising, if Sebastian were in any real sense the author, that Bristol is not marked in England ; that Ireland is made almost to equal Great Britain ; and that the delineation of Newfoundland is so far from the truth ;—a multitude of little islands (many of them obviously conventional) being laid down here as off the coast of Labrador, just as if the draughtsman was working in the dark from some vague narrative which stated 'Here are to be found many islands.' In a word, this map, in its picture of the Old World as well as the New, is inferior to the better Italian, French, Spanish, and Portuguese maps of this time ; even the Mediterranean is much mis-shapen ; while the representation of the La Plata region, which Sebastian unquestionably visited in 1528–1530, contains some serious errors of fact.[1] Once more, whereas in the Columbus lawsuit of 1535 Cabot had declared himself uncertain as to whether north of the Gulf of Mexico America was conti-nental, without any intervening break, or no—in this map the New World is set forth as one mass of undivided land from the Arctic to the Antarctic Seas.

It will not, therefore, appear very probable that Sebastian really designed the planisphere of 1544, or wrote or even revised any part of the legends which

[1] Thus 'the all-important elbow (of the Parana) found near Cor-rientes and carrying the stream eastward, is entirely omitted . . .' Cabot 'continuing the Parana due North, confusing it with the Paraguay' (Harrisse).

accompanied it, except perhaps those two (Nos. 8 and 17) which concerned the place and date of the landfall of 1497(94), and the name and share of John Cabot in the original discovery.   It seems also pretty clear, from the general history we have already recounted, that in these paragraphs, which appear to come more directly from Sebastian himself, the false and the true are inextricably blended.   His father and and himself, we are told, sighted land on the 24th of June, 1494, at Cape Breton, according to the apparent indication of the Prima Vista of the map.   Now all this had not only been suppressed but implicitly contradicted in the maps published in Spain for many years past, under Sebastian's superintendence or during his residence in the Peninsula.   The English share in the Western world had been relegated to the extreme North ; now that Cabot is meditating a return to the Tudor service, that English share is immensely increased by a placing of the landfall, not high up on the Labrador coast, but well to the south of the Gulf of St. Lawrence.   To crown all, a very early date is assigned to the English expedition—too early, as we know now, by three years.   It does not seem, therefore, that we have here anything of great weight in favour of the Cape Breton landfall,[1] granting that the Prima Vista applies to this point.   But it is just possible

---

[1] That is, as against a landfall at Cape Race, Cape Bonavista or Cape Charles.   The question is rather different when we widen the issue, as is discussed a little later.

that these words, written right across the mouth of the St. Lawrence, may be intended to refer to the Northern instead of to the Southern shore, to the lowest point of Labrador (say at Cape Charles) rather than to Cape Breton and Nova Scotia. In any case, the character of the workmanship both in the map and the inscriptions, is not such that any confident theory can be built upon its apparent statements. For the workmanship is not only unskilful and careless, but essentially second-hand; it is not the production of an explorer who was well acquainted with America.

We believe, however, that the indication of the Prima Vista represents, with whatever inaccuracy of detail, the general truth that the first English expedition to America was commanded by John Cabot, and that it reached land in a temperate rather than in a sub-arctic zone, in the latitude of Newfoundland and not in that of the Upper Labrador coast; and we are inclined also to believe that this resuscitation of the (approximately) true landfall, as well as of the true discoverer, after a suppression of forty years, was due to Sebastian's interest in pleasing the English Government and paving the way for his return to our island. On the other hand, if Spanish authorities objected, Cabot might reply that the map was not published in Spain under his supervision, that it was fathered on him without his consent, and that he was not responsible for any of its statements.

We see no reason to believe with M. Harrisse that the

day and month of the landfall (June 24) are spurious, like the year [1] (1494 for 1497) ; still less that the St. John Island near Cape Breton [2] is purely imaginary, originating in a mistaken entry of earlier maps, and that the date of June 24 (St. John Baptist's Day) was 'invented to tally with the name of St. John then existing' in charts of that region. Whether, as Mr. Dawson contends, the St. John Isle of 1497 is Scatari, just at Cape Breton ; whether the same name as placed on the map of 1544 corresponds to the Great Magdalen, discovered by Cartier in 1534, and attached to that point by the draughtsman of our planisphere, who was using French information, each inquirer must judge for himself—these points do not seem to us finally solved, or indeed solvable. Whatever we think, it is surely rash to use this map for establishing any precise theory ; its whole character supports us in depending upon it for nothing but general and vague conclusions.[3]

[1] Which Sebastian ante-dated in almost every reported conversation of his. There is also the possibility mentioned before of a copyist's mistake, IIII. for VII., if the V. was carelessly written **V.**

[2] So important from the 8th inscription, which asserts that it was discovered the *same day as* the landfall. It is in the underlined words that we suspect the exaggeration lies.

[3] Thus when M. Harrisse suggests that the map of 1544 'records, perhaps unconsciously, the mishap of Cartier (when on September 28, 1535, he was unable to cross with his ship the western extremity of the Angoulême or St. Pierre lake, and was compelled to continue the voyage in boats) in the words, ' Here it is not possible to pass,' we can only admire the ingenuity of detraction which elsewhere suggests that because Adams is not known to have learnt map-engraving, therefore he could not possibly have 'cut' the Cabot planisphere (copy of 1549).

The 'Cabot' chart of 1544 seems to have been reissued in 1549, with the Latin version (only) of the Legends, and a rearrangement of their number, as 19 instead of 22. In this form the German scholar Chytraeus (Nathan Kochhaff) apparently saw it at Oxford in A.D. 1565, and Richard Hakluyt at Westminster and London in A.D. 1584 (or earlier)— 'Cabot's own map (in the latter's words) which is in the Queen's Privy Gallery at Westminster and in many merchants' houses in London.' Hakluyt adds that the Queen's copy was 'set out' by Clement Adams, and elsewhere credits the same copyist with 'cutting,' or engraving, examples of this work for English use. If all this be accepted, we have here the earliest English map engraving (by five and twenty years), but even if we refuse to believe that an Englishman could engrave maps so early in the sixteenth century, we may at least agree on the words of Purchas, where he says that the Adams copy of 1549 was 'taken out of Sir Sebastian Cabot's.' In other words, we may admit, as M. Harrisse puts it, that simple impressions from the map of 1544 were imported from the Continent, and that the Legends were set up in Latin only, and printed (twice) by Clement Adams in 1549—first with the date of 1494 as that of the original Cabotian discovery, and afterwards with the true year (1497) as it is definitely stated by Purchas, and probably copied by Hakluyt in his final edition of the *Principal Navigations* (1599–1600),

by Michael Lok in his map of 1582, and by Moly-
neux in the map drawn to illustrate the completed
and corrected Hakluyt of 1599–1600.[1] One or other
of these editions by Adams, we may be pretty sure, is
intended by Richard Willes in 1577, when he writes
of 'Cabot's table which the Earl of Bedford hath
at Cheynies.'

The work of 1544, thus associated with a famous
name, was in some request for a time on the Continent as well as in England;[2] it has been supposed
(without much probability) that this was the Cabotian
map sold among the remains of Juan de Ovando in
September, 1575; it is certainly mentioned by Ortelius
among the authorities for his *Theatrum* of 1570; it
seems to have been a model in the Italian Cartographical School of Gastaldo; and in our own day it
has been studied and argued upon, and its importance
magnified, out of all proportion to its merits.

[1] Hakluyt in the *Principal Navigations*, as edited in 1589, gives 1494;
in the same, as edited in 1599–1600, 1497; and in the *Western Planting* of 1584, 1496, in the last borrowing from Ramusio and Peter Martyr.

[2] Dr. Dee is probably referring to this map when on the back of his
own map of America, A.D. 1580 (B. Mus. Cotton. MSS. Aug. I. 1), he
bases 'the Queen's Majesty's title royal to these foreign regions and
islands' on the discoveries of Cabot, &c.,—one of the earliest formal
statements of this claim. (Thus, *e.g.*, 'Circa an. 1497, Sebastian Caboto
sent by King Henry VII. did discover from Newfoundland so far along
and about the coast next to Laborador till he came to the latitude of $67\frac{1}{2}°$.
And still found the seas open before him.') In the same way Hakluyt, in
dedicating his *Divers Voyages* of 1582 to Sir Philip Sidney, derives the
'title which England has to that part of America which is from Florida
to 67° North . . .' from the letters patent granted to John Cabot and his
three sons.

The present volume is not the place for an elaborate discussion of Sebastian's claims as a scientific geographer, a leading inventor in the seaman's art, or a student of the most mysterious problems of navigation. But it must be said that he owed a great deal of his reputation to these claims, and that he has been freely credited with the discovery both of the declination and of the variation of the magnetic needle, of the line with no variation, and of more than one method of finding the longitude at sea.

Now the declination and variation of the magnetic needle were both observed by Columbus on the night of the 13th of September, 1492, in the Mid-Atlantic, and these first observations were checked by the same great navigator on the 21st of May, 1496, and the 16th of August, 1498.

Similarly the conjecture of a line with no variation, which Livio Sanuto tells us[1] was demonstrated to

[1] Sanuto's language is : ' Being the friend of a certain gentleman named Guido Giannetti di Fano . . . I ascertained from him that the needle of the mariner's compass, rubbed with the loadstone, does not always indicate the meridian of the observer, but a point some degrees from that meridian ; and this place, whatever its distance may be, is indicated by the needle. . . . Sebastian Cabot, a Venetian and admirable pilot, discovered this secret by means of experiments which he undertook when he sailed to the Indies ; and this he afterwards disclosed to the most serene King of England. Giannetti had the honour of being present, as I have understood from others. On the same occasion Cabot showed what the distance was [of the needle's indication from the observer], and [proved] that it did not appear the same in every place.' Sanuto, *Geografia distinta in XII. libri Vinegia D. Zenaro*, 1588, bk. i., fol. 2. The work in question was apparently written within S. Cabot's lifetime, before 1553, and probably ' between 1548 and 1551.' Nothing more is

Edward VI. himself by Sebastian Cabot, is fully expounded by Columbus on May 23, 1496, and in
almost exactly similar language.   Cabot showed the
English King, we are informed, the meridian where
the needle pointed to the North, and inscribed the
meridian (on a chart) as 110 miles west of Flores
in the Azores.   Columbus, fifty years earlier, expressed
his view that the compass in certain parts of the
Atlantic approached nearer to the Pole Star (then
supposed to indicate the true North) in some parts of
the Atlantic than anywhere in the Mediterranean, and
declared his belief that the needle pointed absolutely
North a few days' sail west of Flores.

On the other hand, as we may judge from the
planisphere of 1544, Sebastian did construct maps
exhibiting the magnetic variations, and for all we
know he may have been the first to do so, although
this honour has often been claimed for Alonzo de
Santa Cruz and the year 1536.

But perhaps his most cherished hope was the inven-
tion of an accurate method for finding the longitude
at sea.   This he proposed to do in two ways : first, by
the variation of the magnetic needle ; second, by the
declination of the sun.   Of these the former (which
Sebastian explained to Contarini at the famous interview on Christmas Day, 1522) seems to have been quite

known of Giannetti di Fano.   Biddle is wrong in his conjecture that
Giannetti was ambassador in England at this time.   See Harrisse, *Cabot*,
1896, pp. 465–6.

as fully examined and set forth by Columbus on May 23, 1496; but the second appears to be much more his own speculation, though unfortunately inadequate for its purpose, and is thus explained by Alonzo de Santa Cruz, some time after 1547 :

'The method of Sebastian Caboto, Pilot-Major to his Majesty in England, for obtaining the longitude.

'First, in order to find the difference in the longitude of any points however distant . . . we must know that in a little less than a year the sun . . . passes through all the signs of the Zodiac, taking something more or less than a month to move through each of these divisions. Thus it passes through almost one degree per day.

'Moreover, we must not forget that the Zodiac retreats from the Equator, after cutting it at two points which are the zero-points of the signs *Aries* and *Libri* graduated into degrees and minutes.

'Now the declination of any part of the heavens, whether divisions of the Zodiac or stars, &c., being merely the distance of that part from the Equator, the two points of intersection of ·the Zodiac and the Equator have a declination zero; likewise the declinations of the divisions of the Zodiac increase with their distances from the Equator up to the signs of Cancer and Capricorn, which are at a distance of about $23\frac{1}{2}°$ from the Equinoctial; when in one of these two signs the sun's declination equals $23\frac{1}{2}°$—its greatest possible value. In every other sign its declination is more or less great, according to the position of the sign in the Zodiac, but it is always less than $23\frac{1}{2}°$. Moreover, we must note that as every degree of the Zodiac has a declination of a definite value, so also the sixty minutes of any degree have certain declinations proportional to the distance of these minutes from minute zero.

' Thus the zero-point of the first minute of the first degree of Aries having a declination zero, and the zero-point of the first minute of the second degree of the same sign having a declination of 24', it is evident that these 24' must be distributed proportionately among each of the 60' through which the sun moves in the Ecliptic in a day—the approximate time necessary for the sun to pass through one degree of the Ecliptic. By calculation we see that a movement of $2\frac{1}{2}'$ in the Ecliptic causes a variation of a minute in the declination of the sun.

' Now supposing that on March 10th the sun were at the zero-point of the first minute of the first degree in the sign of Aries, its declination being zero, and that at the same moment it crossed the meridian of Seville —then, when in consequence of the daily rotation of the Celestial Sphere, the sun had come to the 90th degree West of the meridian of Seville, its proper motion in the Ecliptic would have brought it to the 15th minute of the first degree in Aries, and at this moment its declination would be 6'.

' And continuing its course towards the West, in

accordance with the daily rotation of the sphere, when it arrived at 180° West longitude from Seville it would have passed, in its proper motion, through 30′ of the first degree in Aries, and would then have a declination of 12′. Similarly when it reached the point of 270° West longitude from Seville, it would be at the 49th minute of the first degree of Aries with a declination of 18′.

'Again, on returning to the meridian of Seville, it would have passed through 360 degrees by its apparent diurnal motion, plus the 60″ of the first degree in Aries, and its declination will then be equal to the 24′ above stated.

'And now the sun will enter the first minute of the second degree in Aries, moving through the minutes of this degree in its own proper motion, just as has been expounded for the first degree.

'From all this we see that the transit of the sun, over the meridian just described, will give us the power of perceiving what is the sun's declination for the moment of transit, although the difference of the sun's declination from one meridian to another diminishes as the sun approaches the tropics. The difference of declination between two positions of the sun in the Zodiac, being distant one minute from each other, cannot be more than 24′; it is very little indeed when near the tropics; and when the sun is actually at one of the tropics the difference is nil.

'With this principle a book of tables should be constructed, wherein should be inscribed the declination of the sun for every day in the year, reckoned for the meridian of Seville—as that is the starting-point of navigators setting out for the West and North, and is near the meridian of Lisbon, the starting-point for the South and East.

'And to get tables of more precision, the sun's declination should be inscribed for each minute of degree in the Ecliptic, because the differences of declination are not always the same between one minute and another. This Ptolemy shows in his Almagest, where the differences of declination are obtained by arcs and chords from which come angles of precision.

'Thus, knowing the differences of declination for an interval of our degree in the Ecliptic, we now by the Rule of Three get the difference of declination for an interval of one minute in the same degree— arguing : If an arc of a certain number of minutes in the Ecliptic corresponds to a certain chord or difference of declination, then another arc of the Ecliptic will correspond in the same proportion to another chord or difference of declination. . . . Ptolemy noted the declination of the sun for all the degrees of the Zodiac on the assumption that the sun's greatest declination was 23° 53' . . . now this is supposed to be 23° 33' . . . my own observations, made at Seville, with graduated instruments of great precision, gave me 23° 26'.

'On this as a foundation I have reckoned the sun's declination for the Seville meridian, so that by increasing or lessening the declinations as computed, according to the place of observation pilots can get the sun's declination for any meridian.

'The books now used by pilots are very inaccurate in their computation of the sun's declination. And a mistake of one-third of a degree in this, coupled with an error of the same amount in the observation of the altitude of the sun, may give an error of almost one degree in the latitude. . . .

'Eliminating this cause of error, let us suppose our tables to be desirably precise—we should then construct an instrument graduated into 90°, each degree being again graduated into 60'.

'This instrument may be a quadrant with an alidade or ruler fixed at the centre, as in the Astrolabe, and furnished with two pinules for observation of altitudes.

'That done, we must know, for the place of observation, the highest meridian altitude of the sun in Cancer, the lowest meridian altitude in Capricorn, and the mean meridian altitude at the Equator. These being noted and marked on our instrument, the intermediate altitudes will give us the sun's declinations on either side of the Equator.

'Also one of the sides of this instrument of ours (say quadrant) should be fixed to the ground, so that it will be stationary, and not move to either side. . . . And the declination of the sun for the meridian of

Seville being known for all the days in the year, and its declination for any given meridian being obtained by observation, we can deduce the difference of the sun's declination on the Seville meridian and on the meridian in question, and so get the difference in longitude in the way already expounded.'[1]

To all this Santa Cruz objects, that pilots could not use the quadrant suggested at sea because of the great size which would be necessary in an instrument graduated with degrees and minutes ; that the motion of the ship would prevent the stability essential for the proper observation ; and that the sun's declination for the days of the whole year could not be ascertained with the needful accuracy.

Certain French naval experts have also calculated, for the information of M. Harrisse and his readers, the practical working of Sebastian Cabot's method above stated, and have concluded that it would be extremely inaccurate,[2] but in the sixteenth century it was not

[1] In short, as M. Harrisse summarises, with the assistance of Admiral Fleuriais and Lieutenant Bauvieux, the method given is as follows :— The latitude being known, the question is to determine the declination of the sun by observation of its meridian altitude. The sun's declination, at the moment of transit over the first meridian, is also known, for the date of observation, by means of tables established for every day of the year. From the difference of these two declinations is computed the time elapsed between the two transits of the sun over the first meridian and the meridian of observation, viz., the longitude—on the hypothesis that for this interval of time the motion of declination is proportional to the time elapsed.

[2] 'The error in longitude, when following Cabot's method, would . . . have reached 60°, i.e., one-sixth of the circumference of the globe.'

without its merits—‘ a very clever way of finding the longitude at sea,’ (as Contarini says of his other method), albeit not perfect, was evidently the judgment of his best-informed contemporaries.

Lastly, Cabot’s sailing directions, as given in the 17th Legend of the map of 1544, have been criticised by the same French experts in three particulars among others. First, Cabot makes the South-West course magnetic, with one point of easterly variation, correspond to South-West one quarter South true, whereas it really corresponds to South-West-by-West true. Secondly, he appears to state here, as elsewhere, that curves of equal magnetic declination are meridians, bases his sailing directions upon this hypothesis, and with its aid tries to explain the cause of the magnetic declination. Thirdly, he seems to believe that the direction of a face can be circular—‘ For if the needle pointed to the North always . . . it would not vary at all, being then directed in a circular line.’

<hr/>

ADDITIONAL NOTE.

On Sebastian Cabot’s Portrait and alleged Knighthood.

1. There still exist copies of a portrait of Sebastian Cabot, one of which is reproduced as the frontispiece for the present volume. The original referred to was discovered by C. A. Harford, of Bristol, at the Scottish residence of a nobleman in 1792 ; it was identified by him as probably identical with a picture described by Purchas, and brought to London in 1832, whence it was taken to Pittsburg, in Pennsylvania, U.S.A., on becoming the property of Richard Biddle, the author of the *Memoir of Sebastian Cabot* (1831). It perished, however, in the conflagration of Biddle’s house in

1845. After Harford had first obtained possession of it, it was engraved by Rawle for Seyer's *Memoirs of Bristol* (1824). It has also been copied for the galleries of the Massachusetts and New York Historical Societies, and for the Mayor and Corporation of Bristol in 1839. Long believed to be a Holbein, £500 was given for it by Biddle. It bears the following inscriptions : (1) 'Spes mea in Deo est.' (2) 'Effigies Sebastiani Caboti Angli filii Johannis Caboti Veneti militis aurati primi inventoris terræ nova[e] sub Henrico VII. Angliae rege,' which corresponds very closely with the earliest reference, in Purchas, *Pilgrims*, of 1625 (iii. 807 ; iv. 1812) ; 'Sir Seb. Cabota : his picture in the privy gallery at Whitehall hath these words, " Effigies Seb. Cabot, Angli filii Joannis Caboti Veneti militis aurati."' Hence Harford conjectured his find to be the same as, or a copy of, that possessed by Charles I. The portrait in question does not appear in the Harleian catalogue of that king's pictures, drawn up before 1649 (Harleian MSS. 4718), nor in the Ashmolean catalogue of the same, dating from the middle of the eighteenth century. (*Catalogue and description of King Charles the First's capital collection,* 1757.) The Holbein tradition is unreliable (except as referring to the 'School' of that master), for (1) The dress and chain Cabot appears to be wearing is probably that belonging to his office of governor of the Merchant Adventurers, or Muscovy Company—which office he assumed in 1553. (2) Holbein died in 1543, before Cabot's 'second English period' begins, and the former's residence in this country, (*a*) 1526–29, (*b*) 1532–43, is not known to coincide with Cabot's visits to our shores at any point.

A portrait of Sebastian Cabot, conjectured to be also a copy of the 'Harford' picture, is said to have been painted in 1763 for the Sala della Scudo in the Ducal Palace at Venice. The wording of the inscription leaves it doubtful whether Sebastian or John is intended as the 'finder of the New World.' From the position of the words 'filii . . . Veneti,' Humboldt argued that the father was meant ; it may well be that the form is intentionally doubtful.

2. This inscription and Purchas's reference, above quoted, have given rise to the theory that either Sebastian or his father was knighted by the Crown of England. No conclusive evidence of this is forthcoming. The only distinction attached to either Cabot in English records is that of Armiger, or Esquire, given to Sebastian in documents of 1555 and 1557. His name does not occur (nor his father's) in the Cotton MS. (Claudius C III.) list of men raised to knighthood under Henry VII., and his descendants, to the death of Elizabeth.

APPENDICES

APPENDIX I.

*N.B.—Documents relating solely to the foreign life of the
Cabots are in square brackets.*

1476. 1. [The order for John Cabot's naturalisation as
a Venetian citizen, granted on March 28,
1476, in the Doge-ship of Andrea Vendramin. By this the privilege of citizenship 'within and without' is bestowed
on the said John in consideration of
fifteen years of residence.

'Quod fiat privilegium civilitatis de
intus et extra Ioani Caboto per habita-
tionem annorum xv., juxta consuetum.
De Parte (= Ayes), 149; De Non

(= Noes), o ; Non Sinceri (= Neu-
trals), o.'

See Rawdon Brown, Venetian Calendar
State Papers, vol. i., No. 453. Original in
the Senatorial Registers, entitled *Terra*,
for A.D. 1473–77, vol. vii., fol. 109.

See text of this vol., p. 34.]

1472–6. 2. [Decree of Doge Nicolao Trono, of
August 11, 1472, and consequent grant
to Cabot, &c. Original in series of
records entitled *Privilegii*, dealing with
years 1425–1562, vol. ii., fol. 53. See
p. 35 of this vol.]

1496. 3. The petition of John Cabot, and of Lewis,
Sebastian, and Sancto his sons, delivered
on March 5, 1496, and answered by the
First Letters Patent, granted to the
Cabots by Henry VII.

Both (a) the Petition and (β) the
Letters Patent are in the Public Record
Office, London, viz.—

(a) Privy Seals and Chancery Signed
Bill, 11 Henry VII., No. 51, 7th fol. in
packet.

(β) French Roll, 11 Henry VII., membrane 23 (8).

(β) is reprinted in Rymer's ' Fœdera,'

ed. of 1741, vol. v., part iv., p. 89 ;
in Hakluyt's ' Divers Voyages,' and
' Principal Navigations' (see the latter,
iii. 4, in ed. of 1598–1600) ; in Desimoni's 'Intorno a Giovanni Caboto,' p.
47 ; and in some other collections. An
English version in Hakluyt (as above) ;
also in Nicholls, Bristol, iii., 294, and elsewhere. See text of this vol., p. 48, &c.
The date (March 5, 1496) is not that of
the petition itself, but only of the delivery,
and of the grant following thereon.

1496. 4. The despatch of March 28, 1496, from the
Spanish sovereigns to Ruy Gonçales de
Puebla, Senior Ambassador of their
Majesties in England.

This, as already noticed, replies, among
other things, to a letter from Puebla of
January 21, 1496, now lost, but which
evidently gave notice of John Cabot's
projects and compared them to those of
Columbus.

See Bergenroth, Spanish Calendar, i.
pp. 88–9, No. 128 ; text of this vol.,
p. 51, &c. Original at Simancas, Capitulaciones con Inglaterra Leg., 2, fol. 16.

1497. 5. The grant of £10 from Henry VII. to

'him that found the new isle.' Dated August 10, 1497 (British Museum Additional MSS., 7099, fol. 41 ; copy by Craven Orde of original entry in Remembrancer Office). This fixes, more nearly than any other record yet known, the exact time of John Cabot's return from his first voyage. See text of this vol., pp. 55, 92.

1497. 6. The letter of Lorenzo Pasqualigo, in London, to his father and brothers in Venice (August 23, 1497), describing John Cabot's first voyage. Here the duration of the voyage is stated at three months.

See Rawdon Brown, Venetian Calendar, vol. i., p. 262, No. 752 ; and text of this vol., p. 60, &c. (Original in Marin Sanuto's Diarii in Marciana Library at Venice ; printed at Venice 1879, vol. i. pp. 806–8.)

1497. 7. The Despatch of August 24, 1497, from Raimondo di Soncino to the Duke of Milan.

See Rawdon Brown, Venetian Calendar, vol. i., p. 260, No. 750 ;[1] and text of

---

[1] Harrisse misprints, 759.

this vol., p. 62. (Original in Archives of the Sforzas, Milan.)

1497. 8. The pension-grant of £20 a year from King Henry VII. to John Cabot, dated December 13, 1497. The order is addressed to Cardinal Morton as Chancellor, and was sealed on January 28, 149⅞.

In Public Record Office, London, Privy Seals, December 13, 13 Henry VII., No. 40, fol. 22.

'The text of this was first made known by Mr. Deane, who printed it in Winsor's "Narrative and Critical History of America," iii. 56' (Winship). See pp. 92–3 of this vol.

1497. 9. The Despatch of December 18, 1497, from Raimondo di Soncino to the Duke of Milan.

In State Archives, Milan, Potenze Estere, Inghilterra, December, 1497. First published in 'Annuario Scientifico' for 1865, Milan, 1866, p. 700. A careful English version, revised by Prof. B. H. Nash, in Winsor (Deane), 'Narrative and Critical History of America,' iii. 54–5. See text of this vol., p. 62, &c.

1498. 10. The new (second) Letters Patent of February 3, 1498, granted by Henry VII. to John Cabot alone, without mention of his sons.

Latin text in Public Record Office, London, French Roll, 13 Henry VII., No. 439, membrane 1. First printed by Harrisse, 1896, p. 393. A contemporary English version of the same, which is referred to by Hakluyt, is also in P.R.O. Chancery Signed Bill, 13 Henry VII., No. 6 (5th in packet). This is used in text, pp. 95–6. The value of this translation was first pointed out in modern times, by Biddle (Memoir of 1831, pp. 74–5). A 'revised text' is given in Desimoni, 'Intorno,' 56–7. Hakluyt quotes under this form : 'The King upon the 3rd day of February,' &c. ; he prints in his 'Principal Navigations,' as early as 1589, the Rolls Office Memorandum of this license. See text of this vol., pp. 92, 95.

The Latin reads as follows : 'D licencia Caboto. R[ex] omnibus, etc. Sciatis quod nos de gratia nostra speciali ac certis consideracionibus nos specialiter moventibus dedimus ac concessimus . . .

Johanni Caboto Veneciano . . . quod
ipse . . . sex naves . . . portagii ducen-
torum doliorum vel infra . . . pro
salvo conductu earundem navium ad
libitum suum capiendi et providendi
navesque illas ad terram et insulas per
ipsum Johannem nuperrime inventas
conducendi solvendo pro eisdem navibus
et earum qualibet tantum quantum nos
solveremus et non ultra si pro nostro
negocio captæ fuissent . . . Et quod
idem Johannes . . . omnes et singulos
marinarios magistros pagettos ac subditos
nostros . . . qui . . . usque terram et
insulas predictas transire . . . voluerint
. . . recipere possit. . . .'

1498. 11. The authorisation for the immediate payment of John Cabot's pension of £20
first granted on December 13, 1497 (see
above p. 269), which had been delayed.
In Public Record Office, Warrants for
Issues 13 Henry VII., February 22, 1498
(8th in packet). See p. 93 of this vol.

1498. 12. Memorandum of a Loan of £20 from
the King (Henry VII.) to Lanslot or
Launcelot Thirkill of London, 'going
towards the new island,' probably with

John Cabot, dated March 22 [1498].
Also of another loan of £30, on April
1, 1498, to Thomas Bradley and
Launcelot ¹ Thirkill 'going to the new
isle' [apparently one grant of £30 to
the two adventurers, not two grants as
M. Harrisse has understood].

And of a third grant of 40
shillings and 5 pence [not £40 5s. 0d.
as given by M. Harrisse] to John Carter
'going to the new isle.'

B. Mus. Addit. MSS. 7099, fol. 45.

With these may be connected the entry
of June 6, 1501, in B. Mus. Addit.
MSS. 21,480, fol. 35, which states
that Launcelot Thirkill was then 'bound
in two obligations to pay at Whit-
Sunday next coming £20, and that day
twelvemonth 40 marks for livery of
Flemings' lands.' In this bond he is
associated with Thomas Par, Walter
Stickland, and Thomas Mydelton, who
perhaps were his securities. If we can
be sure that Thirkill went with Cabot
in 1498, this would show that he had
returned safely from this voyage, like
his commander. See pp. 102, 109 of
this vol.

¹ Not Thomas Thirkill as given by Harrisse.

1498. 13. Despatch from Puebla to Ferdinand and Isabella, undated, but probably written about 25th July, 1498, warning them of the start of the second Cabot expedition. In Archives of Simancas, Patronato real. Capitulaciones con Inglaterra, Leg. 2, fol. 198. Copy in Public Record Office, London. See text of this vol., p. 100.

1498. 14. Despatch of July 25, 1498, from Pedro d'Ayala to the Spanish Sovereigns, about same expedition. Original in Simancas Archives, Estado, Tratado con Inglaterra Legajo 2. Translated in Bergenroth, Spanish Calendar, i. pp. 176–7, No. 210, with omission of one clause, re Treaty of Tordesillas ('the convention with Portugal') which is supplied by M. Harrisse, p. 396 of his book on the Cabots [1896]. Copy in Public Record Office, London. See text of this vol., p. 101.

1499. 15. The newly discovered memorandum in the Westminster Chapter Archives (Chapter Muniments, 12,243). Endorsed : Brystolle the Acompts of the Custymers Entry No. 2. Bristoll. Arturus Kemys et Ricardus A. Meryk Collectores

s

custumarum et subsidiorum regis ibidem
a festo Sancti Michaelis Archangeli Anno
xiij^{mo} Regis nunc usque idem festum
Sancti Michaelis tunc proximo sequens
reddunt computum de £mcciiij ij ℔
viij^s xj^d ob

De quibus

Etiam in thesauro in una tallia pro
   Thoma Lovell, milite   ...   C ℔
Etiam in thesauro in una tallia pro
   Johanne Caboot   ...   ... xx ℔

Entry No. 3. Bristoll. Arturus
Kemys et Ricardus Ap Meryke Collectores custumarum et subsidiorum Regis
ibidem a festo Sancti Michaelis Archangeli anno xiiij^{mo} Regis nunc usque
idem festum Sancti Michaelis tunc
proximo sequens reddunt computum de
£mccccxxiiij ℔ vii x^d quadr.

De quibus

Etiam in thesauro in una tallia pro
   Johanne Heron ...   xiij ℔ vii^s viij^d
Etiam in thesauro in una tallia pro
   Johanne Cabot   ...   ... xx ℔

This, as already noticed, apparently
proves that John Cabot was alive in the

autumn of 1499, that he had returned from his voyage of 1498, and was drawing his pension a year after our previous knowledge lost sight of him. The memorandum here quoted was discovered by Mr. E. J. L. Scott, Keeper of Manuscripts at the British Museum, in the Chapter Muniments at Westminster, in the course of the year 1897 ; it was verified as an entirely new document by Mr. C. H. Coote of the Map Department in the British Museum, and is here printed for the first time. Announcement of this find was made by the Marquis of Dufferin and Ava, at the Cabot Centenary Meeting in Bristol, June 24, 1897. See pp. 94, 116 of this vol.

1508–9. 16. The entry in the 'Cronicon regum Angliæ

re

1498.
et series Majorum et Vicecomitum Civitatis London ab anno primo Henrici [tertium] tertii ad annum primum Henrici Octavi,' probably written 1508–9, but inserted under date of 1497, presumably refers, as noticed in text (p. 98), to the second Cabot voyage of 1498, though Harrisse is wrong in supposing that the *Cronicon* dates this passage under 1498.

The MS. is in B. Mus. MSS. Cotton. Vitell. A xvi., fol. 173. This is apparent original of statements in Stow, p. 862 of edition of 1580; and in Hakluyt, 'Divers Voyages,' 1582, 'Principal Navigations,' ed. of 1589, and 'Principal Navigations,' ed. of 1598–1600, vol. iii.; p. 9.

On this MS., Mr. James Gairdner reported that it was a quite trustworthy source of contemporary information, its earlier part being derived from a source common to several London Chronicles, such as Gregory's, and its later portions having something in common with Fabyan, but containing a good deal for the reign of Henry VII. not to be found, at least in print, anywhere else.

1500. 17. The La Cosa Map of 1500.

Now in Naval Museum at Madrid. No. 553. A mappemonde on an oval sheet of vellum, measuring 1 mètre and 80 centimètres by 96 centimètres, coloured and illuminated. First described by Alexander Humboldt, who had lighted upon it in the library of Baron Walckenaer (in Paris) in 1842. Sold at Walckenaer's death, April 21,

1853. Bought by Spanish Government for 4020 francs. No degrees of latitude are given in this map. Its Cavo d' Ynglaterra probably marks the landfall of John Cabot, as La Cosa understood it ; this point Kohl identifies (rightly ?) with Cape Race. See text of this vol., p. 104, &c. The best reproduction of this chart is perhaps in Jomard, 'Monuments de la Géographié,' No. xvi.

1502. 18. Entry from Fabyan's lost manuscript chronicle, given by Stow's Chronicle, London, 1580, p. 875, and dated 18 Henry VII., A.D. 1502. This reference to savages brought home by Cabot (probably in 1498) has been construed into evidence for a third Cabot voyage in 1501–2, and is quoted by Hakluyt, 'Divers Voyages,' as being concerned with the eighteenth year of Henry VII. ; by the same compiler in later days, 'Principal Navigations,' vol. iii., p. 9, (Edition of 1598–1600) under the 14th year of Henry VII., Aug. 1498, Aug. 1499. See p. 99 of this vol.

1503. 19. Appropriation for the pension of Fernandes and Gonçales. December 6, 1503.

In the Public Record Office Warrants for issues 13 Henry VII., December 6, 1503. No. 1.

This is an evidence that the earlier grants to the Cabots had now expired. See p. 121 of this vol.

1512. 20. Entry of payment to Sebastian Cabot for a map of Gascony and Guyenne, May, 1512.

Original in Book of King's Payments 1–9 Henry VIII., p. 183; see Brewer, Dom. and For. Calendar Henry VIII., vol. ii. part ii. p. 1456, and p. 126 of this vol.

1516. 21. Letters from Ferdinand of Aragon to (a) Lord Willoughby de Brooke, (β) to Sebastian Cabot; both of September 13, 1512. See in Muñoz Transcripts, vol. xc, fols. 109, 115; also p. 126 of this vol. With these may be taken a letter of Ferdinand's 'concerning Seb. Cabot,' dated October 20, 1512. See Harrisse, 'Jean et Sébastien Cabot,' document xvii. p. 332.

1516. 22. Memorandum in Testament of William Mychell of London, chaplain, under date of January 31, 1516–17 :—

'Lego Elizabeth Filie Sebastini Caboto filiole mee, iijs., iiijd.' See Travers Twiss, 'Nautical Magazine,' London, July, 1876, p. 675 and p. 134 of this volume. Original in Principal Registry of the Probate, Divorce, and Admiralty Division of High Court of Justice.

1518. 23. [Seb. Cabot appointed Pilot-Major of Spain, February 5, 1518. Notice in Muñoz Transcripts, vols. lxxv. fol. 213; lxxvi. fol. 28. See p. 128 of this vol.]

1519. 24. 'A new interlude . . . of the IV. Elements,' *circa* 1519–20? Only copy in British Museum; once belonged to Garrick. Printed by J. Rastell (?) 1519–1520? Press mark C 39 b 17. At the first leaf the following MS. notes, 'An interlude of the IV. Elements, &c., by John Rastell, juxta anno 1519. This interlude was bound with Rastell's abridgment of the Statutes. First impression dated 25th Oct. 11 Henry VIII.' See p. 131 of this vol.

This play seems in part at least designed to pourtray the struggle of 'higher and lower' things for man's attention, as exemplified by Experience, Sensual Appetite, and the Student, who finally refuses to follow the latter any longer. At first Sensual Appetite has it all his own way; then, while he is absent, enters Experience, who enchants the Student with a picture of the countries of the world.

The Student asks him about Jerusalem, England and Scotland, and the countries of Europe; arriving at last in the course of his answers at Norway, his teacher then proceeds to Iceland (as quoted on p. 131). From Iceland he goes West to the new lands, illustrating to what extent he has been 'in sundry nations, with people of divers conditions.'

After the passage (quoted in text) alluding to the discovery of America in the time of Henry VII., Experience continues—

' And what a great meritorious deed
It were to have the people instructed
To live more virtuously.
And to learn to know of men the manner
And also to know God their maker,
Which as yet live all beastly ;
For they neither know God nor the Devil,
Nor never heard tell of Heaven nor Hell,

Writing nor other Scripture.
But yet in the stead of God Almighty
They honour the Sun for his great light,
For that doth them great pleasure.
Building nor house they have none at all,
But woods, cotes, and cavès small—
No marvell though it be so ;
For they use no manner of iron,
Neither in tool nor other weapon
That should keep them thereto.
Copper they have which is found
In divers places above the ground,
Yet they dig not therefore. . . .
Great abundance of wood there be,
Most part fir and pine apple tree.
Great riches might come thereby,
Both pitch and tar and soap ashes
As they make in the East lands
By burning thereof only.
Fish they have so great plenty
That in havens taken and slain they be
With staves withouten sail.
Now Frenchmen and other have found the trade
That yearly of fish there they lade
Above an hundred sail.
But in the south part of that country
The people there go naked alway,
The land is of so great heat,
And in the North part all the clothes
That they wear is but beasts' skins ;
They have none other feet.
But how the people first began
In that country or whence they came
For clerks it is a question. . . .
These new lands, by all cosmography,
From the Khan of Cathay's land cannot lie
Little past a thousand miles.'

Experience finishes his reference to
the New Lands by stating that men can
sail thence ' plain eastwards and come

to England again.' He then describes
other parts of the world, as he has
already dealt with Europe, the Mediterranean, Africa, India, and the New
Lands.

1521. 25. Protest of the London Livery Companies
against the employment of Sebastian
Cabot on an English expedition to the
New World. March 1 to April 9, 1521.
Original in Wardens' Accounts of
Drapers' Company. Reprinted in full in
Harrisse, 'Discovery of North America,'
pp. 747–750. See also W. Herbert's
'History of the Twelve Great Livery
Companies,' i. p. 410, and p. 136 of this
vol.

1522. 26. [Despatch from Council of Ten to Gaspar
Contarini and reward given by same
Council to Cabot's secret messenger,
both of September 27, 1522. Originals
in State Archives, Venice, Capi del
Consiglio dei X. Lettere Sottoscrite
Filza No. 5, 1522. See Rawdon Brown,
Venetian Calendar, vol. iii. No. 557 and
p. 142 of this vol.]

1522. 27. [Despatch from Contarini to (Council of
1523.   Ten and) Senate of Venice, dated

December 31, 1522. Original in
Marciana Library, Cl. vii., Cod. mix.—
(*i.e.*, Contarini's Original Letter-
Book, No. 193 St. Mark's Library)
cart. 281–283. See Rawdon Brown,
Venetian Calendar, vol. iii. No. 607, pp.
293–5, and p. 143 of this vol.]

[With this we must group — (*a*)
Despatch from Contarini of March 7,
1523, to Venetian Senate. Original in
Contarini's Letter-Book, No. 201, St.
Mark's Library. See Rawdon Brown,
Venetian Calendar, vol. iii. No. 634,[1]
p. 304, and p. 149 of this vol.

[(*b*) Letter from Hieronimo de Marino
to Seb. Cabot, dated April 28, 1523.
Original in Capi del Consiglio dei X.
Lettere Sottoscritte Filza No. 6, 1523.
See Rawdon Brown, Venetian Calendar,
vol. iii. No. 670,[2] p. 315, and p. 151 of
this vol.]

[(*c*) Letter from Gaspar Contarini to
the Chiefs of the Ten, dated July 26,
1523. Original in Contarini's Letter-
Book, No. 220, St. Mark's Library.
See Rawdon Brown, Venetian Calendar,
vol. iii. p. 328, No. 710, and p. 150 of
this vol.]

---

[1] Not 632 as in Harrisse.   [2] Not 669 as in Harrisse.

1523. 28. Payment of 43s. 4d. (February 18, 1523)
to John Goderyk of Foly,[1] (Fowey)
Cornwall, for conducting Seb. Cabot to
London some time before, 1519 or 1520 ?
See Brewer, Cal. For. and Dom. H.
VIII. vol. iv. part i. p. 154 ; Harrisse,
' Jean et Sébastien Cabot,' document
xxxii. A and p. 139 of this vol.

This is an item in the will of Sir
Thomas Lovell and the transportation
of Cabot was done 'at our testator's
request.'

We omit the numerous Spanish documents of this period relative to Seb.
Cabot, as they do not bear on his English
career, and are of no great importance in
illustrating our text, except

1533. 29. [Seb. Cabot's letter to Juan de Samano,
June 24, 1533. Original in Archives of
the Indies, Seville, Est. 143, Caj. 3,
Leg. 2. See Harrisse, 'Cabot' of 1896,
pp. 429–430 and p. 208 of this vol.]

1538. 30. Note of Remembrance (December, 1538)
from Sir Thomas Wyatt, English
Ambassador in Spain, recommending
Cabot to Henry VIII. (per Philip Hoby,
on his return from Spain to England)

[1] Not " Tory " as in Harrisse, *Cabot*, p. 405.

B. Mus. Add. MSS. 5498 fol. 8. See
Gairdner Letters and Papers For. and
Dom. H. VIII. vol. xiii. part 2, p. 415,
No. 974; and p. 163 of this vol.

1541. 31. Despatch from Chapuys to the Queen of
Hungary, for information of Charles V.,
May 26, 1541. Original in Imperial
Archives at Vienna Rep. P. Fasc. C. 232
ff. 24–7. See Gayangos, Spanish Calendar,
vol. vi. part i. No. 163, p. 327 and
p. 163 of this vol.

1544. 32. The Cabot Map of 1544. Original in
Geog. Department Bibl. Nat., Paris.
Reproduced in Jomard, 'Monuments
de la Géographie,' Pl. xx., and (at least
in part) in most modern works of good
quality on the Cabots—as Harrisse's,
Deane's, Dawson's, &c. See pp. 218–
53 of this vol.

1547. 33. Warrant of October 9, 1547, to 'Mr.
Peckham' for £100 against expenses incurred in bringing 'Shabot' (= Cabot) to
England. Dasent, 'Acts of Privy Council,' ii. 137. Harrisse, 'Jean et Sébastien
Cabot,' doc. xxxiv. p. 358. See p. 166 of
this vol. The original is on fol. 236 in

MS. No. 2 in the Council Office Series of MS. Registers of Privy Council.

1549. 34. Warrant of September 2, 1549, to Henry Oystryge for £100 expenses incurred in bringing Sebastian 'Sabott' to England. Dasent, 'Acts of Privy Council' (London, 1890), ii. 320. The original is on fol. 578 in MS. No. 2 in the Council Office Series of MS. Registers of Privy Council. See p. 169 of this vol.

1549. 35. Despatch of November 25, 1549, from English Ambassadors in Brussels to Privy Council, conveying demand of Charles V. on Seb. Cabot's services.

B. Mus. Cotton MSS. Galba B. xii., fol. 124. Harrisse 'Jean et Sébastien Cabot,' document xxxiv. A., p. 359. 'Notes and Queries,' 1862. Vol. i. p. 125. See p. 170 of this vol.

1550. 36. Pension-grant (January 6, 1549–50) of £166 13s. 4d. yearly to Sebastian Cabot from Edward VI. Patent Roll. 2 Edward VI., part 2, membr. 10 (32). See Hakluyt, 'Principal Navigations,' iii. 10 (edition of 1598–1600); Rymer, 'Fœdera' (edition of 1741), VI., iii. 170, and p. 166, &c., of this vol.

1550. 37. Answer of Privy Council to Emperor, January 29, 1549–50, and April 21, 1550. See, Dasent, 'Acts of Privy Council,' ii. 374; and p. 170–1 of this vol. The original is on fol. 65 of MS. No. 3 in the Council Office Series of MS. Registers of Privy Council.

1550. 38. Cabot's own answer to Charles V., April 21, 1550. B. Mus. Harleian MSS. No. 523, fols. 6 bis.–7 bis [not fol. 9 as in Harrisse, 'Cabot,' 449]. See also Harrisse, 'Jean et Sébastien Cabot,' document xxxiv., pp. 359–60; and p. 171 of this vol.

1550. 39. Certificated copy of Letters Patent to John Cabot (originally issued in 1496) granted to Seb. Cabot, June 4, 1550. Original in Patent Roll, 4 Edward VI., Part vi., membr. 10. See p. 172 of this vol.

1550. 40. Gratuity of £200 from Edward VI. to Sebastian Cabot. 'ICI li [= £200 ?] by way of the K. M. reward,' 1550. See Harrisse, 'Jean et Sébastien Cabot,' document xxxiv. C. p. 360. This is followed by warrant to Exchequer to pay this sum. Dasent, 'Acts of Privy Council,' iii. 55, June 26, 1550.

Strype, 'Memorials,' ii., 2, 76, probably

refers to this same grant, under wrong date, March, 1551. See p. 173 of this vol. Original on p. 59 in MS. No. 4 of Council Office Series of MS. Registers of Privy Council.

1551. 41. Entry of April 17, 1551, of Cabot drawing his pension. Public Record Office. Tellers Rolls 100. See pp. 166–7 of this vol.

1551. 42. Despatch of September 12, 1551, from Venetian Council of Ten to Sorenzo, Venetian Ambass. in England. (Rawdon Brown, Venetian Calendar, vol. v., No. 711.) Harrisse, 'Jean et Sébastien Cabot,' document xxxv. p. 361.

With this also a despatch of same date from Peter Vannes to Privy Council—in Turnbull, Foreign Calendars, Edward VI. 171 ; Harrisse, 'Jean et Sébastien Cabot,' document xxxvi. Original in Public Record Office ; Foreign Papers of Edward VI., vol. viii. (July–September, 1550–51) No. 444, p. 1101. In the original the following unimportant sentence is added : 'and the said Secretary [Ramusio] hath promised me so to do, and I shall not fail to raise this matter often to be put in his remembrance.' See pp. 173–5 of this vol.

1553. 43. Ordinances, &c. issued (May 9, 1553) by Sebastian Cabot as Governor of Muscovy Company for Chancellor and Willoughby's Voyage in 1553.

See Hakluyt, 'Principal Navigations,' i. 266, Edition of 1598–1600; cf. W. N. Sainsbury, Colonial Calendar, i. 3; and pp. 179, 187, &c., of this vol.

1553. 44. Letter of September 9, 1553, from Charles V. to Queen Mary, pressing for Sebastian Cabot's services.

See Harrisse, 'Jean et Sébastien Cabot,' document xxxvi. pp. 362–63; Turnbull, Calendars, Foreign, 1553–58, vol. i., No. 30, p. 10. 'Notes and Queries,' 1862; vol. i. p. 125. See p. 196 of this vol.

1553. 45. Letter of November 15, 1553, from Sebastian Cabot to Charles V. Original at Simancas, Estado Correspond. de Inglaterra, Legajo, 808. See Coleccion de documentos ineditos para la Historia de España, vol. iii. p. 512; and p. 197 of this vol.

1554. 46. Entry of September 29, 1554, of Cabot drawing his pension (this time on a different footing). See text, p. 195.

T

Public Record Office, Tellers Rolls, 103.

1555. 47. Charter of Incorporation to Merchant Adventurers, February 6, 1555. Calendar Domestic State Papers, 1547–80, vol. i. p. 65. See p. 177 of this vol. Original in Public Record Office ; Domestic Papers, Mary (January–July, 1555), fols. 25–33 ; numbered (4) ; reprinted in Hakluyt, 'Principal Navigations,' ed. of 1598–1600, vol. iii.

1555. 48. Entry of March 25, 1555. Cabot draws half of pension on footing of September 29, 1554—viz., 100 marks. Public Record Office, Tellers Rolls, 103. See p. 195 of this vol.

1555. 49. Entry of September 29, 1555. Cabot draws half of (larger) pension (viz., £83 6s. 8d., the half of £166 13s. 4d.). per William Worthington. Public Record Office, Tellers Rolls, 104.

1555. 50. Pension-grant by Queen Mary to Cabot, November 27, 1555, apparently a renewal of his old pension from Edward VI. (new grant is of same yearly amount

—250 marks or £166 13s. 4d.). See Rymer, 'Fœdera' (1741), VI., iv. p. 40 ; and p. 202 of this vol.

1555. 51. Entry of December 25, 1555. Cabot draws a quarter of his original pension, viz., £41 13s. 4d. Public Record Office, Tellers Rolls, 104 (back of fol. 42, near foot).

1556–7. 52. Similar entries under June 24, 1556 ; September 29, 1556 ; December 25, 1556 ; March 25, 1557 ; June 24, 1557 ; September 29, 1557. Public Record Office, Tellers Rolls, 104, 105, 106.

1557. 53. Retrocession of Cabot's pension of 1555 and new grant of the aforesaid to Cabot and William Worthington, May 29, 1557.

Rymer, 'Fœdera' (1741), VI., iv. 55 ; Harrisse, 'Cabot' (1896), 459, &c. ; and p. 202, &c., of this vol.

Worthington on December 25, 1557, first draws pension without Cabot. Public Record Office, Tellers Rolls, 106. See p. 204 of this vol.

APPENDIX II.

Cabot Literature.

1. Anspach, L. A., 'History of Newfoundland,' London, 1819. See especially p. 25.

2. Arber, Edward, 'First Three English Books on America.' See especially pp. xx–xxi. 'Interlude' passage, xxxvii.

3. 'Archivo dos Azores,' 1894. See especially vol. xii. p. 530.

4. Avezac, M. A. P. d'A . . . Maçaya. (*a*) 'Les Navigations de J. et S. Cabot,' Paris, 1869. (*b*) Various papers in *Bulletin de la Société de Géographie*, Paris, viz., Aug.-Sept., 1857, xiv. pp. 89–368 ; Sept.-Oct., 1856, xvi. pp. 258–312 ; May, 1869, xvii. pp. 406–7 (in last Avezac mentions a Venetian portrait of John and also of Sebastian Cabot). (*c*) *Révue Critique*, April 23, 1870, vol. v. pp. 264–9.

5. Bancroft, G., 'History U.S.A.,' edition of 1883. See i. pp. 9–12.

6. Barrett, W., 'History and Antiquities of Bristol,' 1789. See pp. 171–4.

7. Beaudoin, J. D. (Abbé), 'Jean Cabot,' in *Le Canada Français*, Oct., 1889.

8. Belleforest, 'Cosmographie Universelle,' Paris, 1575. See ii. p. 2175.

9. Bergenroth, Calendar of State Papers, &c., relating to Negotiations between England and Spain, 1485–1543, London, 1862–95. See especially vol i. pp. 88–9, 176–7 ; vol. ii. p. 68.

10. Biddle, Richard, 'Memoir of Sebastian Cabot,' 1831.

11. Bourinot, J. G., 'Cape Breton,' &c., in *Transactions of Royal Society of Canada*, May 27, 1891, vol. ix., pt. ii., pp. 173–343.

12. Brevoort, J. Carson, 'John Cabot's Voyage of 1497.' In *Historical Magazine*. Morris. New York, March, 1868. 2nd Series, III. (xiii.), pp. 129–135.

13. Brewer, 'Letters and Papers . . . of Reign of Henry VIII., 1509–1540,' London, 1862–96. See especially vol. i. p. 694 ; vol. ii., pt. ii., pp. 101, 1456 ; vol. iv., pt. i., p. 154.

14. Brown, Rawdon. (*a*) 'Ragguagli sulla vita et sulle opere di Marin Sanuto,' Venice, 1837. See especially pt. i. pp. 99–100. 'In the Boston Public Library copy of this work (Library Call No. 4196–9, V. 1) is inserted a MS. note, "Mr. Rawdon Brown will gladly show Mrs. R. E. Apthorp what he considers documentary evidence of John Cabot's English origin, and of his never having come to Venice (where he married a Venetian woman, who bore him

Sebastian and his other sons) until the year 1461. Casa della Vida, Thursday, 2 p.m." The same copy contains (i. 100-103) another marginal MS. note : "I printed this in the year 1837 ; but in 1855–6 it became manifest, through documents discovered in the Venice Archives, that John Cabot really owed his birth to England." ' (*b*) Calendar of State Papers, &c., . . . relating to English Affairs in the Archives of Venice, &c., vol. i., A.D. 1202–1509, continued in nine vols. down to 1591. See especially vol. i. p. 260 ; vol. iii., Nos. 557, 558, 607, 632, 634, 635, 666, 669, 670, 750, 1115 ; vol. v., No. 711, p. 264.

15. Bullo, Carlo, ' La vera patria di . . . Giovanni Caboto,' Chioggia, 1880. See especially pp. 22, 61–70.

16. Campbell. (*a*) ' Navigantium Bibliotheca,' London, 1743–8, enlarged from Harris's Collection of 1705. See ii. p. 190. (*b*) ' Lives of the British Admirals,' London, 1748 and 1817. See i. pp. 312–16, 373–387 of later edition.

17. Cespedes, A. G. de, ' Regimiento de Navegacion,' Madrid, 1606. See fols. 137, 148, 149.

18. Chauveton, ' Histoire Nouvelle de Nouveau Monde,' Geneva, 1579. See p. 141 (Peter Martyr is credited with the summary of Cabot's voyage here made).

19. Chytraeus (Nathan Kochhaff), ' Variorum in Europa itinerum deliciae,' Herborn, 1594.

20. 'Coleccion de Documentos ineditos para la historia de la España.' See especially iii. pp. 512, &c.

21. 'Coleccion de Documentos ineditos de las Indias.' See especially xxxii. p. 479; xlii. p. 481.

22. Coote, C. H., Notices of 'Sebastian Cabot,' and 'Richard Hakluyt,' in the 'Dictionary of National Biography.'

23. Correa, Gaspar, 'Lendas da India,' Lisbon, 1858-62. Speaks of Sebastian Cabot as a Basque in iii. p. 109.

24. Cortambert, 'Nouvelle histoire des Voyages,' 1883-4. See pp. 207-17.

25. Crowley, Robert, 'Epitome of Chronicles,' London, 1559. See sub. ann. 1552. *See* Lanquet.

26. Daly, 'Early History of Cartography,' in American Geographical Society's Journal, New York, 1879. See xi. pp. 1-40.

27. Dasent, J. R., 'Acts of Privy Council,' London, 1890, &c. See vol. ii. pp. 37, 320, 374; vol. iii. pp. 55, 487, 501, 531.

28. Davis, John, 'The World's Hydrographical Description,' London, 1595.

29. Dawson, Samuel, 'Voyages of the Cabots,' in *Transactions of the Royal Society of Canada*, May 22, 1894, xi. pp. 51-112.

30. Deane, Charles. (*a*) 'On Sebastian Cabot's Mappemonde,' in American Antiquarian Society's Proceedings, October 20, 1866, pp. 10-14; and in

same for April 24, 1867, pp. 43–50. (b) 'Voyages of the Cabots,' in Justin Winsor's 'Narrative and Critical History of America,' iii. pp. 1–58.

31. Dee, John, 'Map of America,' in B. Mus. Cotton MSS., Aug. I. 1, art. i. (MS. dated 1580.) See especially inscription re Sebastian Cabot on back of map.

32. Desimoni. (a) 'Scopritori Genovesi in Giornale Ligustico,' Genoa, 1874. See pp. 308–16. (b) 'Intorno a Giovanni Caboto in Atti della Soc. Lig. di Storia Patria,' Genoa, 1881, xv. pp. 177–239. Also separately printed.

33. Dexter. (a) 'Early European Voyages in Massachusetts Bay,' in Winsor's 'Memorial History of Boston,' i. pp. 23–36. (Boston, 1880.) (b) 'Testimony of Fabyan's Chronicle to Hakluyt's Account of the Cabots,' in American Antiquarian Society's Proceedings, New Series, 1882, i. pp. 436–441.

34. Dionne, Review of Harrisse's 'Cabot' (of 1896), in *American Historical Review*, July, 1896. See vol. i. pp. 717–21.

35. Doyle, J. A., 'English Colonies in America,' 1889. See especially chap. iii. pp. 20–41.

36. Duro, Fernandez, 'Arca de Noe.' See p. 521.

37. Eden, Richard. (a) 'Treatise of the New India . . . after . . . Sebastian Munster,' London, 1553. See especially Dedication preceding pt. v. (b) 'Decades of the New World . . . translated from Peter Martyr,' London, 1555. See especially Preface,

leaf c. 1, and folios 249, 255, 268, 324. (*c*) 'Book
Concerning Navigation . . . translated from John
Taisnierus (Jean Taisnier).' See especially Epistle
dedicatory. London, about 1575.

38. Fox, 'North-West,' 1635. See pp. 31–37 of
Hakluyt Society reprint, 1894.

39. Gairdner, James, 'Calendar Henry VIII.'
(continuation of Brewer). See especially vol. iii., pt. i.,
p. 415.

40. Galvano, 'Discoveries of the World,' 1563,
translated by Hakluyt, 1601. See pp. 87–9 of Hakluyt
Society's reprint of latter, 1862.

41. Ganong, W. F., 'Cartography of Gulf of St.
Lawrence.' In *Transactions of the Royal Society of
Canada*, May 8, 1889, vol. viii., pt. ii., pp. 17–58 (also
in 1887, vol. v., pt. ii., pp. 121–136).

42. Gayangos, Pascual de, 'Spanish Calendar.' See
especially vol. vi., pt. i., p. 327.

43. Gilbert, Humphrey, 'Discourse of a Discovery
for a New Passage to Cathaia,' London, 1576 (written
in or before 1566). See fol. iii.

44. Godwin, 'Annals of England,' London, 1630.
Speaks of 'Sebastian Cabota a Portugal.'

45. Gomara, Francisco Lopez de, 'Historia General
de las Indias,' 1553. See especially chap. xxxix.

46. Grafton, Richard, 'Chronicle,' London, 1568–9.
See especially vol. ii. p. 1323.

47. Hakluyt, Richard. (*a*) 'Discourse on Western
Discovery' (Western Planting), 1584; first printed,

Portland, 1870, in vol. ii. of 'Documentary History of Maine.' See especially p. 126. (*b*) 'Divers Voyages touching Discovery of America,' 1582, reprinted Hakluyt Society, 1850. See especially Dedication and pp. 23, 26, 93, 176 of latter. (*c*) 'Principal Navigations,' 2nd edition of 1598–1600 (1st edition of 1589). See especially pp. 4–11, 498–9, 509–516 of vol. iii.

48. Hale, E. E. In *Proceedings of the American Antiquarian Society*, 1866, pp. 14–53, and in same Proceedings for April 25, 1860, pp. 36–38.

49. Hamersley, J. H., 'John Cabot,' in *Century Magazine* for May, 1897.

50. Harrisse, H. (*a*) 'Bibliotheca Americana Vetustissima,' 1866. See especially pp. 59–60. (*b*) 'Jean et Sébastien Cabot,' Paris, 1882. (*c*) 'Discovery of North America,' 1892. See especially pp. 1–50, 107–8, 406–8, 706–8, 747–50. (*d*) 'John Cabot and Sebastian his Son,' 1896. (*e*) Contributions to the *Révue de Géographie*, Paris, 1894 and 1895. See vol. xxxv. pp. 381–8, 474–81 ; vol. xxxvi. 16–23, 19–104, 200–7. (*f*) Paper in *Forum*, New York, June, 1897, 'When did John Cabot discover America ?' (*g*) Diplomatic history of America, 1897.

51. Hart, A. B. 'American History told by Contemporaries,' New York, 1897. See especially chap. i. pp. 69–72.

52. Hellwald, F. von, 'Sebastian Cabot,' Berlin, 1871.

53. Herbert, William. 'History of the Twelve Great Livery Companies of London,' London, 1837. See especially vol. i. pp. 410–11.

54. Herrera. 'Historia general' (1492–1531), Madrid, 1601–15. See especially Decade I., bk. ix., chap. xiii. ; Decade II., bk. i., chap. xii. ; Decade III., bk. iv., chap. xx: ; bk. ix. chap iii. ; Decade IV. bk. viii., chap. xi.

55. Higginson, 'Book of American Explorers,' Boston, 1877. See pp. 55–9.

56. Holinshed, R., 'Chronicles of England,' &c. London, 1577. See vol. ii. p. 1714.

57. Horsford, E. N., 'John Cabot's Landfall,' Cambridge, Mass., 1886.

58. Howley, M. F., 'Cabot's Landfall,' in *Magazine of American History*, New York, October, 1891, vol. xxvi. pp. 267–88.

59. Howley, J. P., 'Landfall of Cabot,' in *Bulletin of Geographical Society*, Quebec, 1886–9, No. v. pp. 67–78. Quebec, 1889.

60. Hugues, Luigi, 'Navigazioni di G. e S. Cabotto,' in *Mem. Soc. Geog. Ital.* Rome, 1878, vol. i., pt. iii., pp. 275–313.

61. Hunt, W., 'Bristol' ('Historic Towns'), London, 1887. See pp. 126–35.

62. Jomard, 'Monuments de la Géographie,' Paris, 1855–62. See Nos. xvi. and xx. for the Cosa and Cabot Maps.

63. Jurien de la Gravière, J. B. E., 'Les Marins

du XVI. Siècle,' Paris, 1876, &c. See especially vol. i. p. 215.

64. Kidder, F., 'Discovery of America by John Cabot,' Boston, 1878. Reprinted from *New Engl. Hist. Gen. Reg.*, Oct. 1878.

65. Kohl, J. G. (*a*) ' Descriptive Catalogue of Maps relating to America,' Washington, 1857. See pp. 11–16. (*b*) ' Die Beiden altesten General-Karten von Amerika.' Weimar, 1860. (*c*) 'History of . . . Discovery of . . . East Coast of North America and particularly of Maine' ('Documentary History of Maine'), Portland, 1869, &c. See especially chap. iv., pp. 121, 163, and pp. 199, 219, 362–3, 506.

66. Lanquet, Thomas (with Robert Crowley and Thomas Cooper), 'Epitome of Chronicles,' London, 1559. *See* Crowley.

67. La Roque, ' Armorial de la Noblesse,' Montpellier, 1860. See ii. pp. 163–5.

68. Lemon, Calendar of Domestic State Papers, 1547–80. See vol. i. p. 65.

69. Lok, Michael, Map dedicated to Philip Sidney, 1582, published in Hakluyt, ' Divers Voyages,' 1582.

70. Madero, E., Study on Cabots, Buenos Ayres. See Prowse, Newfoundland, 30 (1st ed.).

71. Major, R. H., 'True date of English Discovery of America,' reprinted from 'Archæologia,' 1871, xliii. pp. 17–42.

72. Markham, C. R. (*a*) ' Journal of Columbus,' with documents relating to the Cabots and Cortereals,

London Hakluyt Society, 1893. See especially pp.
ix–xliv., 197–226. (*b*) Paper read at Roy. Geo.
Soc., London, June, 1897.

73. Martyr, Peter M. d'Anghiera, 'Decades of the
New World' (De orbe novo decades). First three
decades published 1516 at Alcala, trans. by R.
Eden, 1555. The whole eight decades, 1530,
Alcala. See especially Decade III., bk. vi., fol. 46,
&c. ; Decade VII., bk. vii., fol. 97.

74. Mason, J., 'Newfoundland described by J. M.,
an Industrious Gent,' 1626. Has a map giving Cabot
landfall at Cape Bona Vista.

75. Navarrete. (*a*) 'Coleccion de los Viajes,'
Madrid, 1825–37. See iii. pp. 308, 319 ; iv. p.
339 ; [v. p. 333]. (*b*) 'Disertacion sobre la
historia de la Nautica,' Madrid, 1846. See especially p. 134. (*c*) 'Coleccion de opusculos,' Madrid,
1848. See i. pp. 65–6. (*d*) 'Bibliotheca Maritima
Española,' Madrid, 1851. See ii. pp. 697–700.

76. Nicholas, Harris, 'Excerpta historica,' London,
1831. See especially pp. 113, 126.

77. Nichols, J. G., 'Literary Remains of Edward
VI.,' London, 1857.

78. Ortelius, 'Theatrum Orbis terrarum,' Antwerp,
1570.

79. Oviedo, G. F. de, 'Historia General de las
Indias,' 1535. Best edition, Madrid, 1851–5. See
bk. vi., chaps. xxxv., xlii. ; bk. xxiii., chaps. i., ii.

80. Peschel, Oscar. (*a*) 'Geschichte der Erdkunde,'

Munich, 1877. See pp. 287–319. (*b*) 'Geschichte der Zeitalters der Entdeckung,' Stuttgart, 1858 (1877, 2nd ed.). See pp. 274–282.

81. Pezzi, 'G. Cabotto,' Venice, 1881.

82. Prowse, D. W., 'History of Newfoundland,' London, 1895. See chap. ii. pp. 4–17, 29–30.

83. Purchas, Samuel, ' Pilgrims,' 1625. See especially iii. pp. 806–9 ; iv. pp. 1177, 1812.

84. ' Raccolta Colombiana,' vol. i., pt. iii., p. 137.

85. Ramusio, G. B., 'Navigationi,' &c., 1550, vol. i., Venice. Complete ed., 1563–5. See vol. i. p. 374 ; vol. iii., preface, and fols. 4, 35, 55, 374, 417 ; cf. Eden, ' Decades,' fol. 255, Hakluyt, ' Principal Navigations,' vol. iii. pp. 6–7.

86. Reumont, A, 'I due Caboto,' Florence, 1880.

87. Ribaut, Jean, ' Discovery of Terra Florida,' English trans., London, 1563. See Hakluyt, ' Divers Voyages,' in Hak. Soc. reprint, p. 92.

88. Romanin, S., 'Storia Documentata,' Venice, 1853–61. See iv. p. 453.

89. Ruge, S., ' Entwickelung der Kartographie von Amerika, bis 1570.' In supplement No. 106 to Petermanns Mittheilungen.

90. Rymer, ' Fœdera,' ed. of 1741, vol. v., pt. iv. pp. 55, 89, 186; vi., pt. iv. pp. 40, 55 ; vi., pt. iii. p. 170.

91. Santa Cruz, Alonzo de (*a*) 'Islario' MS. in Besançon Library, fol. 56. (*b*) Libro de Longitudes, Madrid National Library, Aa, 97.

92. Sanuto, Livio, 'Geografia . . . 1588." See i. fol. 2 ; ii. fol. 17.

93. Sanuto, Marino, 'Diarii, 1496–1527.' Best ed., Venice, 1879–95. See especially i. pp. 806–8 ; iv. p. 377.

94. Seyer, S., 'Memoirs of Bristol,' 1821–3. See ii. pp. 208, 210.

95. Stevens, Henry. (a) 'Historical and Geographical Notes, 1453–1530' (1869). (b) 'Sebastian Cabot minus John Cabot = 0' (1870).

96. Stow, John, 'Chronicles of England,' London, 1580. See pp. 862, 872, 875.

97. Strachey, W., 'History of Travel into Virginia . . . 1612,' pp. 6, 139 of Hak. Soc. reprint, 1849–51.

98. Strype, 'Ecclesiastical Memorials,' ed. of 1721. See ii. p. 190 ; ii. p. 402.

99. Tarducci, 'Giovanni e Sebastiano Caboto,' Venice, 1892, English trans. Detroit, 1893.

100. Thevet, A. (a) 'Le Grand Insulaire, written before 1558,' Paris, Bibliothéque Nationale, Fonds Français, Nos. 15, 452, vol. i. fol. 143. (b) 'Les Singularités de la France Antarctique,' Paris, 1558 ; Eng. trans. London, 1568. See chap. lxxiv. fol. 148. (c) 'Cosmographie Universelle,' Paris, 1575. See bk. xxiii., chap. vii., fol. 1022.

101. Thorne, Robert, in Hakluyt's 'Divers Voyages' (map) and 'Principal Navigations,' vol. ii. pt. ii.

102. Turnbull, W. B. (*a*) Foreign Calendar, Edward VI., p. 171. (*b*) Foreign Calendar, Mary, vol. i. p. 10.

103. Tytler, 'Progress of Discovery,' Edinburgh, 1823. See pp. 417–44.

104. Varnhagen, Adolf de, 'Historia . . . de Brazil,' Madrid, 1854. See i. p. 439.

105. Verreau (Abbé), in *Memoirs of Royal Society of Canada*, 1891–2, iii. pp. 103–152 ; ix. pp. 73–83.

106. Weare, G. E., 'Cabot's Discovery of North America,' 1897.

107. Weise, 'American Discoveries . . . to 1525,' London, 1884. See chap. vi. pp. 186–204.

108. Willes, Richard, 'History of Travel,' London, 1577. See fols. 232–3.

109. Winsor, Justin. (*a*) 'Narrative and Critical History of America.' Especially iii. pp. 1–58 (Deane's contribution), London ed., 1886; also viii. p. 384. (*b*) 'Christopher Columbus,' Boston, 1892. See pp. 339–46. (*c*) Contributions to *Nation*, September 29 and October 6, 1892 ; also December 7, 1893. (*d*) 'Cabot Controversies' in Massachusetts Hist. Soc., 2nd Series (vi.), reprinted, Cambridge, Mass., 1896.

110. Woodbury, 'Relation of Fisheries to Discovery . . . of North America,' Boston, 1880 (claims that Basques preceded Cabot).

111. Zeri, 'G. e S. Caboto,' Rome, 1881. From 'Rivista Maritima,' March, 1881.

112. Ziegler, J., 'Opera Varia,' Strasburg, 1532.

See fol. xcii. Copies Martyr. See Eden, 'Decades,' fol. 268 ; and Santo Cruz, ' Islario.'

113. Zurla, D. Placida, ' Marco Polo,' &c., Venice, 1818–19. See ii. pp. 274–86.

INDEX

Appendix II. being arranged alphabetically is not indexed.